CHRISTIANITY IN THE SOUTHERN HEMISPHERE

CHRISTIANITY IN THE SOUTHERN HEMISPHERE

The Churches in Latin America and South Africa

BY

EDWARD NORMAN

CLARENDON PRESS · OXFORD
1981

Oxford University Press, Walton Street, Oxford OX2 6DP

OXFORD LONDON GLASGOW
NEW YORK TORONTO MELBOURNE WELLINGTON
KUALA LUMPUR SINGAPORE HONG KONG TOKYO
DELHI BOMBAY CALCUTTA MADRAS KARACHI
NAIROBI DAR ES SALAAM CAPE TOWN

Published in the United States
by Oxford University Press, New York

British Library Cataloguing in Publication Data

Norman, Edward
  Christianity in the Southern Hemisphere.
  1. Church and state in Latin America
  2. Church and state in South Africa
  I. Title
  322'.1'098   BR660   80–41308
  ISBN 0–19–821127–9

Phototypesetting by Parkway Group, London and Abingdon
Printed in Great Britain by Richard Clay (The Chaucer Press Ltd.,)
Bungay, Suffolk

Preface

The Birkbeck Lectures, which I delivered in Cambridge during November 1979, and the Prideaux Lectures, at Exeter, in March 1980, examined four themes in the relationship between the ecclesiastical developments and the political and social histories of two apparently quite different areas of the world—Latin America and Southern Africa. At the time that I received the invitations to give the lectures my research interests had already been centred for some years on the religious histories of these regions, and the opportunity of presenting a parallel analysis was especially attractive. The lectures were therefore planned from the start as sections of a comparative study, the basis of the interpretative introduction which this book comprises. These seemingly incomparable areas soon disclosed some important common features—looked at as enormous and complicated examples of what happens to European religious institutions when transplanted and re-cultivated in unfamiliar circumstances, and in contact with peoples of alien indigenous cultures.

There has been surprisingly little writing of ecclesiatical history in both areas. Some Latin American countries are without a single account of the Catholic Church; in some others there are only minor writings concerned with individual dioceses or the work of particular religious orders. In South Africa there are a few denominational histories—those of the Dutch Reformed churches are exclusively in Afrikaans, those of the English-speaking churches are all in English—and no study of Christian developments which includes both. In addition to its inherent intellectual importance, however, religious consciousness of wider contemporary issues is today leading a number of activists from both continents to examine their common inheritance. As the Final Communiqué of the Conference of Third World Theologians (held in Accra, December 1977) declared: 'African theology concerns itself with bringing about the solidarity of Africans with black Americans, Asians, and Latin Americans, who are also struggling for the realisation of human communities.' Comparative analysis of their various past developments can only help to clarify such undertakings.

As the main substance of this book was originally delivered orally, I thought it appropriate to restrict the notes to the identification of quotations, and since the point of quotation is anyway to secure precision of meaning, I have left them in the language of the sources from which they are taken. Translations are provided in the footnotes. There is also a full bibliography, intended to serve as a general guide to further printed sources. In the course of a great amount of travel I have received the help of many people, amongst whom I would especially mention the following: Señora Carmen Gilabert of the Ministerio de Culto, Monseñor Serra and Monseñor Liden, in Buenos Aires; the staff of the Santuario de Santa Rosa in Lima; Señor L. H. Jowett in Santiago de Chile; Mgr. Severino Nogueira in Recife; the staff of the Museo Colonial de Santa Mónica in Puebla; Miss C. J. Schmidt and the staff of the Information Service of South Africa, Professor A. König, Dr H. Cronjé and Professor C. W. H. Boshoff, in Pretoria; Professor P. A. Verhoef in Stellenbosch; Mrs Rosa du Toit in Cape Town; Bishop Barnabas Ramarumo of the Zion Christian Church, and Professor J. A. van Wyk, of Pietersburg; Miss Carol Smythe, and Bishop Manas Buthelezi, in Johannesburg; the Revd M. S. Tladi in Soweto; Bishop Koppman, and the Revd P. Strauss, in Windhoek; Professor E. Shils in Chicago; Mr E. Mcdermott in New York City; Mr S. A. Otto in Toronto; Miss Ronelle Henning, Mrs Louise Purslow, Mr G. Fischer, Mr I. McIntrye, and Mr P. Ducker, in London.

E. R. N.
April 1980

Contents

Latin America

1

Church and State

Latin-American historians have directed so much attention to the nineteenth-century liberals' assault upon the influence of the Catholic Church, and to the formal separations of Church and State in some of the republics, that one of the most remarkable features of the ecclesiastical history of the hemisphere has passed virtually without comment: the survival of established Churches at all. The men who made the Independence movement at the start of the last century were imbued with the ideas of the European Enlightenment. They were the intellectual kin of those who in revolutionary France, and in the emergent United States, had regarded it as an article of political reason to provide for the legal separation of Church and State. The Radical Clubs in Britain, too—whose ideals were often adopted by South American leaders during periods of exile—were insistent upon the freedom of conscience which only a full separation of religious belief and public life could, they argued, guarantee. Yet in the Latin-American Independence struggle there was no attack upon the Church as a visible embodiment of colonial administration—despite its close relationship to the old order and the opposition of the bishops to Independence. The organic laws of the new republics without exception provided for the legal establishment of the Catholic religion. Statesmen who were rigorously committed to the idealogy of Philosophical Radicalism in most other aspects of their political outlook were nevertheless anxious to secure Catholicism as a public expression of the new nations' moral identity, as well, of course, as respecting its utility as a social cohesive.

Thus Francisco de Miranda, in his advocacy of a liberal scheme of government before the *cabildo* of Caracas in 1810, included the Roman Catholic Church as the national religion. He was a man noted for his espousal of religious toleration. The translator of Rousseau's *Social Contract*, Mariano Moreno, when secretary of the Buenos Aires *junta*, contended consistently for the maintenance of an established religion. Opponents of the Independence movement, in fact, pointed to the rationalist ideology of its leading figures as if that, in itself—as so often in Europe—made them enemies of religion. Bishop Rodríguez Zorilla of Santiago de Chile described the rebels as 'impenitent Voltaireans'.[1] He was later expelled by Bernardo O'Higgins— himself a strong supporter of the union of Church and State. Bolívar was the great exception; he really did fit the rationalist model feared by the conservative churchmen. Indeed, his desire for a separation of religion and government was one of the things which lead to differences with San Martín. His 1819 Constitution for Great Colombia—the Constitution of Angostura—contained no article on religion. The original 1826 Constitution for Bolivia did not recognize the Church either.

Both were against the grain of popular sentiment, and were outside the terms of reference acceptable to the élites who had made the revolution. So in the 1821 Constitution of Cúcuta there was provision for Catholicism as the state religion of Great Colombia, and in Bolivia the assembly ignored the founder's opinions and set up a State Church in the organic laws finally adopted in 1826. Bolívar himself shifted ground, and later came to recognize the expediency of enlisting the clergy within the machinery of the state. This was especially noticeable after his assumption of dictatorial powers in Great Colombia in 1828.

It is necessary to ask why the Catholic Church, which was weak both institutionally and politically at the end of the Colonial period, was regarded by the founders of the new republics as so essential a part of their schemes of government. In some large measure, no doubt, the Church, which was stronger in the rural areas than in the towns, was seen to fulfil an important function of social control. The loyalty of the priests guaranteed the adhesion of the peasantry to the new order. But the matter was scarcely and urgent one. The wars of Independence had not elicited any serious divergences between the aspirations of town and country. The peasantry and the urban radicals did not, it is true, share a common ideology of politics, or have very much in common at all. The revolution, however, was not—except, perhaps, among the followers of Hidalgo and Moreno in Mexico— led by a series of *jacqueries;* and the interests of the urban élite and

[1] J. Lloyd Mecham, *Church and State in Latin America,* revised edn, University of North Carolina Press, 1966, p. 202.

the leaders of rural society, the priests and the *hacendados*, were able to coincide. There was no need for the new governing groups to seek the aid of the Church in order to contain a disaffected peasantry. The reason why the men of the Enlightenment in Latin America made choices about religion different from those made among European and North American political rationalists lay more deeply in their Hispanic inheritance, in their understanding of the nature of the state itself.

Here there were profound differences from experience elsewhere, and here also were preceding examples of the possibility of rationalizing government without destroying the continuity of inherited values. For the rationalist political schemes of the new republicans had followed royalist alterations to the administration of the colonies which were, in their way, no less rationalistic. The Bourbon reforms in Spanish America, and Pombal's reconstruction of the government of Brazil, had replaced some of the old political structure and the system of influence with which *criollo* society was familiar, with arrangements which were quite a break with the past. These changes also explain the support of so many of the lower clergy for the Independence cause. They distrusted the higher dignitaries of the Church because the bishops had supported the reforms of the Crown. The parish priests reflected the attitudes of those who not only saw their influence threatened by the hated *gachupines*, but who looked back to an idealized colonial society of the past, to a half-mythical world of harmonious social relationships and traditional authority before the alien rationalization of the *peninsulares*. In the Independence movement they sought a work of restoration. That is the sense in which the clergy who supported the revolutionary movements were conservative. The secular leaders of the Independence movement, on the other hand, shared and extended the reasoned ideals of the Enlightenment; they were not so conservative. Quite early in the nineteenth century the logic of the different social visions of these two interests worked through, and the way was prepared for the inevitable clash of liberal anti-clericalism and Catholic traditionalism. At first, however, that did not appear a likely outcome, and the union of patriotism and popular religiosity which marked the Indpendence period seemed a hopeful sign for the new era. The Colonial bishops' change of policy towards Independence

came as a direct result of their awareness that rationalist politics
were more conservative at home than they were in the mother
country. In 1820 the liberal Spanish *cortes* approved its anti-
clerical reform. The ecclesiastical *fuero* was abolished, some
religious were suppressed, tithes were confiscated. In Spanish
America, the bishops joined the lower clergy in welcoming
Independence.

There has been, in the ecclesiastical history of Latin-American
countries, a considerable emphasis on the question of patronage
as the major determining consideration in the conflict of Church
and State. Patronage was, indeed, of the greatest importance:
the *real patronato* was the symbol as well as the actual means by
which the Crown's supremacy over the Church was exercised.
But when it passed to the independent republics an arrangement originally intended to cement the union of Church and
State behind the purposes of a Christian social order became,
instead, the ground of discord. Differences of opinion on the
question, however, were again to be found within the Church.
There is little evidence to suggest that the parochial clergy were
unhappy about the continued control of ecclesiastical appointments by the state. They had no relationship with Rome at all,
and those who served churches on the great *haciendas*—as many
did—had scarcely any relationship even with the nearest
urban church authorities. The bishops, for their part, had been
content enough with political appointment until the Independence period. They had received large benefits from the Crown,
and shared the general administrative outlook, and the sympathy for enlightened reform, characteristic of the public life of
the later eighteenth century. In the bull *Sollicitudo Ecclesiarum*, of
1831, Gregory XVI recognized the political legitimacy of the
new republics and allowed traditional rights of the Crown over
patronage to be continued by them, *de facto*. But the principle
was never formally conceded, and Rome continued to insist
that with the termination of royal sovereignty the right of
appointment legally reverted to the Papacy. Rome's initial
intransigence had been broken in the end by the Papal calcula-
tion that a schism in South America—should the Churches,
bereft of episcopal appointments for many years, act on their
own—was worse than the hostlity of the Spanish Crown to any
recognition of the new republics by the Vatican. But the problem

of the *patronato*, with its enduring legacy of friction, was not in
itself the major cause of Church and State conflict in Latin
America in the nineteenth century—though it was often the
occasion. That conflict derived, on the side of the state, from the
growth of the secularization ideology of the liberal politicans
and *pensadores*, and, on the side of the church, from the growth
of ultramontanism among the higher clergy—a development
exactly corresponding to its spread in Europe, and, as there,
providing some classic confrontations between ecclesiastical
autonomy and the claims of the modern state. Particular controversies over patronage, in the different republics, led to the
foundation of Catholic defence organizations, and it was these
which often sharpened the conflict with liberal ideology by
furnishing clear propagandist statements of developing Catholic
autonomy. In the 1850s, for example, the Chilean clergy formed
an association 'para defender la libertas de la Iglesia' which
they called *La Sociedad de Santo Tomás de Cantorbury*.[2] It was
explicitly intended to defend Catholicism against the improper
exercise of patronage by the state—which had just made a
controversial appointment to the staff of the cathedral in
Santiago.

The new governments regarded the exercise of ecclesiatical
patronage not only as a public indication of their legitimacy but
also, more practially, as helping to guarantee a measure of
control over the only institution in each country which had a
truly national existence—whose influence upon the people,
despite the weakness of the Church, was still much more extensive than that of the state itself. One after another, the republics
claimed to use the powers held by the Crown under Papal
concessions going back to the bulls of 1493, 1501, and 1508. The
Catholic hierarchies in the various countries, anxious to avoid a
breach with the Papacy—which had demanded the powers
back again—consolidated their opposition. In Mexico, a committee of bishops, convened at the invitation of the Regency
government in 1821, reported that patronage had indeed reverted to the Papacy. Congress disagreed, and claimed the
patronato for the nation. There it remained until in 1831 Presi-

[2] Jaime Eyzaguirre, *Historia de las instituciones políticas y sociales de Chile*, Santiago, 1967, p. 118.

dent Anastasio Bustamante, under the influence of his Foreign Minister, Lucas Alamán, who had developed ultramontane sympathies, abandoned the state's claims. But they were resumed in 1834. Elsewhere the state's assumption of the *patronato* was equally durable: Chile in 1818, Argentina in 1819, Great Colombia in 1824, Bolivia in 1826, Uruguay, Venezuela, and Ecuador in 1830. In some countries the interference of the state over ecclesiastical appointments was actually extended beyond the former practice of the Crown. In Colombia, under the presidency of the anti-clerical José Hilario López, a law of 1851 gave the *cabildos* the right to nominate parish clergy. In 1824 the Central American Federation had required all appointments of parish priests to have government approval. For thirty years after Independence, President José Gaspar Rodríguez of Paraguay controlled the Church to such a degree that the President declared himself its head. He had been a theological student as a young man, and sought an ecclesiastical polity like that of Henry VIII in England. In Brazil, patronage was in 1824 vested in the new Imperial government, and under Pedro II was greatly extended until in 1854 the state claimed the right of nomination to all benefices. At this time, according to Professor Bruneau, the Church became 'nothing more than an ordinary bureau of government'.[3] Venezuela, under President Juan Vincente Gómez, actually extended the *patronato* in 1911 so that it included non-Catholic churches too.

'In Latin America', as Frederick B. Pike has written, 'vexatious problems that had concerned Europeans for centuries were resolved in the course of a few short years.'[4] The question of Church appointments—often the centre of European discord between Church and State—was a case in point. In the longer perspective, the patronage issue had the effect of forcing the clergy themselves to separate temporalities and spiritualities in a way which allowed secularizing politicians to distinguish between the social and economic influence of the Church (which they were able to represent as temporal accidents merely) and the spiritual substance of religion, which they regarded as the

[3] Thomas C. Bruneau, *The Political Transformation of the Brazilian Catholic Church*, Cambridge, 1974, p. 23.
[4] Frederick B. Pike, *The Conflict between Church and State in Latin America*, New York, 1964, p. 14.

only legitimate concern of the clergy. In this manner they could attack the influence of the Church without antagonizing the Catholic masses. The separation of temporalities and spiritualities, in fact, assisted the more permanent Latin-American legacy of divorcing religious sanction from public political life. There were also more formidable causes of Church and state conflict. In the nineteenth-century world, the leaders of the Catholic Church in Latin America found themselves cut off both from the political past and the political future. The Hispanic regalist tradition had meant state control but with privilege in return. Control had remained but not the reward, and the growing ultramontanism of the hierarchies regarded most connections with the civil power as inappropriate. The liberalism and secularism of Latin America's erratic nineteenth-century political development demanded the progressive reduction of ecclesiastical influence as a necessary condition for the construction of the modern state. The Church was a victim not so much of its own ideological adhesion to conservative political forces, or of its own political ineptitude, as of the conditions demanded by unsympathetic politicians for the growth of the state. The Church was, in this sense, an involuntary ally of conservatism: it had no choice. The resulting attrition became almost constant—between the traditional role of the Church as a guarantor of social harmony, particularly in the rural areas, and the emergent, liberal, urban élites, seeking alternative, seclar, social cohesives. Like earth-plates in collision, there were periodic adjustments of their relative positions; ruptures in the relations of Church and State were the signs that this was taking place.

Because of the nature of Catholicism, with its own universal explanations of human society—for so long supported by the authority of government in Latin America—the advocates of secularization themselves became more doctrinaire in their counter-Thomism. It was this exaggeration of their position, as well as the undoubtedly unique features of the Iberian political characteristics of South American society, which have inhibited comparisons with conflicts of Church and State in Northern Europe or in North America. But the ingredients are actually the same: an expanding demand for freedom of conscience and for the removal of civil disabilities based upon religious profession, an increased level of state activity in administrative and social areas formerly regarded as within the exclusive province of the Church, urban population growth (allowing advocates of change to point to the inadequacy of the Church's parochial system, which broke down in the new urban expansion, as a social cohesive), the association of the Church with conservative social practice. These conditions existed in Britain, too, during the nineteenth century, and some instructive parallels may be drawn—provided it is always remembered that the political context and the political tradition were enormously different, and that comparisons are valid solely in relation to the impact upon ecclesiastical institutions of the forces creating the modern state. In Britain, too, there was an influential (but not so powerful) 'anti-clerical' interest in the nineteenth century. It became an element in evolving liberal politics, a crucial catalyst in the reduction of the privileges of the Established Protestant Church. In Britain, reform proceeded by stages, each particular issue inexorably bringing forward a severance of legal connections between religion and government. There, also, was the ideology of secularization, hidden, sometimes, with the contentions of those who were Christian believers but whose liberal political principles required a neutral or secular state for their fulfilment. There was a background of erastianism, itself not too dissimilar from the ecclesiastical control of the Iberian regalist tradition. In Britain, of course, the political adjustments by which the Church was progressively removed from the centre of political society were characterized by a greater pragmatism than in Latin America. But the issues were the same ones. In any analysis of the Latin-American experience of change in Church and State relations it is worth keeping this external comparison in mind.

Statistical evidence about the composition of society is an essential prerequisite of the modern state, and social reform, whether it is empirical, as in Britain, or paternalistic, as in South America, needs prior social knowledge. The Church in both places was stripped of its function as the compiler of the statistics of births, deaths, and marriages. And in both places the clergy were in general unhappy about the change—correctly sensing that a reduction of their administrative duties presaged greater secularization. Civil registration was introduced to

Venezuela under anti-clerical influence in 1834, although it was not made effective for some years. In Mexico it came as part of the secularizing code of Juárez in 1856. In Chile it was enacted in the *reformas teológicas* of Balmaceda, in 1884. In England, civil registration came in 1836. The ending of the monopoly of the Church over marriage was similar. It was not demanded by the Latin-American liberals solely as a measure intended to weaken the control of the Church, however, but was required anyway— because of the increase in population, the shortage of priests, and because of the existence, especially after the mid-century, of small numbers of influential Protestants. Civil marriage, despite strong protests from the Church and from Catholic politicians, came to the Central American Federation in 1822, to Uruguay in 1837, to Chile in 1884, to Argentina in 1888, and to Brazil in 1890. In England, the civil marriage law was passed in 1836.

The secularization of the cemeteries was also vehemently contested by the Church, as another reduction, carried out for ideological reasons, of the social role of religion. But there was also a pressing need, in view of the parochial inadequacies of the Church in the expanding urban areas, for more burial facilities anyway: there was, that is to say, again a reason for the change related to the growth of modern society, quite separate from the ideals of the liberals. Cemeteries were secularized in Mexico in 1856, in Chile in 1883, in Brazil in 1890. In England, cemeteries were in practice secularized by Gladstone's legislation in 1883— a measure regarded at the time as a reward for the political activity of the radical Nonconformists who had campaigned for the Liberal Party in the preceding election.

Tithes were another symbol of the old order. They had been granted to the Spanish Crown by Alexander VI in a bull of 1501, but the Colonial administration had collected them and returned them to the Church. Arrangements after Independence at first continued without interruption. This was also the case in Brazil. But as a tax on land they were particularly vulnerable to liberal assault and they were among the first of the Church privileges to fall before the liberals' militancy. Modern society, according to the liberals' creed, required the creation of a rural middle class. The destruction of tithe would assist this, and in addition it would diminish the local resources, and therefore the influence, of those guardians and symbols of traditional rural society, the parish priests. Tithes were duly abolished: in Argentina in 1822, Chile in 1825, Mexico in 1833, and Venezuela in 1834. In England an Act of 1836 began the gradual abolition of tithes, and in 1868 a Liberal government abolished the compulsory payment of Church rates.

The landed wealth of the Catholic Church was also seen as an impediment to effective modern government, by those who contended not only that it preserved a level of ecclesiastical influence that was detrimental to progress, but that the wealth of the Church should as a matter of right belong to the nation. The Spanish Crown itself provided a precedent for state interference with ecclesiastical property, when in 1804 it compulsorily redeemed mortgages belonging to charities and chantries in the South American colonies. In many of the Latin-American countries — though not in Chile, Peru, or Argentina — the last century and half has seen considerable confiscations or redistributions of Church property. The most well-known expropriations took place in Mexico with the *Ley Lerdo* of 1856 and the policies of Juárez, in the nineteenth century, and with the enforcement by Calles, in 1926, of the 1917 Constitution, in the twentieth. Juárez was motivated both by progressive anti-clericalism and by his need for money; Calles by a determination to destroy forever a survivor — as he saw the Church — of the old Mexico whose values he so completely rejected. In Britain, it need hardly be said, the attack upon ecclesiastical property was rather more restrained and much less successful. But there were similarities of motive: the nineteenth-century middle-class liberals and Nonconformists who demanded the disendowment of the Established Church did so because of their political objection to its symbolic representation of the values of landed society. In legislation of 1833 and 1869 property of the Irish Church was regulated, and some was confiscated, by the State; and in England ecclesiastical property was removed from the control of the Church, and placed in the hands of a Royal Commission, in 1836.

All the Latin-American republics were anxious to restrict or to abolish the ecclesiastical *fuero* — the legal immunities of the clergy, and the exercise of jurisdiction over the laity. Reform here was slightly more hazardous, since the military also enjoyed comparable rights in their own *fueros* and were sometimes unprepared to countenance damaging precedents created by too summary treatment of the Church. Yet the *fuero eclesiástico* was first reduced—as in Colombia in 1836, when ecclesiastical tribunals were subordinated to civil courts—and then altogether abolished—as in Argentina in 1822, Peru in 1856, or Mexico in 1857. In England, the abolition of ecclesiastical jurisdiction in civil causes also proceeded by stages, of which the most seminal was the appointment in 1830 of the Royal Commission on Ecclesiastical Jurisdiction.

The general issue of religious toleration was another item on the agenda of Latin-American liberals from the start of Independence. In Argentina, liberty of conscience was guaranteed in the first constitution of La Plata. Elsewhere it was won, largely against clerical opposition, through political agitation which quite deliberately sought to undermine the position of Catholicism by recognizing its religious opponents. Toleration was achieved in Brazil in a limited form in 1824, fully in Uruguay with the Constitution of 1830, and in Paraguay in 1870—where, as in other later examples, the concession of civil liberties to Protestants was associated with the need to encourage immigration, a policy which some progressive liberals, with characteristic Social Darwinism, believed essential in order to preserve European culture against the Indian. The classic conflict over the issue of religious toleration occurred in Chile. The *Ley Interpretativa* of 1865 was only one, if the most significant, of a series of liberal reforms which in the second half of the nineteenth century removed the exclusive protection afforded the Catholic Church by the State under the various constitutions enacted since Independence. Foreign Protestants, and especially the Revd David Trumbull, an American evangelist who worked in Valparaíso for over forty years after 1845, took a leading part in allying Protestantism to the liberals' political agitation. In England, also, this association of dissent and liberal politics had helped to secure the concession of religious equality, from the repeal of the Test and Corporation Acts in 1828 to the Religious Disabilities Removals Act of 1891.

Another area in which reform diminished the rights of the Church was education. Again, the reasons were mixed: liberal dislike of clerical influence in the schools, and the insufficiency of the Church's own resources, in terms both of finance and manpower, for the task of continuing as the national agent of education—in societies where both the size and the expectations of the population were expanding. In many Latin-American countries, as a result, the State extended its own schools and universities. A wide variation of practice resulted. In some countries, like Costa Rica, or Colombia after the pro-clerical changes made by Núñez in 1886, the teaching of the Catholic religion was compulsory. In some others, like El Salvador after 1962, religious teaching became optional, or, as in the case of Brazil after 1891, was only permitted outside normal school hours. Some, like Cuba after 1899, prohibited the teaching religion altogether. A few countries extended the state's interest to include the supervision of Church schools: Venezuela and Bolivia have done this. The variations are not even constant. Argentina, which did not allow the teaching of religion in the public schools after 1884, reintroduced it under Perón in 1943. It disappeared again in 1955. It has now reappeared in the educational curriculum as 'Formación civico'—a more broadly-based, comparative study of Argentina's Christian values. Brazil brought back religious teaching in 1946. The general pattern, however, is clear enough. The creation of a State interest in education has radically diminished the Church's national role, even though Catholic schools have in most countries continued to have a disproportionately large educational influence as a result of the upper classes and the emergent middle sectors sending their children to them for social reasons. In Britain the state also created its own school system; in Ireland in 1831, and in England after 1870. The demand made by liberals and Nonconformists that state education should be secular became one of the most important political agitations of nineteenth-century English popular politics, although it was not successful.

Now these evidences of similarity in the chronology and typology of adjustments in the relationship of Church and State, between Latin-American and British experience, are not offered in order to suggest that they shared a common political or religious heritage. They certainly did not. The development of the two areas was entirely different. Apart from the absorption of some of the anti-clericalism implicit in the writings of the English Philosophical Radicals of the early years of the nineteenth century, the influence of English religious history upon Latin-American liberalism has been slight. These pointers have been added to the analysis of Latin-American developments in order to demonstrate another underlying feature: the effect upon the position of the Church of the growth of the state. It is that phenomenon, and the accompanying claims of the state to omnicompetence—reinforcing, as it did in Latin America, existing traditions of paternalism—which have determined both the extent and the nature of Church and State conflict.

The symbolic success of the state's exclusivism came with the various disestablishments. In three cases—Brazil, Uruguay, and Chile—the separation of Church and State was attained without a political upheaval. Brazil's disestablishment, in 1890, followed the overthrow of the Empire, and was in fact prepared by the attrition between the Ultramontanist bishops—themselves a minority within the Brazilian episcopate—and the state, following the religious crisis of 1874. Despite the separation, however, the Constitutions of 1934 and 1946 continued to invoke the name of God. Uruguay's disestablishment was largely the work of José Batlle y Ordóñez, and was carried out in the furtherance of his political commitment to the ideology of secularism. Nevertheless the separation, which took place in 1919, was not greatly opposed—partly because of the institutional weakness of Catholicism in Uruguay, and partly because Uruguayan society was, already, the most secular in Latin America. Chile's disestablishment was preceded by years of gradual adjustment in the relationship of Church and State, with the main arguments taking a developed form during the presidency of Santa María, after 1883. By 1925, when the formal separation was accomplished by Alessandri's administration, opinion was well prepared and little controversy occurred.

In some of the republics adjustments in the relations of Church and State did not proceed so far as complete disestablishment; in some the Church continues to have structural links with the state—in Peru, for example, and Argentina, Nicaragua, and Costa Rica. With the exception of Peru, it has been those countries most notable for their Catholic fervour which have endured the most contentious problems in the separation of Church and State, a sign, doubtless, of the greater polarization of opinion that has occurred between the Church and the liberal secularists in societies with the strongest surviving traditionalist elements. The first Latin-American disestablishment took place in Colombia in 1853. Juárez's government in Vera Cruz carried out the Mexican separation of 1859, in what proved to be the prelude to the most bitter conflict. It was a characteristic irony that the 1860 laws, which confirmed the Mexican separation, were formally enacted in 'the name of God.' Guatemala's disestablishent was carried out with great rigour as part of the anti-clerical legislation of President Justo Barrios in 1879. It, also, was accompanied by immense hostility between the Catholic and the liberal parties.

It was precisely because the liberals who attacked the position of the Church did so in furtherance of a rival view of human society that hostility and political controversy were so great over ecclesiastical issues, and why the governments tended to retain strong state supervision of the Church even after disestablishment—anticipating the practices of twentieth-century socialist states in Eastern Europe and in the Soviet Union. Again, the need was seen to be greatest where Catholicism retained the strongest hold upn the popular affection. In Colombia under President Tomás Mosquera it was decreed in 1861—eight years after disestablishment—that no member of the clergy could exercise his religious functions without government permission. In Guatemala the state continued to interfere in ecclesiastical appointments despite its formal abandonment of the *patronato* in the Concordat of 1884. El Salvador separated Church and State in 1962, yet most of the anti-clerical legislation which had accumulated over the preceding century remained, including a legal prohibition of monastic orders. But it is once again Mexico which provides the clearest example. Each legislative reduction of the position of the Church was accompanied by legal restrictions upon its social influence and institutional autonomy. Article 123 of the Constitution of 1857 gave the federal government the right to intervene 'in matters of religious worship and outward ecclesiastical forms'.[5] It is instructive that under the French occupation of Mexico, after 1863, the Emperor

[5] For this text of this and other provisions of the Juárez period, see A. Toro, *La Iglesia y el Estado en México, estudio sobre los conflictos entre el clero católico y los gobiernos méxicanos desde la independencia hasta nuestros días*, Mexico City, 1972.

Maximilian, himself a liberal, did not dismantle the anti-clerical code and did not attempt to re-establish the Church.

Control even of the number of church buildings permitted to remain open for worship, and of the numbers of priests to serve them, has also been a feature of Mexican anti-clericalism. Carranza resorted to this in 1916, so did Calles in 1925, and Portes Gil in 1931. The Constitution of 1917, with its strict regulation of religious institutions, its prohibition of ecclesiastical property, its state suervision of the clergy, its requirement of state permission for any new church, and its refusal to allow political parties to have any religious association, was the most advanced of all the attempts to secularize modern society through state regulation of religion. Its enforcement in 1926 led to the most well known of all Latin-American Church and State confrontations—to the suspension of religious services by the Catholic hierarchy from July 1926 to June 1929, and to actual warfare, the rebellion of the *Cristeros*. In Mexico, the determination of anti-clerical politicians that Catholicism should not impede the creation of a progressive society even went, on two occasions, to the extent of trying to set up a rival state church. Juárez had in 1868 proposed that the Episcopal Church of the United States should consecrate a bishop for an independent Mexican national church. And in 1925 Calles supported the so-called Mexican Catholic Apostolic Church—a schismatic enterprise begun at the instigation of Ricardo Treviño and socialist labour organizers who had supported the occupation of the Church of La Soledad in Mexico City. Ten priests joined the Church. Calles, when Governor of Sonora, had sought to replace the Catholic priests he expelled from their parishes with others prepared to set themselves up independently of the official hierarchy. Mexican Catholicism was too well established for such attempts to have more than an ephemeral appeal.

The terms of the relationship of Church and State have usually decided the form that the political involvement of the Catholic Church has taken in Latin America. Yet it is important to notice that the embracing claims of the modern state were not entirely without familiar features. The Spanish and Portuguese colonial systems also made universal claims upon institutions within their own boundaries. The expulsion of the Jesuits in 1767 is explicable largely in the light of the State's exclusive claims, for the Jesuits were the only part of the machinery of Catholicism which had an effective independence of the Council of the Indies. The political clashes of religion and government in the modern period have not been caused by the existence of a state power with universal claims as such, but by the *sort* of social ideology the liberal and then the socialist politicians built into their programmes as essential conditions for their success. Indeed, Latin-American Catholicism has, if anything, a more consistent record as an opponent of the atomistic state—as envisaged by many nineteenth-century liberals—than it has as an opponent of universalist concepts of government. The organic and the corporate state have, in the present century, found much Catholic support in Latin America, and that has not been because of their supposed conservative political character—such a conclusion would not, for example, account for the Church's support of the corporate state under Perón in Argentina or under Velasco in Peru. As Professor Stepan has pointed out his study of Peru, the South American organic state is not to be identified with the established order and sometimes demands quite 'rapid structural change'.[6] The difficulty lay in the discontinuity of the Independence period. With the removal of the Crown no universalist concept of sovereignty came to take its place which was satisfactorily accommodated with the surviving Hispanic insistence that political power requires a moral basis for its legitimation. The rational schemes of the Enlightenment—the sovereignty of the people, the checks and balances, and so forth—were quite inadequate as political myths, as cohesives of the new order. It is not surprising that, in this situation, the Church should tend to ally itself to what remained of Hispanic traditionalism, and, because it appeared as the most authentic and stable embodiment of Hispanic virture, to the landed society whose conservative politics put the Church at variance with the emergent liberalism of the urban élites.

At this point some mention must be made of Ivan Vallier's distinguished analysis of the relationship of Catholicism and political power in Latin America. In his view, it has been the Church's attempt to preserve its religious monopoly that has determined the nature of its political involvements: it has needed

---

[6] Alfred Stepan, *The State and Society. Peru in comparative perspective*, Princeton, 1978, p. 34.

to establish itself within the structures of influence. 'Because of the special historical and institutional conditions that prevailed from the time of the conquest in the sixteenth century up to the independence period,' he has written,
the Church had not consistently pursued policies aimed toward building religious solidarity or the deepening of lay spirituality. Consequently, when basic changes occurred in the political sphere, the Church did not possess bases of autonomous religious stength. It could not resist the strategy of realigning itself with political power, and turned energetically to the task of securing both the legal bases of privilege and the support of political elites. In short, political guarantees emerged as the basis of adaptive action which, in turn, set into motion a whole range of traditional forms of behaviour that are still a central part of the political-religious complex in Latin America.[7]

In Vallier's model typology of the development of the motivation there are a number of stages. Most characteristic, earliest in time, and still everywhere present, are those churchmen who seek the creation or presentation of what he calls the 'monopoly church' — the institutional indentification of Catholicism with the aims of political society in a form which is more conventionally described as the 'Christendom' ideal. Then there is the 'political church' — which mostly emerged in the second half of the nineteenth century as the Church, under liberal assault, forged alliances with conservative politics. The 'ghetto church' indicated a withdrawal from a society increasingly given over to alien secularist political influences. Here there was an emphasis on the training of lay groups for social penetration. Next came the 'servant church' — this was the sign of a re-entry into political society through the pursuit of social changes on behalf of the socially deprived. Finally, there is what Vallier calls the 'pastoral church' — this is the Church born of the radical upheavals of the 1960s, and with the inspiration of the Second Conference of Latin-American bishops held at Medellín in 1968. In this stage, the Church is linked to the secular goals of radical politics.[8]

As a typology of ecclesiastical involvement with the political order Vallier's thesis clearly has enormous merits. Where it may require some adjustment is in the attribution of motiva-

[7] Ivan Vallier, *Catholicism, Social Control, and Modernization in Latin America*, Santa Cruz, 1970, p. 7.
[8] For a summary of these stages, see Ivan Vallier's essay in *The Church and Social Change in Latin America*, ed. Henry Landsberger, Notre Dame, 1970, pp. 14–27.

tion. For if the origin of Church and State conflict lay in the exclusive claims of the modern state to be the institutional representation of inherent human values and of the materials of social progress, then the political responses of churchmen have acquired the character not so much of those seeking monopoly influence 'as of those seeking protection for the purpose of survival. The difference is rather more than one of tone and emphasis. The Church was confronted with militants whose alternative social objectives were expressed with great ideological pointedness and whose political vision, if ever accomplished, would create societies—or so churchmen supposed—in which the conditions for religious belief would be drastically reduced. The Church did not enter the business of political influence as part of a mission whose ultimate objective was the preservation of its own monopoly. In the close union of sympathy between the Church and conservative regimes, which have formed the most typical instances of the 'monopoly church' model, the influence of the Church as an institution has usually been very low in fact. It was the avoidance of a state whose doctrinaire materialism would preclude the spirituality of the people from sustaining itself that motivated Church involvement. The liberalism of the nineteenth century was anathema not because it was a harbinger of change, as such, but because of its actual ideology. The Catholic bishops at the end of the eighteenth century had been open enough to the reasoned reforms of the Bourbon Enlightenment. One of the consequences of Independence was that they now had, for the first time, effective access to the world outlook of the Vatican. The secular values for which the Latin-American liberals contended were all condemned by the *Syllabus of Errors* in 1864. Latin-American churchmen had a counter-ideology to the advocates of liberalism around them. Theirs was not a comfortable acceptance of the old order for its own sake. They saw a wide battle around them, for the possession of men's souls. The socialist exponents of *Indigenismo* appealed against the Church of the *Conquistadores* to a pagan, pre-Hispanic social order; theirs was a serious attempt to replace Catholicism with alternative sets of values for the people. The liberals and the later Communists have also had clear and rival alternatives to Catholicism. In this perspective, the Church's involvement with politics became, at times, a matter—as they saw it—of survival. Forever conscious of their institutional weakness, leaders of the Church naturally supported the political groups whose adhesion to the *status quo* appeared less lethal than the reforming ideologies. With some important exceptions, the Latin-American Church has in general had a pragmatic approach to politics, in fact; just as the normal relationship of Church and State, again with some important exceptions—and ones which have tended to set the agenda for entrenched positions on both sides—has been characterized by harmonious and unrecorded coexistence. It is interesting to notice that the existing conservative political order to which the Church has, in many countries, lent its support is not the ideological creation of those who laboured for a traditionalist Catholic society. It is the survival of the society fashioned by the nineteenth-century secularizing liberals; pluralistic, capitalist, and with all the bourgeois freedoms which Catholic leaders once rejected as hazardous to the maintenance of faith.

It is in this sort of perspective that systematic explanations of Catholic political action have to be set. The Latin-American world before Independence represented a single experience of social order, promoted by both Church and Crown, within which the Hispanic inheritance and the Indian subculture existed together. The Church's mission in human society was coextensive with the political order. This 'Christendom' model, as Vallier rightly points out, is still retained in the present thinking of many South American Catholics, in varying degrees of adaptation to contemporary circumstance. This of course involved churchmen in the unconscious sacralizing of all kinds of political forms whose real purposes were far removed from the promotion of a Christian polity. The extent to which the Church's involvement with politics corresponded to the pursuit of influence, in the Vallier sense, and the extent to which it derived from the less ambitious object of survial, may perhaps be calculated by considering the reasons for which the 'Christendom' models have been promoted. One of the difficulties in the application of the first explanation is that the 'Christendom' model has much more typically been promoted by statesmen, in the pursuit of political stability through conciliation of the Catholic masses, then it has by the Catholic hierarchies. This was the case with Diego Portales in Chile

during the 1870s; with Garbriel García Moreno in Ecuador in
the 1860s and 1870s; with Getulio Vargas in Brazil, in the 1930s
and 1940s; with Alvarado Velasco in Peru after 1968; with
Augusto Pinochet in Chile after 1973. President García Moreno's
strongly pro-clerical government of Ecuador, from 1860, in
fact, assembled a state structure whose correspondence to the
'Christendom' ideal, sealed in the Concodat of 1863 and in the
dedication of the nation to the Sacred Heart in 1873, probably
exceeded anything the Church leaders had expected. The rising
tide of *Hispanidad* sentiment, at the start of the twentieth century,
also favoured the idea that Catholicism and national integrity
were related. This was the world of the Uruguayan José Rodó
and of *Ariel:* a world in which a revived Christian order, allied to
classical virtues, was seen as essential to the civilizing of modern
society. It was the intellectual atmosphere which encouraged
the interpretation of Catholicism in new universalist categories,
of comprehensive explanations of culture, of the neo-Thomism
of Jackson de Figueiredo in Brazil. One of the most successful
renewals of the 'Christendom' ideal was actually formed in
Brazil: in the alliance of Cardinal Leme and President Vargas's
Estado Nôvo, declared in 1937. The 1934 Constitution, with its
extensive favours to the Church—financial aid, religious instruction in the schools, the exclusion of divorce—had prepared the way. But Vargas was himself a freethinker. The
'Christendom' features of his regime were promoted for reasons
of national cohesion. Perón's use of the Church in Argentina
was similar, particularly his declaration in 1945 that his new
social policies were inspired by the encyclicals of the Popes, and
his provision of religious instruction in the schools. The symbols
of the 'Christendom' model were the religious parades in the
streets of Buenos Aires—something virtually unknown before
Perón—and it has been truly said that 'within the administration itself, the role of the clergy became an important one'.[9]
Unlike Vargas, Perón was a believing Catholic. So was Velasco
in Peru, another whose social reformism cemented an alliance
with the Church. In all these examples the Church did not
initiate the 'Christendom' pattern; it was the grateful beneficiary.
The 'Christendom' model cannot therefore be seen on all occa-

---

[9] Robert J. Alexander, *Ther Perón Era*, New York, 1951, p. 126.

sions—and perhaps not on most—as the successful accomplishment of ecclesiastical strategy.

Some of the most familiar instances of Catholic backing for conservative political regimes turn out to be evidences of the acceptance, by the ecclesiastical leaders, of a supportive role defined for them by the state. In Argentina, under the dictatorship of Juan Manuel de Rosas, between 1835 and 1852, the Church willingly resorted to a marked political subservience in order to maintain a stability which was preferable, so the bishops believed, to the anti-clericalism of Rivadavia. The Church, the military, and the landed oligarchs stood together under Rosas in a union of interests that historians of Latin America have conventionally taken as the sign not of mutual expediency but of inherent ideological affinity. In 1906, the Chilean conservatives cast themselves as the champions of the Church against radical attempts at disestablishment—just as the conservatives had increasingly, in the nineteenth century, taken upon themselves the defence of ecclesiastical interests against liberal anti-clericalism. The radicals were quick to depict the association of conservatism and Catholicism as one of indelible compatibility; in their propaganda they brought the point to a vivid general interpretation of the nature of Catholicism, and it has stuck, as successful propaganda does, in the collective memory. But the Church's institutional weakness was so great that its responsiveness to political protection was, in fact, quite random. It offered legitimacy to political forces representing various political interests which seemed friendly; and the politicians, for their part, sought out the Church because of its office as keeper of the religiosity of the masses. It was that sentiment which, in the absence of other national links, was in many countries the only link which bound the Indians to the rest of society, and the provinces to the capital. When the Mexican radicals tried to break the Church, precisely because of its social influence, they broke the link also and society came near to dissolution. Hence the bitter legacy of the years after 1910.

In Brazil, after Independence, the clergy gave their support to the Emperor and his political society not because they were inherently given to conservative political beliefs but because the government offered them protection in return for their political subservience. They were willing partners to the arrangement. Most were Freemasons, and, until the mid-century advance of ultramontanism, the clergy were markedly liberal in politics. The force of nationalism has often assisted the Church leaders in their supportive role. In March 1938, the Mexican bishops, still recovering from a decade of militant persecution, publicly supported Cárdenas over the petroleum nationalization crisis. Recent examples are more ambiguous, however, because ecclesiastical support for radical politics has, especially since the Medellín Conference of 1968, come to express individual rather than corporate commitments by Church leaders. And ideological loyalty on a pan-hemispheric basis is replacing older nationalist loyalties among those most sympathetic to Catholic support for radical politics. Nationalism and political reformism were mixed, however, in Cardinal Silva Henríquez's statement to Cuban journalists, following the election of Salvador Allende to the presidency of Chile in 1970, that the Church supported the basic programme of the Marxist *Unidad Popular*. Socialism, he remarked, had 'enomous Christian values which in many ways make it superior to capitalism'.[10] The Church's acceptance of the revolution in Cuba, however, and the conciliatory policies of Mgr Cesare Zacchi, apostolic nuncio in Havana after 1960, perhaps domonstrate more an older tradition of expediency, and of the Vatican's diplomatic realism, than they do any ideological shift of ground by the Church. It was Zacchi who said that Castro was, from the ethical point of view, a Christian. The preparedness of contemporary Catholic radicals in Latin America to embrace the goals of socialism is motivated by ideological conviction and not by expediency, however. It also suggests a renewed essay in 'Christendom' polity—this time as the initiative of Church leaders. In their vision of a just social order, Catholicism and socialism are to stand together against international capitalism and regimes of 'Seguridad Nacional'.

Independent Christian political parties have not achieved much support in Latin America. The reason, again, is to be found partly in the Church's weakness in relation to the intelligentsia and in its long tradition of political dependency. The most successful has been Christian Democracy, with the election

[10] Hugo Latorre Cabal, *The Revolution of the Latin American Church*, Oklahoma, 1978, p. 168.

of Rafael Caldera to the presidency of Venezuela in 1968, and of Eduardo Frei in Chile in 1964. Frei has been the great intellectual advocate of Christian Democracy, and his writings owe much to the thought of the French Catholic theorist, Jacques Maritain, with all its universalizing categories, and to the Latin-American neo-Thomists. His rejection both of liberal capitalism and of Marxist collectivism has affinities with the papal encyclicals, and clears the middle ground, not for a diluted compromise, however, but for a highly ideological model of an ethical, organic state which is nevertheless pluralistic. Frei's Christian democracy, in fact, looks like a version of the 'Christendom' ideal in a particular well-adapted form, disguised beneath its insistence upon social diversity. For its inner life is inspired by a very prescriptive reliance upon exact social principles, and the obligation of the state to educate its citizens into acceptance. The new social polity is to be based firmly in Christian values.[11]

In many countries there has been a long tradition of non-involvement by the Church in party politics, interrupted only by exceptional conditions of national dislocation or ecclesiastical controversy. Non-involvement has been the practice of the Church in Paraguay under Stroessner, and Cuba under Batista: both conservative regimes. In some cases the Vatican has advised the clergy to keep out of politics—as under the terms of the 1937 *modus vivendi* in Ecuador. But it is important to notice that the Church's participation in political organization does not invevitably result in conflict: the cases of Mexico and Colombia, though well known and well documented, are not in fact typical. Peru's long practice of clerical involvement has been peaceful. On two occasions, in 1880 and in 1912, the presidency of the Dominican Republic has actually been held by ecclesiastical dignitaries, and that country has had a peaceful history of Church and State relations. In other places, the state has itself sometimes banned the clergy from participation. This has happened periodically in Guatemala and Mexico.

These variations of practice should not be allowed to obscure some general conclusions which may be adduced about the relations of Church and State in Latin-American history. The terms of the association have been set by the needs of government, by the expanding functions of the modern state. The

---

[11] See Eduardo Frei Montalva, *Sentido y forma de una política*, Santiago, 1951, p. 8.

Church has followed each change with a preparedness to adapt to circumstance where this has not involved assault by hostile political ideology. It has willingly supported the *status quo* when the alternative political forces have regarded its own demise as essential for schemes of social reconstruction. And occasionally, as in the twentieth-century alliances between Catholicism and the corporate state (though these have tended to be ephemeral), it has projected a clear political ideology of its own—only to find that the corporate state, in seeking out its support, has motivations which are not immediately related to Catholic ideals. And despite many characteristics which are obviously derived from peculiarities of Latin-American culture, the salient features in the relations of Church and State have been familiar enough, viewed from a European perspective. When Dwight Morrow arrived in Mexico City in November 1927, as ambassador of the United States, his immediate task was to seek an accommodation between Calles and the Church. In preparation, he had read classic works on the relations of Church and State: Stubbs, Creighton, Acton. It was the right thing to have done.

2

The Liberal Critique of Catholicism

'Anti-clericialism', although it was the word used by contemporaries as well as by subsequent writers, very inadequately describes the extent of the assault made upon Catholic values by nineteenth-century progressives in Latin America. The clergy, certainly, were the object of attack; not because the Church they represented was itself particularly strong, either institutionally or politically—as in European examples of anti-clericalism—but because their role as the guardians of traditional social order seemed to impede the accomplishment of the new society the liberals sought to create. Latin-American anti-Catholicism, therefore, did not involve merely the mechanics of shifting the influence of institutional religion to the periphery of a political order which was, anyway, in the process of change— as was, again, the case in Europe. It was made to stand at the very centre of the definition of social value; it was a symbolical role that it occupied in the liberals' world-picture. Some of the most important features of the emergent modern state in Latin America directly issued out of conflict with the traditional society of which the Church was—or was made to appear— the embodiment.

It is arguable that the result was as unsatisfactory for the state as for the Church. The content and social legitimacy of the new liberal values were often founded upon very insubstantial social and moral diagnoses as a result of exaggerating or misinterpreting the real nature of Catholic commitments in the social and political spheres. And although the attempt to destory the allegiance of the masses to their local priest was not particularly successful—where it has been accomplished, indeed, it owes more to the secularization of urban circumstance than to ordinary ideological subversion—the liberals' changes did tend to take away the culture of the masses and put nothing in its place. The values of liberalism were bourgeois and urban: the Latin-American history of anti-clericalism is the history of an assault by an élite of progressive thinkers upon the only social and ideological cohesive that the peasantry had known how to recognize.

More than fifty years before Max Weber produced his best-known thesis, Latin-American liberals already regarded it as self-evident that Protestantism was more compatible with capitalism than Catholicism. Soaked in the ideas of the British Political Economists, they promoted the notions of self-help individualism, and what they regarded as the capitalist ethic, in direct opposition to their native Catholicism. They looked for the material and moral advances of the Latin-American republics and considered a drastic curtailment of Catholic influence an essential prerequisite. Their version of the relationship between religion and the rise of capitalism contained virtually all the ingredients later to be found in European and North American commentary upon that theme. As in the modifications later made in that classic debate, an analysis of their contentions and assumptions must proceed with considerable caution. The capitalist enterprise to which the Latin-American liberals appealed, for example, was rather different from the vigorously *laissez-faire* version depicted in the Weber thesis. The Iberian inheritance of government paternalism meant that the various economies of the South American republics were subject to much more central scrutiny and control than was usual in Europe or North America in the nineteenth century. Latin-American liberals showed themselves to be much more concerned with the *social* effects of the destruction of the influence of the Church than there were with the economic consequences of capitalism, and they assumed that a measure of central control was necessary for the effective development of their progressive social polity. Paradoxically, furthermore, it was the very economic success of Catholic institutions before Independence which figured in the liberals' anti-clerical demonology.

The Church was attacked for its domination of large areas of economic enterprise, yet this had been achieved—though the liberals do not seem to have been quite aware of the fact—by capitalist means. The Church, and especially the religious orders, had employed both capitalist devices and capitalist attitudes in their landholding and in their industrial activity. It was, indeed, the enormous economic influence of the Jesuits which had contributed to their expulsion by the Crown in 1767. They had extensive rural estates in Peru, Chile, and Mexico, ranches in the area of the River Plate. They introduced irrigation, new crops, and agricultural improvements; and their organization of the market for the sale of agricultural produce disclosed very sophisticated capitalist instincts. The first colonial industries were mostly conducted by the religious orders: the manufacture of lime, medicines, and household furnishings. Their mills and tanneries were, again, linked to highly capitalistic marketing arrangements. At the time of the expulsion, the Jesuits had more in common with the bourgeois elements in society than they did with the traditional world of the landowners and the administrators. The spirit of capitalism was not as foreign to Catholicism as the nineteenth-century liberals liked to argue. As intellectuals, they were too impressed by the rejection of capitalism in classic Iberian theology and not attentive enough to the actual economic conduct of the Church. Spanish Catholic divines had certainly been hostile to those who had tainted Christianity with financial practice, especially the Italians and the Flemings. Writers like Solórzano y Pereira, in the seventeenth century, had combined an appraisal of the economic wealth of the Spanish Colonies with emphatic and explicit rejection of the capitalist spirit.

In the middle years of the nineteenth century, many Latin-American liberals looked to the United States as the exemplar of the progressive virtues derived from the link of capitalist enterprise and political liberty. This was actually quite a novel reversal of things. For at the end of the eighteenth century it was South America, with its urban civilization, its seats of learning, cultured élites, trade and wealth, which seemed so much more advanced than the rural Anglo-Saxon society to the north. To explain the sudden change of fortunes, Latin-American liberals turned upon the social effects of the Catholic faith: the source of the southern hemisphere's stagnation compared with the new vigour to the north. Most influential exponent of this view was the Chilean writer Francisco Bilbao. Exiled in Europe following a blasphemy prosecution in the courts, he published two works in the 1850s which depicted the South American as retarded by the medieval outlook of the Catholic Church, in contrast to the capitalist vitality of North American Protestants—*La America en Peligro* and *El Evangelio Americano*. The United States was a monument to the successful questioning of dogma and obedience; a nation with no established Church and whose religion encouraged reason and individualism. This was a scheme of things repeated time and time again in the writings of the Latin-American anti-clerical liberals. Thus in Argentina, the most successful of the republics in adapting to European and North American Economic development, the link of Protestantism and progress was a central theme in the writings of the liberal politicians and *pensadores:* Sarmiento, Mitre, and Alberdi. Only a radical reduction of the influence of Catholicism, they argued, could prepare the creation of a modern society. In Chile, too, another country where there was a significant amount of foreign influence, advocates of progress connected the advance of the United States with its Protestantism. In the great debate about religious liberty, in the Chilean Congress during 1865, for example, this was the central theme in the main speech of Benjamin Vicuña Mackenna.

Some attempts were actually made to introduce Protestantism as a matter of government policy—in the belief that this would, in itself, hasten social and economic progress. The Liberal President of Ecuador, Vincente Rocafuerte, tried this in the 1830s. It was also attempted by President Guzmán Blanco as part of his extensive campaign of anti-clericalism in Venezuela in the 1870s. Recognizing that the Catholic religiosity of the masses was not easily displaced, he sought to spread Protestantism among the upper social groups and the educated classes. The policy was not successful. Nor was the similar attempt in Mexico, when Obregón and Calles gave their support to Protestant missions and to the YMCA in the hope that this would help to undermine the Catholic loyalty of the peasantry. One of the symptoms of their miscalculation was the *Cristero* rebellion of 1926: to the Catholic insurgents, Calles's favour of Protestantism was clear proof—if that was still needed—that his values were fundamentally alien. The Protestantism of twentieth-century Latin America is not numerically significant enough to be particularly relevant in judging the anti-clericals' contentions. Protestants have certainly been disproportionately successful in commerce and industry—but they hae been, in most cases, foreigners or recent immigrants. It is certainly true, however, that Catholic working people believe that their Protestant co-workers are more successful because their religion encourages sober and ordered habits. 'There is', as Professor Emilio Willems has observed, 'a folklore of economic success attached to Protestantism.'[1]

As if to complement the liberals' diagnosis, Catholic thinkers of the nineteenth century themselves began to represent medieval economic institutions and practices as ideal embodiments of Catholic faith and order. In Latin America the romanticizing of the medieval guild—the *gremio*—and the idea that the Protestant Reformation had destroyed a just social and economic order, were well developed by the middle of the century, anticipating, in fact, the Pre-Raphaelite idealizations of the culture and crafts of the medieval world made in England. Catholic thinkers in Latin America were heirs to the undoubted medievalism of Iberian Thomism and to a surviving body of moral theology which was deeply antipathetic to departures from medieval ideas about usury. When anti-clericals like Bilbao denounced the Church for perpetuating the Spain of feudal times—'the body and soul of Catholicism'[2]—there was some justification for his opinion in contemporary Catholic writings. In the first decades of the twentieth century, Latin-American Catholics tended to parallel their European co-religionists in criticizing Protestantism for its association with capitalism—a theme found not only in Papal encyclicals but also in Catholic appraisals of the corporate state, whose institutions were so readily made to correspond to idealized medieval models. By the 1930s, for example, the writings of the Brazilian Fr Leonel Franca became influential statements of this position. Some of his writings were actually a reply to Eduardo Carlos Pirena, a contemporary exponent of the doctrine that Protestantism encouraged social progress.

Hostility to the capitalist ethos became a major part of the Catholics' rejection of nineteenth-century liberalism—especially as, through positivism and its variants, liberalism developed sophisticated intellectual and moral alternatives to Catholic universal explanations of culture. Catholic thinkers were not

[1] Emilio Willems, *Followers of the New Faith. Culture Changes and the Rise of Protestantism in Brazil and Chile*, Vanderbilt, 1967, p. 198.
[2] Francisco Bilbao, *La sociabilidada chilena*, Santiago, 1941, p. 76.

alone in finding the materialism of classical liberalism in Latin America unsatisfactory, but reversions to traditional Hispanic culture, or to non-materialistic social visions, like Krausism and Arielism, did not involve a revival of Catholic ideals. Many versions of the new thought were still deeply antipathetic to Catholicism. A few leading figures, it is true, did once again espouse the Catholic faith: Luis Alberto de Herrera in Uruguay, José Vasconcelos in Mexico, José de la Riva Agüero in Peru. They joined themselves to the rivived Catholic intellectualism of the early twentieth century, with its re-emphasis of social paternalism and its renewed rejection of the atomism and individualism of capitalism. The leaders of the new school were often very militant—men like Laureano Gómez in Colombia in the 1920s, and Manuel Gálvez in Argentina. Ideas like theirs easily translated into defence of the corporate state, and drew a direct inspiration from developing Iberian fascism. Thus Agüero supported an ideological union of Catholicism and fascism; he denounced American capitalism, and looked for the return of a medieval harmony destroyed at the Reformation. Perhaps equally well known and influential as a theorist of right-wing Catholic nationalism, Fr Julio Meinvielle, in Argentina, began his interpretation of the values of Christendom with the Protestant Reformation also. The nineteenth-century liberals were the direct descendants of the reformers, he argued; the pre-capitalist social order could only be restored by the action of Catholic social teachings. 'En la década del treinta sentó las bases de una vasta interpretación católico-tradicionalista del nacionalismo,' Professor Cristian Buchrucker has written 'problamente el edificio doctrinario más completo que pueda encontrarse en la derecha argentina. . . . Su influencia en las primeras y aún en las más recientes generaciones del nacionalismo doctrinario ha sido muy notable.'[3]

Catholic opponents of materialism and capitalism were not the only enemies of liberalism who sought the restoration of a preceding order of economic relationships. In the Marxism of

[3] *Criterio*, No. 1829–30, 23 February 1980 (Buenos Aires), 'La visión de la historia contemporánea en cuatro nacionalistas de los anos 30', by Cristian Buchrucker. (In the thirties the essentials of a large interpretation of nationalistic traditionalist Catholicism were felt, probably a doctrinal structure more systematic than it is possible to encounter on the Argentine Right. . . . Its influence on the first and even on more recent generations of nationalistic doctrine has been very considerable).

Mariátegui and the *Aprista* thinkers of Peru, in the art and literature of the Mexican Revolution after 1910, and in the Bolivian intellectual socialists of the 1920s, the ideals of *Indigenismo* included the rehabilitation of Pre-Conquest economic and social values and a complete rejection of nineteenth-century captalist individualism. In that, if in little else, Catholicism and early Latin-American Marxism shared some common ground. They were not to find it again until the *socialcristianismo* of the present times. The Church, in fact, had historically operated as the preserver of rural social values, locked up in the prevalent syncretism of Catholicism and Indian beliefs and cultic practices. Against the nineteenth-century liberals, the parish priests worked quite consciously to retain traditional rural culture. But this meant the survival of the fatalism of Indian society, and gave substance to the liberals' contention that Catholicism operated against progress. Nineteenth-century attempts at the redistribution of ecclesiastical land, especially in the Mexican *Ley Lerdo* of 1856, were in large part inspired by the liberals' belief that a rural middle class would awaken the *campesinos* from their social resignation and wrench them from the control of the priests. As it happened, the land reforms were not a capitalist revolution. It was the existing landowners, the *hacendados*, who gained—at the expense of the Indian *ejidos*. But, as Dr Brading has shown, by the start of the present century, 'many of the *hacendados* were as much in debt to the banks as they had once been to the Church',[4] and that, at least, must have furthered some aspects of the capitalist nexus and so fulfilled the liberals' expectations. The Indian peasants, however, remained outside capitalist society until their drift to the cities in the twentieth century. In them, the Church found an authentic medieval, pre-capitalist world of values. But *Indigenismo* was not a strong feature in Catholic apologetics, however much the local priests might operate to protect traditional society. For it was alien to the Hispanicism of Catholic theology in Latin America; its version of genuine medievalism was not what the Catholic opponents of capitalism had in mind.

---

[4] David Brading, 'Hacienda profits and tenant farming in the Mexican Bajío, 1700–1860', in Kenneth Duncan and Ian Rutledge, eds, *Land and Labour in Latin America. Essays on the the Development of Agrarian Capitalism in the Nineteenth and Twentieth Centuries*, Cambridge, 1977, p. 54.

The reappearance of the anti-capitalist tradition of Latin-American Catholicism within recent radical Christian thinking is not restricted to the school of 'Liberation Theology' nor to those who consciously seek to represent a Christian understanding of social order with Marxist analytical apparatus. It has a wider currency with Catholic advocates of change. Nor is it found only among the clergy. Eduardo Frei's Christian Democracy is as opposed to capitalism as it is to Marxist collectivism, in a balance of opposites notable for having itself a stongly universalist ideology which, even though Christian Democrat parties are not tied to the Church, is very distinctly Catholic in atmosphere. And Peru under General Juan Velasco Alvarado, after the left-wing military *coup* of 1968, furnishes an example of Marxist-orientated political forces, with the support of the Catholic Church, adopting an anti-capitalism which is clearly of pre-Marxist Catholic pedigree. Critics of the Latin-American Church, contemporary successors of the anti-clerical tradition, are as scornful of the modern rejection of capitalism by Catholic apologists as their predecessors were, but for rather different reasons. They see it as a false radicalism, the means by which the Church seeks to further its deeply unprogressive view of man and society. Juan Rosales has written: 'El social-cristianismo aparecerá, aquí y allá, por su lenguaje "anti-capitalisata", sus arengas moralizantes, sus aspiraciones a modificar los aspectos hirientes de la sociedad, como un movimiento de renovación y avance; pero se trata de una ilusión, en todo caso de uno de esas buenas intenciones de que está empedrado el camino del infierno . . .'[5]

The nineteenth-centry ideology of anti-clericalism did not have popular roots. Such opposition as existed to the influence of the clergy among the rural peasants and the urban artisans expressed antipathy towards the less than perfect morals of some of the priests. The clergy, that is to say, were criticized for not being Christian enough; for not faithfully representing Catholic values. But the educated élites who promoted anti-

[5] Juan Rosales, *Los Cristianos, los Marxistas y la Revolución*, Buenos Aires, 1970, p. 236. (Social Christianity will appear, here and there, through the language of 'anti-capitalism', with its moralistic rhetoric, its aspirations to modify the hurtful aspects of society, with a movement of reform and progress; but it is all about an illusion, in any case one of the good intentions with which the way to the inferno is paved.)

clericalism rejected the values themselves. Some liberals, indeed, went on to contrast them with 'real' Christianity—which they defined in coldly ethicist language, worlds removed from the folk religion of the masses. The liberals acquired most of their ideas from European, and especially from Spanish and French, rationalism, and from British Philosophical Radicalism. Young men from the upper classes completed their education with European travel, and there they absorbed at first hand the intellectual atmosphere of liberalism. Many of the works formally banned by the Inquisition in the years before Independence were anyway familiar enough, through privately printed editions and smuggled copies brought home by travellers. In the first half of the nineteenth century, anticlericalism gained much from a knowledge of the works of Lamennais—whose insistence on religious democracy greatly influenced Bilbao. Similarly, the works of Saint Simon reinforced the inclination to associate Catholicism with social stagnation and reactionary politics, especially as they influenced Esteban Echeverría, and also the whole group of Argentinian intellectuals whose opposition to the conservative dictatorship of Juan Manuel Rosas characterized the so-called 'Generation of 1837'. Sarmiento also drew upon European rationalism in his opposition to ecclesiastical traditionalism. To him, Latin America was a bulwark of ignorance, medievalism, of the lack of freedom of thought.

The impact of British Philosophical Radicalism was of equal importance. To the European abstract freedoms, it added the individualism and progressivism of Political Economy. The resulting mixture regarded Catholicism as not only inhibiting the intellect and restricting free inquiry but as impeding material and social advance. The formative influences in the Latin-American absorption of this outlook were, of course, Adam Smith—whose *Wealth of Nations* achieved considerable popularity among the intellectuals, following the Spanish translation of Carlos Martínez de Irujo in 1792—and Jeremy Bentham. The exact nature of Bentham's influence is difficult to determine because, as in England itself, 'Benthamism' came to be an extremely loose term employed to describe virtually any philosophical or radical objection to existing society. As in England also, however, the economic doctrines of the Political Economists appealed to the intelligentsia in general, whatever

their political identities. Conservatives as well as liberals became convinced of the value of the new science to society. Thus
Lucas Alamán, the Mexican conservative who, up to his death
in 1853, sought a monarchical restoration, was a convinced
advocate of capitalist development and of Political Economy.
Bolívar and Santander admired Bentham's works, though they
knew him mostly only as a codifier of law. Bernardino Rivadavia
had Bentham's principles taught in 1821, at the new university
of Buenos Aires. As First Minister of Governor Rodríguez, in
1822, he carried out the regulation of the Argentinian monastic
houses and other anti-clerical reforms which owned much to
what he considered to be Bentham's reasoned explanation of
religious phenomena. José María Luis Mora, the great Mexican
anti-clerical *pensador* and politician, also regarded himself as a
disciple of Bentham, seeking to apply his reformist spirit to
ecclesiastical institutions. Mora believed that a progressive
society could create nearly perfect men, once the control of the
Church over men's lives had been broken. Men needed to
recognize individual interest and to give up their dependence
upon religious authority. In 1831 he wrote a work on ecclesiastical property favouring its reduction and secularization—a
reform which he rightly supposed corresponded to the recommendations of English Philosophical Radicalism—a work which
became one of the major intellectual justifications of subsequent
Mexican anti-clericalism. Andrés Bello, a Venezuelan whose
political life was largely expended in England, where he was the
agent of a number of Latin-American revolutionary movements, and then in Chile, had been greatly influenced by both
Bentham and James Mill, whom he had met in London. His
advocacy of liberal education in Chile was seen as being in direct
opposition to the Catholic values and existing practice. In
Central America, José Cecilio del Valle infused Bentham's
ideas into his political conservatism, giving his belief in ecclesiastical reform a basis in Political Economy. Fernández de
Lizardi, in Mexico, was another prominent Benthamite: he
favoured not only a reduction of the Church's social influence
but also wanted the clergy to forced by law to teach the principles
of civil liberty and free enquiry. These thinkers and politicians
were mostly active in the first half of the century, but as late as
1867 Ezequiel Rojas attempted to get the Colombian senate to

require Bentham's ideas to be taught in the nation's schools as a matter of obligation. It is curious that Bentham's influence on Church reform, which in England was so indirect and diffuse, should in Latin America have acquired such importance. Latin-American liberalism was less pragmatic, less based in popular politics, and more the formulation of intellectuals, than England's. Yet even Bentham's anti-Christian polemicism, disguised within a nearly respectable Deism, was better known in Latin America than its English reputation would suggest as likely. Bilbao's central contention that Christianity represents the great moral teaching of Christ, and is a progressive force for mankind, but that the Church represents an ecclesistical tyranny, a reactionary direction engineered by Saint Paul, itself derives from an anonymous work published by Bentham in 1823.[6]

To this original deposit of intellectual anti-clericalism, Positivism added a new secular idealism in the second half of the nineteenth century. The intellectual vogue of Positivism was much stronger in Latin America than in Europe or North America. Initially it reinforced the existing orthodoxy of Political Economy. The *científicos* expressed a materialist view of society which, just as much as the preceding Political Economy, required the destruction of the influence of the Church. The intellectual life of the Díaz period, in Mexico, was dominated by them—by men like Francisco Bulnes, José Yves Limantour, and Justo Serra—men whose anti-clericalism lacked the crude anti-ecclesiastical vituperation of the earlier part of the century, but who, nevertheless, looked to educational and social change to eradicate the influence of Catholicism. Some were attracted to quasi-Comptian alternatives. In Brazil, Miguel Lemos and Raimundo Teixeirra Mendes founded the *Templo da Humanidade*—a Postivist church—in 1881. Benjamin Constant, when Minister of education in Brazil after 1889, followed up the constitutional separation of Church and State by seeking a thorough reform of national education. The new scheme was intended to reduce religious influence and propagate scientific

---

[6] Bilbao, *La sociabilidad chilena*, p. 82. See Gamaliel Smith [Bentham], *Not Paul, but Jesus*, London, 1823, p. 73, where Saint Paul's object was described as the securing of 'an empire over the minds of his converts, and, by that means, the power and opulence to which he aspired'.

attitudes to society and morality. Luis Pereira Barreto provided Positivist materials for just such an enterprise. In fact the spread of secular alternatives to religious teaching, which so marked educational advance in the different republics towards the end of the nineteenth century, itself provoked the opposition of the Church, making Catholicism, once again, appear as the enemy of all reasoned inquiry. And that, in turn, heightened the determination of the reformers. The most crucial moment in the attempt to destory religious influence through education came in the Mexican Constitution in 1917, with its prohibition of religious instruction. In 1934, Article 3 was amended to read— 'Education imparted by the State shall be socialistic, and in addition to excluding all religious doctrine shall combat fanaticism and prejudices, for which purpose the school shall organize its teachings and activities in a manner to permit the creation of a rational and exact concept of the universe and social life in the mind of the youth.' In some of the Mexican states, teachers were required to make an 'Ideological Declaration' to oppose religion. Atheist textbooks were provided, and so was sex education—a deliberate affront to Catholic faith and morals. In the resulting popular rejection of atheist education a hundred schoolteachers were assassinated in three years. In February 1936, Cárdenas recognized the force of Catholic religiosity and withdrew the State from the direct attempt to educate the masses out of their beliefs—'No hay propósito de atacar el sentimiento religioso, ni debilitar el cariño, ni la veneración de los hijos a sus padres y solamente se indican como factores que deben combatirse el fanatismo y la superstición . . .'[7]

Just as in England, the orthodoxy of Political Economy came under attack in the later decades of the nineteenth century from those who sought a greater collective responsibility for social change. The gradual abandonment of *laissez-faire* ideology by the intelligentsia was followed by the adoption of several philosophical positions which have the common theme of a greater role for the state, and a renewed emphasis on the cultural and moral basis of social order. The influences were seen in develop-

---

[7] Roberto Blanco Moheno, *Tata Lazaro. Vida, obra y muerte de Cárdenas*, Mexico, 1972, p. 385. (There is no intention of attacking religious sentiment, nor to weaken the love or the respect of children for their parents, but only to indicate factors which combat fanaticism and superstition.)

ments within Positivism, and in Krausism and Arielism, in the revival of Hispanicism, and, inside the Catholic Church, in the Latin American adoption of the social idealism of the Papal Encyclicals after Leo XIII's *Rerum Novarum* (1891). But the new rejection of materialism and individualism, and the insistence upon the need for a universalist basis for social morality, was established in a rigorous humanism and a secular ethicism which was as much at variance with Catholicism as the older liberalism of the first half of the century. It was precisely because Latin American Catholicism was itself so universalist—so faithful in its Iberian Thomism—that it lacked the pragmatism to accommodate atomistic philosophical outlooks like Political Economy. The new secular universalism was no better: it was a direct rival. It became, indeed, the new vehicle of anti-clericalism. Krausist ideas inspired the followers of Madero and the Mexican Revolution of 1910; they influenced the militant secularism of Batlle in Uruguay. In contrast to the integrated explanations of culture which characterized the successors of utilitarianism, Catholicism still appeared superstitious and obscurantist, with its baroque Christs and its folk devotions. Worse: to many who sought a revival of Hispanic ideals, the Catholic religion appeared as a built-in defect which required elimination in order to render the main cultural tradition acceptable. The superstitious aspect of popular Catholicism has always figured heavily in Latin-American anti-clerical literature, and the secularists of the new idealism produced some classic examples.[8] The thought of the Mexican Justo Serra Méndez shows the sort of horror of Catholic superstition experienced by the educated objectors to the Church. At a more popular level there were itinerant lecturers and preachers. Juan B. Canut is a good example: he propagated a vehement anti-Catholicism in Chile. Canut was a Jesuit who had left the Order and become a Protestant in 1878. His attack upon Catholicism was extremely bitter and very colourful, upholding a simple Biblicism and a religion for independent men—who could stand upright in Christian truth without the need for the priest-craft of Rome and its superstitious machinery of control. After

[8] See Guillermo Dellhora, *La Iglesia Católica ante la Crítica en el Pensamiento y en el Arte*, Mexico, 1929. This official government publication, intended as propaganda against the Church, consists of extracts from anti-clerical sources.

re-conversions, first back to Catholicism and then, finally, to Protestantism, he died in 1896. This sort of anti-Catholicism is at once recognizable to students of British and North American religious history of the nineteenth century. Canut is the Latin-American equivalent of Fr Gavazzi or Fr Chiniquy.

The Catholic Church, then, continued to be regarded by secular *pensadores* as a survival from the feudal order, a pillar of illiberal politics and reactionary social groups, and an impediment to progressive change. When contractors arrived from the United States to begin the construction of the Panama canal, in 1903, they first began a campaign of sanitary reform, to remove health hazards in the area. Among more obviously decisive measures, they removed holy water from the receptacles at church doors: the breeding-place of mosquitoes. Nothing so exemplifies, as this small action, the notion that Catholic practices were a hindrance to science, enlightenment, and modern society. Those working for change required the defeat of the Church by real assault. It would not merely wither away beneath the sun of reason, for it was protected by the superstitious awe of the peasantry: its roots needed to be dug out. It is this militancy of the Latin-American anti-Catholic tradition that accounts for the sacrilege which accompanied the victories of the secularists in Mexico—the desecration of churches by General Pancho Villa in 1913, the smashing of religious statues and the abuse of the Sacrament by Federal soldiers fighting the *Cristeros* in 1927. It made even more remarkable Zapata's defence of Catholicism in 1916, especially as his own religious position was decidedly liberal. He had a sense for the values of the rural society he represented. The Mexican Revolution, he declared, was basically anti-feudal, not anti-religious or anti-clerical. Persecution of the Church, he added, would only 'awaken more vividly the superstitions'.[9] These were not the sort of distinctions the anti-clerical militants were accustomed to making.

The idea that Catholicism, unlike Protestantism, encouraged a low moral sense was a central theme in the anti-clerical tradition. It had clear social implications—not only for improving the quality of family life but also for creating a com-

    [9] Robert P. Millon, *Zapata. The Ideology of a Peasant Revolutionary*, New York, 1969, p. 73.

munity of reasoned moral order, the sort of thing Latin-American reformers tended to assume prevailed in Protestant countries. It was often said that Catholicism was more concerned with devotional spirituality than it was with moral behaviour. Foreign observers made the point frequently. In 1912, for example, two Protestant missionaries, George Allan and Charles Wilson, both New Zealanders, were journeying through Bolivia, only to be brought to a halt when their horse fodder was stolen. An Indian was accused. He denied the charge very self-righteously, on the ground that being a pagan, and not a Catholic, he did not steal 'It was', as the recorder of the incident remarked, 'a sad commentary' on the fact that the prevalent form of Christianity 'had no moral or ethical content at all'.[10] Now that is, perhaps, rather an interested perspective. But the same point was made by James Bryce in his account of South American travels, published in 1912. Bryce was careful to explain that his observations concerned qualities of Spanish-American Catholicism— not the very different Catholic life of France or Germany. What he noticed was that the moral standards of the more developed Latin-American countries were quite divorced from religious considerations. Catholicism had been so insistent upon a subservient laity, he believed, taking away their moral freedom, that with the decline of the Church's influence moral influence had gone too. 'This absence of a religious foundation for thought and conduct is a grave misfortune for Latin America,' he observed.[11] It is certainly the case that educated opinion was in general little influenced by distinctly Catholic attitudes, but Bryce rather underestimates the importance of the various secular moral alternatives. These did not, it is true, become effective political or social cohesives, both because they lacked an agreed basis in educated opinion, and because they lacked sanction. They were also hopelessly remote from the social and moral values of the masses. But moral alternatives to Catholicism existed throughout the educated classes, in abundance. The anti-clerical tradition was itself, through all its developments, essentially a *moral* objection to a false ideology. It did, however, share one belief with the masses; the notion that Catholicism

[10] Margarita Allan Hudspith, *Ripening Fruit. A History of the Bolivian Indian Mission*, Harrington Park, New Jersey, 1958, p. 26.
[11] James Bryce, *South America. Observations and Impressions*, London, 1912, p. 583.

was a religion for women, that men could leave the devotional and moral life for women to look after. Bilbao remarked that this was because the Church could dominate women more easily: a classic statement of one of the anti-clericals' leading contentions. But it is also widely evidenced in the practice of Latin-American men. A sociological survey of Catholic attitudes among working people in southern Chile, published in 1963, found that men commonly remarked that the Church was 'for the rich and the women'.[12] It is not a recent phenomenon. In 1877 a Methodist missioner, the Revd William Taylor, described a visit he made to a Catholic Church at Arica, Chile's northern port. Mass was being said, and about sixty women knelt for more than an hour while, as the missioner recorded, 'a few men stood round about gazing at the performance'.[13]

This aspect of Latin-American Catholicism—that it is not manly—has figured largely in the Freemasons' antipathy to the Church. In the history of Latin-American anti-clericalism, Freemasonry has played a prominent part. Most of the liberal intellectuals have been members and so have many politicians in the parties of reform. Outside Brazil, where the nineteenth-century respectability of Freemasonry was such that large numbers of the clergy were themselves members, the link between the Freemasons and the ideology of secularism has been close. In fact, as Mariátegui perceptively noticed, Freemasonry in Latin America became 'a kind of spiritual and political substitute for the Reformation'.[14] It has provided an institutional as well as an ideological continuity within anti-clericalism, acting as a sort of spearhead in the assault upon the claims of Catholicism. Opposition to the religious orders has been especially marked. Indeed, it was Freemasons who turned the famous 'secret convent' of Santa Monica, in Puebla, into a museum of atheism. This place, discovered and disbanded in 1934, was visited and described by Graham Greene during his Mexican travels, seeking to observe the godless state at work.[15]

[12] Émile Pin, *Elementos para una Sociologia del Catolicismo Latinoamericano*, FERES, Bogotá, 1963, p. 65.
[13] G. E. D. Pytches, 'Foreigners and Religious liberty in Chile, 1800–1900', unpublished thesis (written in Santiago, while the author was Anglican Bishop of Chile), Section 2, chapter 7, p. 3.
[14] José Carlos Mariátegui, *Seven Interpretive Essays on Peruvian Reality*, Austin, 1974, p. 146. From 'The Religious Factor' (1928).
[15] Graham Greene, *The Lawless Roads* [1939], London, 1971, p. 202.

During the Juárez attack upon the Church, in 1863, it had been proposed that the convent should be demolished and the site turned into a gasworks. But it managed to survive, in complete isolation from the world—though situated in the centre of the city—until the Freemasons got it in 1934.

Throughout the modern period of Latin-American history there has been a steady insistence by anti-clericals that their quarrel is not with Christianity but with the Catholic Church. Sometimes the claim has been made for reasons only of expediency, by politicians seeking to change the nature of society who nevertheless thought it unrealistic to upset the religiosity of the masses. Ignacio Ramírez, the Minister of Justice and Public Instruction under Juárez—the man who carried out most of the anti-clerical reforms of the later 1850s in Mexico—was almost certainly an atheist. But he found it necessary to declare himself a friend of genuine religion, as he put it. Francisco Mújica, chief author of the anti-Catholic articles in the Mexican constitution of 1917, was probably also an atheist, yet he, too, denounced the priests for perverting true Christianity rather than for holding religious opinions as such. This deference to the deeply entrenched Catholicism of the masses is found at the other end of the political spectrum too. Conservative dictators with dubious religious belief have nevertheless found it politically helpful to act as public defenders of Catholicism—where they have seen it as a valued ingredient of national sentiment. President Getulio Vargas of Brazil was a freethinker, but he carefully defended the Catholic faith in public. His sons, however, bore the signs of his real antipathy to Catholicism: he called on Luther and another, who subsequently changed his name, Calvin.

Probably most of those who claimed to approve of 'real' Christianity, rather than Catholic superstition, as they put it, were genuine. Their bitterness towards the Catholic Church was actually heightened by the conviction that it had betrayed the true purposes of Christ. This, they variously identified; but it always resembled a sort of ethicist religion of humanity with a Deistical animating spirit. The religious opinions of Echeverría and Rivadavia, in Argentina, were certainly like that. Both regarded Christianity, when properly understood, as a force for progress and civilization, the moral basis for social development. Similarly, Bilbao, in Chile, saw Christianity as a liberating vision for humanity, if it could be released from the control of the priests. His own depths of spiritual understanding were actually disclosed in the serenely moving account of the life of Santa Rosa of Lima, which he wrote when exiled in Peru, and published there in 1852.

Politicians in the throes of legislating against the Church were nevertheless perfectly sincere in their defence of the spiritual role of the clergy. This was the contention of Gómez Farías and the Mexican reforms of 1833, and of Justo Rufino Barrios and the reforms of the Guatemalan liberals after 1871. During the present century, however, anti-clericalism has become increasingly associated with Marxist and radical socialist critiques of society, and the entire basis of religious belief has come under political attack. This first became clear in Mexico. By the 1930s, the assault upon Catholicism had gone far beyond the external accidents of its social or moral influence. More recent radical Catholicism with its clamours against the conservative regimes, stands in paradoxical contrast. The anti-clericals' arguments have changed hands. It is now those who see themselves as defenders of traditional Catholic values—in the regimes of 'Seguridad Nacional'—who are attacked by some radicalized ecclesiastical authorities. It is now the traditionalists' attempts to undermine the influence of the Church—because of its political radicalism—which have to be carefully distinguished, by them, from assaults upon what they regard as authentic Christianity. This was the situation as represented by Perón when he turned against the Church in 1954. Though not a traditionalist, his regime had come increasingly under the hostile scrutiny of the Church because of its growing totalitarian character. Clearer examples are provided by Stroessner in Paraguay, Romero in El Salvador, Pinochet in Chile, and Videla in Argentina—all of whom have encountered opposition from Catholic priests committed to radical changes. In each case, governments have justified their countermeasures by distinguishing between Catholicism and dissident elements within the official Church structure.

The actual laws against the influence of the Church, imposed by anti-clerical reformers in the years since Independence, had European antecedents. But reforms in northern Europe or

Britain were often the result of a quite broad agreement within
political society that some adjustment of the position of the
Church was required. They disagreed among themselves about
the extent of the reforms, and often about their exact nature; but
the inclination to suppose some change was necessary was often
a feature of those whose political views otherwise differed. In
England, opponents of particular measures of state interference
with religion went to great lengths to represent them as highly
partisan, in their polemical depictions, but this ignored the real
consensus for some reform which existed within political society.
In Latin America, however, where the pragmatism of the English
political tradition was lacking, reform of the Church was frankly
partisan. The atmosphere of accommodation was not evident,
and legislation to curtail ecclesiastical influences became a
symbol of the liberals' defeat of conservative opposition when-
ever they formed an administration. The result was an unstable
history of adjustment. There was not an accumulating wave of
reform: each particular law could be and often was, reversed by
conservatives on return to the control of government. This kept
highly divisive issues alive for decades. It made issues of ecclesiastical reform the very centre of political controversy—and
exaggerated the real influence of religion in society.

There have been three main periods of anti-clerical legislative activity but they do not very neatly separate for analysis.
The first, in the 1820s and 1830s, was inspired by the early
liberal successes in the new republican governments. They
were the first essays in utilitarianism. Typical examples were
the Venezuelan reforms—the concession of religious toleration
in 1834, civil registration in 1836, and the suppression of the
monasteries in 1837. These years saw also the anti-clericalism
of Rocafuerte in Ecuador and Farías in Mexico.

The second period was the 1870s and 1880s: this indicated
the strength of Positivist critiques of traditional society, of the
influence of the *científicos*. In Chile, the 1870s saw the drift of
President Errázuriz to increasing hostility towards the clergy,
causing the departure of the conservatives from the coalition of
1873, and some success for the liberals' campaign to secure 'la
laicización de las instituciones'.[16] This was also the decade of

[16] Jaime Eyzaguirre, *Historia de las instituciones políticas y sociales de Chile*, p. 148.

Guzmán Blanco's reforms in Venezuela which were, according to Lloyd Mecham—whose account of the anti-clerical laws in Latin America remains the best in the English language—'one of the most complete and devastating attacks ever directed against the Catholic Church in Latin America'.[17] In 1873 the cemeteries were secularized, church marriage ceased to be legally valid, state financial support of the Church was terminated, Church schools were abolished, ecclesiastical seminaries were suppressed, and all religious and monastic institutions were closed and their property confiscated. Monasteries and convents were frequently subject to state control in periods of anti-clerical ascendency. As in European anti-Catholic ideology, they most visibly appeared to symbolize the medievalism of the Church, attracting also the alluring prospect of throwing open the monastic cell and revealing the abuses which a vivid popular literature insisted took place within it. In Latin America, furthermore, the religious orders were also much more wealthy than the secular clergy—who were often not too displeased to see the regular orders wound up—and they were subject to foreign authority, which easily made them appear anti-national. But suppressions were often short-lived. In the case of Venezuela, the religious orders were restored and the seminaries were reopened after the overthrow of Guzmán Blanco in 1888. Other laws remained, but were not enforced. In Guatemala, after the close sympathy between Church and State under President Rafael Carrera, anti-clericalism returned with the liberals in 1871. The religious orders were expelled, the ecclesiastical *fuero* was abolished, tithes were ended. In 1873, with the presidency of Justo Barrios, the policy was extended: convents were abolished, cemeteries were secularized, civil marriage was introduced, and the clergy, in an attempt to diminish their social dominance, were forbidden to wear clerical dress in public. In 1879 the Church was deprived of all juridic personality; it could not own property, even the Church buildings. In Uruguay, too, this period was marked by anti-clerical legislation. There was civil registration in 1880, church marriage became illegal in 1885, and state financial aid to the Church was radically diminished. This all prepared, as it turned out, for the first attacks upon the Church of Batlle and his newspaper *El*

[17] J. Lloyd Mecham, *Church and State in Latin America*, p. 107.

Día. In Chile, the 1880s saw a continuation of the earlier anti-clericalism. This was the work of José Manuel Balmaceda, Minister of the Interior. He had been, like so many anti-clericals, a candidate for the priesthood himself, and had studied at the seminary of Santiago before espousing the principles of Philosophical Radicalism.

The third period in which examples of anti-clerical legislation bunch together has less chronological precision. The twentieth-century attacks by the state have been randomly distributed, but it is possible to divide them between the socialist assaults—largely earlier in the century, as in the case of Batlle in Uruguay or Carranza and Calles in Mexico—and the Conservative attacks—as in the case of Médici in Brazil or Romero in El Salvador, which fell later in time. In the first case, the blanket attempts to destory the influence of the Church by legislative controls continued as the usual pattern. In the latter, the Catholic nationalism of the military or conservative dictatorships has not in general allowed this, and controls have been selective and *ad hoc.* The Mexican experience, furthermore, is exceptional for the entire modern period, not only in its ferocity but because it escapes from the chronological model which applies elsewhere. Juárez's vigorous anti-clericalism in the 1850s took place at a time when most of the continent was inactive over the issue—though Colombia, another deeply Catholic society, also had a history of anti-clerical politics in that decade. And in the 1880s, when legislation was proceeding elsewhere, the Mexican Church enjoyed a period of relative repose, in the years of the *Pax Porfiriana.* It is curious that the most Catholic and relgious and most Indian of Latin-American societies—Mexico, Colombia, and Peru—have had such differing religious histories. The first two are clearly comparble, but Peru has had no significant record of anti-clericalism. The Church has supported political regimes of widely varying ideology. It is a warning—as is the difficulty in applying an exact chronological model to anti-clerical legislation—against expressing Latin-American ecclesiastical history in too precise a manner.

Despite the turbulence of Mexico and Colombia, there has been a general decline of anti-clericalism in the present century, itself, no doubt, indicating the successful elimination of much ecclesiastical influence. But this has been brought about much more by the secularization of opinion and values in general, and by the related effects of urbanization, than it has by legislative controls placed upon the Church. In most Latin-American countries, only 10 to 15 per cent of the population actually go to mass. Assailing ecclesiastical organization, in the light of such statistics, is hardly the most productive way of seeking to bring about a decline of religious influence. Religion is established in family and local custom, not in the strength of ecclesiastical apparatus. The social influence of the priest is in the rural areas, which were always the main target of the liberals. But the rural areas are changing rapidly, as the populations move to the cities, and as rural education and the impact of television slowly work to bring new secular values to the *campesinos*.

For the Church, the past history of anti-clericalism has not been particularly damaging. Through a long and close experience of hostile political ideologies, in fact, the Latin-American Church has, if anything, acquired some of the techniques and psychology of survival. The mid-twentieth-century advance of Marxism within the intelligentsia—which traditionalist Catholics see as the contemporary representation of the anti-clericalism of the past—actually encounters a Church which is effectively vaccinated against antipathetic power. As already suggested, it might, indeed, be argued in reverse that the radical Catholics of contemporary *social-cristianismo* are themselves the new anti-clericals, in occupation before the real Marxists get to the door. They use precisely the same rhetoric of vituperation against the social stagnation and the wrong political sympathies of traditional Catholicism as their liberal predecessors did and as current Marxists do.

For the Latin-American republics, the legacy of anti-clericalism is also still discernible. Some writers have seen the preoccupation of nineteenth-century liberalism with its war against the Church as a negative influence—as having given emergent secular politics an insubstantial basis through seeking legitimation in the narrow references of a dispute with the Church. But that is perhaps to ignore the sophistication of the secular ideologies to which the liberals variously appealed: to allow their real understanding of Political Economy, of

Positivism, and of the ethicism that succeeded it, to go un-recognized. For it was, in this sense, not engagement with ecclesiastical power which made secular political ideology an unsatisfactory national cohesive: that resulted from the internal divisions among the educated élites themselves and from their separation from the culture and beliefs of traditional society. The battle with the Church perhaps postponed the closing of that gap, for the emergent parties of change quarrelled with the one institution that linked the urban and the rural worlds.

3

Frontier Religion and Sectarianism

One of the most remarkable features of Latin-American religious history has been the stability of the Catholic Church. Until the entry of Protestantism in the nineteenth century the Catholic Church remained unchallenged and apparently monolithic in its dominance of public religion. Locally integrated with the surviving practices of preceding Indian beliefs, and centrally built into the structures of Spanish and Portuguese colonial administration, Catholicism seemed confident in its role. The Crown carefully controlled immigration to South America, partly in order to preserve the purity of the ruling groups where these were not, anyway, composed of *peninsulares,* partly to guarantee access to mineral wealth, but above all to keep the New World free of heresy. Immigrants had to establish *limpieza de sangre:* an incontrovertible record, for three generations, of freedom from heretical, Islamic, or Jewish elements in the family history. From the earliest years, furthermore, the Crown had intervened to establish the nature of settlement, as the adventurers moved further away from the first conquered territories in the pursuit of precious metals. The Church came directly under the control of government; the Franciscan missions, employed as the primary instrument of advance into the Indian lands, undertook temporal as well as spiritual duties. Stipends of the friars were paid by the government; soldiers were allocated to the missions to guarantee the work of pacifying the Indian converts. In 1543 the Crown fixed a period of ten years for the friars to perform their labours in each place of advance, before they moved on to the next frontier and their original mission was taken over by the civil authorities. It was all very systematic. These arrangements were confirmed in the Ordinances of 1573. In 1583 the religious orders were subordinated to episcopal authority and Catholicism began to settle down, after its first extraordinary achievements, to the stability that marked its course for three centuries. The Jesuits, arriving in Brazil as early as 1549 and in Spanish America in 1568, resumed some of the frontier advance formerly undertaken by the Franciscans—pushing from Quito towards the Amazon in the 1630s, and from the Brazilian coast into the hinterland. Their settlements in Paraguay were more systematic than anything the friars had attempted. At the time of the expulsion of the Jesuits, in 1767, their missions were still very active in many parts of the continent. Around the same time, in 1769, Junipero Serra established the last of the great Franciscan missions: in Upper California. It was, altogether, an extraordinary extension of Christianity—'not since the pagan peoples of northern Europe were brought to the Christian faith in the early Middle Ages has there been a missionary enterprise so vast in its scope.'[1]

The mission was, in the phrase used by Herbert Bolton, a 'Frontier Institution'. Bolton wrote on 1917, under the influence of Frederick Jackson Turner's celebrated application of frontier experience to explain the development of democratic practice in the expansion of the United States.[2] There has been a recent attempt to explore the 'frontier' characteristics in Latin-American history—the 'sequential frontier pushes'[3] that have marked population advance much more typically than the continuous westward wave of settlement which described North American expansion. There are some similarities; phenomena produced by social upheaval and adaptation. But the dissimilarities are also very marked, especially the failure of the South American frontiers to elicit a democratizing ideology. There has been no Jeffersonian myth of idealized rural society in Latin America. Indeed, the liberal intelligentsia of the nineteenth century looked to European social models, which were urban, and this rejection of the native rural South American, characterized in Sarmiento's *Juan Facundo Quiroga*, was a complete one. Spanish-American expansion was essentially urban; its virtues were sophistication and culture—not the backwoods dynamism of the Saxon frontiersmen to the north. The great

[1] William Lytle Schurz, *This New World. The Civilization of Latin America*, London, 1956, p. 250.
[2] Herbert E. Bolton, 'The mission as a frontier institution in the Spanish American Colonies', *American Historical Review*, 23, Oct. 1917.
[3] Alistair Hennessy, *The Frontier in Latin American History*, London, 1978, p. 12.

rural landowners lived in circumstances which perpetuated
the Iberian ideal of the gentleman; the *haciendas* were minia-
ture courts, hierarchical and authoritarian. By the middle of
the sixteenth century, the main cities of Latin America had
already been established, and in succeeding centuries they
remained the centres of national life. When rural parties of
caudillos came to dominate the political life of one of the
republics—as in Argentina under Rosas in the 1830s and
1840s, or in Venezuela with the success of the *pardos* in the
Federal War which ended in 1863—development was not
characterized by democratization. The Brazilian frontiers
were, in contrast, rural rather than urban, but the distinctive
virtues of North American frontier experience did not appear.
In fact the frontiersmen who operated from São Paulo in the
seventeenth and eithteenth centuries were notorious for their
barbarous conduct, earning the special condemnation of the
Papacy for their slave raids upon the Jesuit Reductions in
Paraquay. This sort of general picture of Latin-American
frontier experience, and the systematic nature of the missionary and political establishment of the Catholic Church, on the
whole make it seem unlikely that the religious history of the
hemisphere will yield examples of 'frontier religion' in the
tradition of North American revivalism, or of the democratization of ecclesiastical authority.

Yet the frontier experience of Latin America did produce
other religious phenomena which, whilst not exclusively characteristic of social or cultural change, are often associated with
demographic upheaval and with alterations in social expectations. Apocalyptic messianism and millenarian speculations
were a feature of Latin-American Catholicism in the early
years, though they were successfully contained within the
official Church. They were not the vehicles of radical religious
protest, as so often in Christian history. The only occasion
on which Latin-American Catholicism ever looked like disintegrating into separate units was not marked by religious
heterodoxy: it was early in the nineteenth century, when the
political independence of the new republics went unrecog-
nized by the Vatican and there was a real fear that in order
to provide for their own continuation the national churches
would start appointing their own bishops. The Vatican changed

its policy and the danger passed. Millenarian hopes in Latin America were not a symptom of impending social disintegration either. Spanish and Portuguese colonial society remain strongly traditional at all levels: there were no movements for social change of the appropriate radicalism. This was, perhaps, a result of ther dual culture. The Indians constituted the only element that, over a long period, comprised a depressed layer in which apocalyptic hopes for a transformed terrestrial order might have appeared. But they did not do so, because the fatalism of the Indians inhibited the growth of rising expectations. The white settlers and their successors enjoyed a status and an economic advancement which was greater than they could have achieved in Spain or Portugal. South American millenarianism did not derive from social discontent. Nor was it inspired by a sense of imminent terrestrial catastrophe, another condition typically accompanying its appearance in religious history. It seems, on the contrary, to have flourished in an atmosphere of optimism. The drama of the discovery and occupation of the New World inspired Spanish Catholics with the vision of an earthly paradise created among the Indian peoples—whose innocence seemed as if especially reserved by God for the restoration of a harmonious social order. Professor Humphreys began his Creighton Lecture in 1964 by drawing attention to the comparison, commonly made by thinkers in the period following the Conquest of South America, between corrupted Europe and unspoiled America: an 'unpolluted' land for which Providence held a more perfect future.[4]

The apocalyptic messianism of the early Colonial period actually had its origins in Spain itself. It has often been noticed that the South American frontier was a continuation of the campaign against the Moors in the Iberian peninsula. The combination of religious crusading fervour and the systematic establishment of Catholicism, which had characterized the Reconquest in the peninsula, was extended directly to the colonies. Apocalyptic mysticism also revived in Spain during the reign of Ferdinand and Isabella, and the contemporaneous reform of the religious orders, carried out by Cardinal Cisneros,

[4] R. A. Humphreys, *Tradition and Revolt in Latin America*, London, 1965, p. 1.

prepared them for the effective conveyance of this spiritual enthusiasm to the New World missions. The events of the Conquest were given Biblical significance. Hernán Cortés was seen as a new Moses—at least by Gerónimo de Medieta, a theoretician of the prevalent millenarian speclations. Martín Fernández de Enciso compared the Conquest with the entry of the Jews into the Land of Canaan: South America belonged to the Christian monarchy of Spain just as Joshua had claimed Jericho. Columbus himself had believed that the Orinoco was one of the four rivers of Eden. In this atmosphere of spiritual anticipation of some great new departure in human experience, millennial ideas acquired a ready acceptance—even amongst some of the Indian tribes. The Apapokuva-Guaraní of Brazil had undertaken recurrent migations in the years before the Portuguese arrived, in the search for a perfect land free of evil and suffering. Their religious mythology indicated an inpending destruction of the world, with the salvation only of those who reached this land or repose. The Spanish friars were influenced by Joachimite Spirituality, a surviving tradition of mystical millenarianism which had at times, since the death of Joachim of Fiore in 1202, slid into heresy, but which, among the Franciscans of the New World, became an orthodox adjunct to the growing anticipation of a new Christian order. The Joachimites believed in a Third Age of mankind—a perfect community beyond the coercive requirements of existing human institutions. In its South American form, a number of Franciscans translated the vision into a transformed role of the Spanish monarchy: the divinely appointed agent of the new Kingdom of Christ. Other quasi-mystical ideals moved to the same sort of conclusion. Mendieta expressed a widely held conviction that the Fifth Monarchy was about to be set up in the New World by God, with the Spanish Crown as its guardian. The earth itself was nearing its end. In America, by divine dispensation, human history was about to be brought to its last and most perfect order.

An eschatology of colonialism existed among the Portuguese in Brazil, too. It was of slightly later appearance, no doubt because the Portuguese settlers and officials lacked the crusading and mystical sense of the Spaniards. Their campaign against the Moors had been successfully accomplished two centuries before the discovery of the New World; there was no immediate continuity of the two theatres of military and religious advance as in Spain. But the myth of Sebastianism, beginning in Portugal at the end of the sixteenth century, developed rapidly in the coastal regions and in the backlands of Brazil. It offered the hope of the return to earth of an ideal kingdom in which the poor would be raised up and endless peace would reign. Like the Fifth Monarchy ideals of the Spanish orders, Sebastianism acquired theoretical explanations—in the writings of the Jesuit, Fr Antonio Vieira, in the middle years of the seventeenth century. As it matured among the coastal settlements, this sort of apocalyptic vision coalesced into a belief that the Portuguese Crown would establish universal monarchy with the New World as its centre. In the Brazilian backlands, however, Sebastianism survived to modern times in a form less sympathetic to existing political institutions—as a mixture of religious egalitarianism and Catholic folk spirituality. It had the characteristics of a classic sect, of the Church of the poor. In the later nineteenth century, Sebastianism merged with the other apocalyptic movements which by then thrived in the economically declining parts of the Brazilian North-East.

It would be tempting to identify the ideal communities of the religious orders as examples of millennial thinking, and many have done so. In some parts of the early Colonial frontier the ordinary mission stations of the Franciscans, where they were directed by friars who were particularly influenced by the religious excitements of the time, took on the features of an ideal community. In Mexico, Vasco de Quiroga, subsequently Bishop of Michoácan, planned an ideal settlement of the Indians, in utopian communities, under close religious supervision. In his experiment, the Indians were gathered into collective landholdings, with a prescribed regimen of exercise and work. It was a species of social paternalism, with communal activity and social welfare. But it was, of course, the Jesuit Reductions in Paraguay which have served best as examples of social utopias, seen by some as an anticipation of the socialist ideal communities of Saint Simon or Fourier, and by others, including thinkers of the European Enlightenment like Voltaire, as proofs that human rationality could successfully accomplish social order, that 'intellect could create society according to given plans.'⁵

By the end of the seventeenth century there were thirty Reductions with a combined population of some hundred thousand Guaraní Indians. Each settlement consisted of housing, storage buildings, a school, and a church. Land was held in common, no money was used, and white men were prohibited from entering the communities. Jesuits acted as overseers in each. The Reductions were not, however, examples of primitive socialism. They were an attempt, not at the creation of an ideal society for the Indians, but at preserving them unchanged, uncorrupted by the bad habits of the settlers. The Jesuits had a low estimate of the Indians' potential for education or social improvement. The Reductions certainly came to resemble a 'Jesuit state', but their purpose was educative and economic, not ideal and certainly not millennial. Conflict with the ecclesiastical and colonial hierarchies—like that with Bishop Berardino Cárdenas of Asunción, between 1644 and 1668—were characteristic of the disputes over jurisdiction and wealth that were typical of colonial society. They were not provoked by any peculiar ideological quality in the nature of the Reductions themselves. Far from being examples of primitive agrarian socialism, in fact, the marketing outlets were run on strictly capitalist lines, and this helped to determine the economic organization of each community. The element of social protest, which was so important in later attempts at socialistic ideal communities, was absent. The only protest came from the Jesuits themselves, concerned at the evil consequences of settler life upon the customs of the Indians. Theirs was an exercise in regimented paternalism, on a massive scale. Most of the Reductions endured successfully until the expulsion of the Jesuits in 1767. Despite the efforts of colonial officials to keep them in existence, the Indians thereafter deserted to the cities or reverted to the forests. Thirty years after the departure of the Jesuits the Reductions were in ruins.

The authentic millenarianism of early colonial Catholicism appears to have passed away with the end of frontier expan-

⁵ Magnus Mörner, *The Political and Economic Activities of the Jesuits in the La Plata Region. The Habsburg Era*, Stockholm, 1953, p. 195.

sion. The South American continent was Christianized with astonishing rapidity, and within fifty years was mostly accomplished—leaving only stretches of inaccessible land still in Indian control until the second half of the nineteenth century. The stability of ecclesiastical institutions after the conversion period was not conducive to apocalyptic speculation. In the succeeding century, the ratio of clergy to lay settlers and officials moved decisively in favour of the latter, and the influence of religion became more clearly defined within conventional social models—it no longer seemed as if a new Christian order was impending. It is interesting that in Peru Christianization was accomplished rather more slowly than elsewhere. Indian culture proved more resistant, the missions were less successful in their first dynamic zeal, and Pizzaro's influence during the Conquest lacked the Catholic moral seriousness of Cortés in Mexico or Valdivia in Chile. Peru eventually became a country of very staunch Catholicism—and also one most notable for its syncretism with Indian religious belief and practice. But the fusion took a long time: the emergent Catholic ecclesiastical order did not have the exclusive control of social custom it achieved in Mexico. This may explain, at least in part, the very different history of Church and State relations in two countries which are otherwise comparable.

The Christianization of the few remaining frontiers, towards the end of the nineteenth century, was, as in the early colonial period, sometimes carried out with direct government assistance. In 1891 the Venezuelan State supported the Capuchin mission among the Indians of the Orinoco; in 1902 the Colombian government granted financial aid and tracts of land to Catholic missions in the Indian districts. But the last frontiers did not produce any distinctive religious phenomena: there were no revivals of apocalyptic mysticism. Indeed, in one of the most difficult of the final advances, in Southern Chile, it was Protestantism which gained a foothold, and not a millennial version either. German settlers began to move into Mapuche territory from the 1840s, taking with them an orthodox Lutheranism. In 1844 the Patagonian Missionary Society, with headquarters in Brighton, was founded by Captain Allen Francis Gardiner—who was martyred by the hostile Indians of Tierra del Fuego in 1851. Temuco was established in 1881: a frontier town in which Protestantism made rapid advances, with Baptists and the Pentecostal congregations being particularly successful. The Lutheranism of the German farmers was not expansive and remained an immigrant religion. In the 1890s the Catholic missions to the Mapuche began to extend themselves, with Franciscan schools and centres for adult instruction. The Catholicism of *La Frontera*, like the Protestantism, however, did not bear the fruits of millenarianism, though there is no doubt that the appeal of Protestantism to the Chilean converts on the frontier was closely related to their own sense of uprootedness from traditional society.

What, then, of the religious expression of social protest—of the 'Churches of the disinherited'—as categorized by Ernst Troeltsch and H. Richard Niebuhr? It must initially seem as if the stability of Catholic institutional Christianity has left no room for this religious phenomenon among the poor of Latin America; as if the history of Catholicism there must be composed in terms of negatives, of reasons why the peoples of the sub-culture did not seek to create a Christianity for themselves. Is it, then, to be concluded that the first appearance of religion of the disinherited occurred only in the twentieth century, with the removal of populations to the cities: that it is to be located exclusively in the fringe Protestant sects and the almost millennial appeal of radical politics?

Latin America does, however, have a continuous and consistent experience of 'Churches of the disinherited', but it has been too familiar to be recognized as such. It has stared into the face of virtually every parish priest since the first Christianization of the continent. For the religion of the disinherited is the popular cultic faith of the ordinary Catholicism of the rural areas, carried, in the present century, into the expanding towns. It is the syncretism of Catholicism and Indian religious practices: a permanent social protest against cultural assimilation of the *Hispanidad* values of the Church of the white men who have run the public life of the continent since the Conquest. One of the most useful contributions which recent radical theology has made to an understanding of Latin-American religious experience lies precisely in its recognition, if sometimes for somewhat doctrinaire reasons, that popular religion, for so long regarded with suspicion by the ecclesiastical hierarchies because of its pagan associations, is in fact the authentic spirituality of the exploited and the dispossessed. *Religiosidad Popular* has been almost unchanged for centuries, for it conveys the social values of a people who have been resistant to change. Here is the judgement of Gustavo Gutiérrez, the Peruvian theologian who has become the most distinguished of the advocates of Liberation Theology—whose methods of analysis, often informed by Marxism, have correctly identified the true nature of popular religion.

El pueblo latinoamericano es un pueblo cristiano sí, pero también es un pueblo explotado. En ese doble carácter están las ambivalencias de la religiosidad popular, pero también sus potencialidades liberadoras. No es posible omitir recordar que las clases dominantes, opresoras de ese pueblo, usan lo cristiano parajustificar sus privilegios, pero no es posible olvidar tampoco que en las expresiones populares de la fe se revela el sufrimiento de un pueblo sojuzgado: hay en ellas una resistencia y una protesta contra la dominación que se ejerce sobre las clases populares, así como una vigorosa manifestación de esperanza en el Dios de la Biblia.[6]

There has been a great amount of interest in popular religiosity—folk religion—in Latin-American Christian thinking in recent years, and a considerable literature is being produced, though none of it in English. The second general conference of bishops, held at Medellín, Colombia, in 1968, both encouraged further study of the phenomenon and also advised that it be evaluated not in terms of westernized bourgeois academic categories but as the authentic product of the proletariat: 'Al enjuiciar la religiosidad popular no podemos partir de una interpretación cultural occidentalizada, propria de las clases

---

[6] Gustavo Gutierrez, 'Sobre el Documento de Consulta Para Puebla' in *La Iglesia de America Latina de Medellín a Puebla, Dossier IDOC—Chile America*, 1978, 43-44-45 (Junio-Julio), p. 89. (The Latin-American people are certainly a Christian people, but they are also an exploited people. In their double character are the ambivalences of popular religion, but also its potential for liberation. It is not possible to forget that the dominant classes, the oppressors of the people, use Christianity to justify their privileges, nor is it possible to forget that the popular expressions of the faith reveal the sufferings of a subjugated people: there is in it a resistance and a protest against the domination that is exercised against the popular classes, as well as a vigorous manifestation of hope in the God of the Bible.)

media y alta urbanas, sino del significado que esa religiosidad tiene en el contexto de la subcultura de los grupos rurales y urbanos marginados.'[7] The subculture, of course, had been there since the beginning of the Colonial period. Indeed, the Spaniards themselves inherited preceding Indian subcultures, each with their own surviving religious practices, because the extension of the great Indian empires before them—the Incas, the Aztecs—had only imperfectly assimilated the peoples they had subjugated. The Franciscan missions suppressed the public expression of the native religions and removed their priests. But the influence of the Church was thinly spread across the vast territories of the Conquest, and in each place the existing cults continued alongside the official Church, a condition of things long recognized as one of the leading features of Latin-American Catholicism. This is the land of the 'idol behind the altar'. Syncretisms of Catholicism and rural pagan cults are familiar enough developments in Spanish and other European experience. But in South America the resistance of the Indians to cultural assimilation lodged the surviving religious beliefs into a partially hidden but permanent place in family and communal custom, 'la Iglesia ha de encarnarse en la cultura de los pueblos.'[8]

This, then, was the real 'Church of the disinherited'. Mariátegui rightly noticed that 'any study of religious feeling in Spanish America therefore must begin with the cults found by the conquistadores.'[9] This is also why it is so important to notice that for most of the rural and the new urban populations religious values and religious authority are primarily derived not from the institutional Church—not even from the local parish priest, despite the esteem in which he is held—but from the materials of syncretism disclosed within family custom. The approach of the individual to God is conveyed through the externals of Catholic worship, but inwardly it

---

[7] *Segunda Conferencia General Del Episcopado Latinoamericano. Medellín. Septiembre de 1968. Documentos Finales*, sixth edn, Buenos Aires, 1972, p. 95 (6.4). (In our evaluation of popular religion, we may not take as our frame of reference the Westernized cultured interpretation of the middle and upper classes; instead we must judge its meaning in the context of the subcultures of the rural and marginated urban groups.)

[8] CELAM, *Iglesia y Religiosidad Popular en America Latina*, Buenos Aires, 1976, p. 55.

[9] José Carlos Mariátegui, *Seven Interpretive Essays on Peruvian Reality*, p. 125. From 'The Religious Factor' (1928).

comprises a varied texture of ancient beliefs. Latin-American
folk religion is a religion of popular devotions and cultic rites,
whose values are increasingly being recognized as a positive
help to official Catholicism—'La religiosidad popular etonces
y en principio, en lugar de un obstáculo será una condición
favorable a la fe.'[10] The peasantry and the urban poor attend
mass at special junctures of their lives when particular sancti-
fication is required, but they do not look to the Church as the
source of their deepest spiritual values. Ninteenth-century
liberal intellectuals who objected to the Catholic priesthood
because it emphasized formal worship to the exclusion of
social development mistook the real authors of the spritual
modes they sought to change. It was the peasantry who set the
terms of the Church's influence, not the priests. It was they
who expected a religion of awesome indifference to the ways
of change, and who looked to a religion of magic as the
externalization of their ancient folk beliefs. This 'Church of
the disinherited' always exhibited, and still does, immense
local variation. But everywhere the micraculous element is
strong, and only occasionally has the official Church been able
to legitimize it. 'La figuras del santoral eran familiares se
conocían sus milagros y poderes especiales', as Professor
Marciano Barrios Valdes has written of folk Catholicism
in Chile: 'Cada familia y cada individuo tenía uno o varios de
su devoción.'[11] Some recent writers have regarded Latin-
American folk religions as essential embodiments of the
peoples' virtue—'los actos y gestos religiosos populares ex-
presan la fe del pueblo y constituyen a la vez las "palabras"
populares con que esa fe se va transmitiendo.'[12] Inarticulate,
and politically unable to gain access to positions of even

[10] Gerardo T. Farrell *et al.*, *Comentario A La Exhortacion Apostolica De Su Santidad Pablo VI 'Evangelii Nuntiandi'*, Buenos Aires, 1978, p. 278. (Popular religion, actually and in principle, instead of being an obstacle is a condition favourable for the faith.)
[11] Marciano Barrios Valdes, 'La Religiosidad Popular en Chile', in *Historia y Mision. Ponencias, aportes y experiencias del II Encuentro Latinoamericano de Religiosidad Popular, celebrado en Santiago de Chile, mayo 1977*, Santiago, 1977, p. 31. (The Saints in the sacred calendar are familiar and well known for their miracles and special powers. Each family and each individual adheres to one of the devotions.)
[12] Fernando Boasso, *¿Qué es La Pastoral Popular?* Buenos Aires, second edn, 1976, p. 59. (The religious ceremonies and acts of popular religion express the peoples' faith and constitute at the same time the popular 'word' with which the faith is transmitted.)

humble influence, the poor have expressed their social values in a religion of their own.

Of all the cults gathered within popular Catholicism in Latin America it is devotion to the Virgin of Guadalupe that has most consistently expressed the hopes of the disinherited—which has at times revealed almost all the characteristics of apocalyptic mysticism. Hidalgo dedicated the Mexican revolt of 1810 to the Virgin of Guadalupe; standards bearing her dark image were carried by Zapata's Indian followers as they entered Mexico City in 1914, and by the *Cristero* soldiers in the uprising of 1926. The miraculous apparition of the Virgin occurred in 1531, just a few years after the Conquest of Mexico. It was at Tepeyac Hill, to the north of Mexico City—a place venerated by the Indians because of its association with female fertility rites—that the Virgin appeared several times to Juan Diego, a converted Indian. So the new and old religion were joined. 'Los mitos paganos de la maternidad y fecundidad', as Professor Alberto Methol-Ferré has written, 'fueron purificados y transfigurados. La Virgen Mestiza de Guadalupe es como el gran signo de este proceso de evangelización y aculuración de la fe cristiana en el continente.'[13] From among the rocks of the hillside, the Virgin told Diego to gather roses in his cloak and take them to the Bishop of Mexico. The miraculous *serape* bearing its imprint of the Virgin—her Indian features, graceful and dark, framed by a sunburst design—still hangs above the altar in the shrine of Guadalupe, where each day hundreds of Indians come from all over the country to pay their homage. In his study of the social life of a Mexican village, Gregory G. Reck has described the long and excited preparations made each year in honour of the feast day of the Virgin of Guadalupe.[14] And nothing so testifies to the class and cultural separation of the contemporary progressive, urban thought of the Catholic leadership from the values of Catholic folk religion than the Bishop of Cuernavaca's opposition, in 1969, to the construction of a new

[13] Alberto Methol-Ferré, 'Apuntes para una historia de la Religiosidad Popular en America Latina', in *Historia y Mision*, p. 23. (The pagan myths of birth and fertility were purified and transfigured. The mestizo Virgin of Guadalupe was a great sign of this process of evangelization and acculturation of the Christian faith on the continent.)

[14] Gregory G. Reck, *In the Shadow of Tlaloc. Life in a Mexican Village*, London, 1978, p. 37.

basilica at Guadalupe—on the grounds that the money would have been better spent on social projects. Pope John Paul II was rather more sensitive to the values of popular religiosity when he visited Mexico for the Puebla Conference of Latin-American bishops in January 1979. Calling the Mexicans 'the people of God', he placed them under the protection of the Virgin of Guadalupe[15]—at whose shrine he made his own devotions.

The cultural tenacity of *Religiosidad Popular* has almost perfectly served the religious needs of a rural society already noted for its submission to existing conditions—for its lack of aspiration, at least until very recent times, to social improvement. There has simply been no need for the poor to create their own churches at moments of national or regional dislocation. The result has been a very low incidence of rebellion against the official Church. But there are a few examples: they reflect occasions when the poor of particular areas have felt betrayed by the Catholic leadership and have resorted to independent action. The 'Little Holy Cross' movement in the Yucatán in 1850 disclosed signs both of sectarian revivalism and of apocalyptic millenarianism. It was associated with a Mayan uprising. The north-east of Brazil has been a fertile area for religious discontents. The economic hardships following the great drought of 1877 prompted quite an extended series of religious excitements which overflowed the boundaries of official Catholicism. All the classic ingredients were present: economic upheaval, a large itinerant population of displaced workers, a local miracle at the town of Joazeiro, which became a cult centre with a shrine attacting thousands of worshippers, and a leader capable of inspiring the absolute loyalty of the masses. This was Fr Cicero Romão Batista, the parish priest of Joazeiro. His gradual involvement in politics led in 1913 to a sort of military campaign whose popular crusading zeal had enormous appeal. He was excommunicated by the Church. Two other contemporaneous movements also testify to the disturbed social condition of the Brazilian backlands. The rebellions of Canudos in 1897, led by Antonio Conselheiro, and in the Contestado, led by José Maria, had strong millennial characteristics. Both looked to the creation of ideal societies of equality and religious order, both swept up the social discontents of large numbers of those whose loyalty to the Catholic leadership had been broken by the allurement of an earthly paradise. Similar in its way was the schismatic movement of the 'Wooden Cross', formed in the Mexican region of Coalcomán by a group of *Cristero* purists after the defeat of their movement. Disgusted by the acceptance of the compromise with the atheist state made by the Catholic hierarchy in 1929, these men and women regarded the official Church as having apostatized. So they set up their own community, in which there was complete social equality and no priests. Their religion was based upon the Sermon on the Mount, and they expected the imminent return of Christ to the earth.

The Afro-Catholic cults, however, which have flourished among the black populations of the coastal regions of Brazil, Colombia, Venezuela, and Central America and the Caribbean, are also examples of protest against the official Church. Macumba, Xangô, and Candomblé, and the thriving Spiritist sects, are more thoroughgoing black equivalents of the Indians' *Religiosidad Popular*—they are syncretisms of Catholicism and preceding religious beliefs and practices imported from the tribal customs of the African regions, particularly of Angola, whence many of the slaves came. 'Throughout the period of slavery the black gods were forced to hide behind the statue of the Virgin or a Catholic saint,' as Roger Bastide remarked. 'This was the beginning of a marriage between Christianity and the African religions in the course of which, as in all marriages, the two partners would change more or less radically as they adjusted to each other.' [16] And as Professor Emilio Willems has observed, 'nonconformity did not begin with the mergence of Protestantism.' [17]

Yet it is Protestantism that in recent Latin-American religious history has provided the clearest examples of sectarianism, particularly in the urban areas. As is well known, the recent rate of urban growth has been extraordinarily rapid: in

[16] Roger Bastide, *The African Religions of Brazil. Toward a Sociology of the Interpretation of Civilizations* [1960], Baltimore, 1978, p. 260.
[17] Emilo Willems, *Followers of the News Faith, Culture Change and the Rise of Protestantism in Brazil and Chile*, p. 33.

thirty years the share of the population living in urban areas
has increased from 30 per cent to around 60 per cent. It is for
those who migrate to the towns that the conditions of *anomie*
most produce the possibility of religious change. The weakening of traditional social controls, the sense of confusion and
helplessness in the anonymity of city life, the shock to values
sometimes accompanying the adaptation to industrial work,
the absence of familiar community loyalites and of the encompassing paternalism still characteristic of rural employment:
all these conditions favour the growth of acute crises of personal identity for some urban immigrants. But the scale is not
to be exaggerated. Most of those who go to the cities do not
change their patterns of religious practice; most retain
the orthodox, or nominal or folk, Catholicism of their rural
origins. For every person who changes allegiance there are
very many who do not. The consolation of the familar Catholic
worship is a much more typical response to the conditions of
anomie than the exchange of old religious values for new
ones. It is among the next generation of urban dwellers that
change is more likely to occur. But even here there is a need
for very careful assessment. Latin-American urban society is
not yet secularized, at least among the working classes, even
though the rate of church attendance is low. The observance
of some elements of folk religion survives and flourishes, with
families preserving veneration for particularly saints, and with
feast-days continuing to form familiar demarcations in the
domestic calendar. There are signs that the rate of secularization is increasing, with the materialist expectations of better
economic circumstances, with suburban life-style, with the
acquisition of secular ideas through the process of embour-
geoisement, and, for some, the attraction of Marxism. This
last point, also, has to be made with great caution. The
adoption of radical politics may certainly be one of the means
by which the new urban dweller may express his revolt against
the cultural monopoly of the Catholic religion. But the pervasive use of Marxist intellectual rhetoric, and the adoption of
radical social idealism, which have characterized the leadership of Latin-American Catholicism in the last two decades,
while they are certainly unlikely to prove popular with the
ordinary Catholic believer, may well retain within the Church

a significant number of proletarian aspirants to social transformation who might otherwise have regarded the espousal of
Marxism as requiring the rejection of Catholicism. The position is an unstable one, however, and predictions can only be
very tentative. What is clear is that for most of the new urban
populations, the sacred and the secular are not yet so divorced
as they are in the urban societies of the developed world.

The attaction of Protestantism, therefore, is to a minority
of a minority; to a few among the relatively small numbers
whose assimilation to urban society involves a real crisis of
values. But Protestantism is important for introducing an
element of sectarianism into Latin-American Christian history
which scarcely had a continuous existence before. In the
nineteenth century the growth of Protestantism was extremely
slow. It was associated with peripheral social groups and
linked to the existence of foreign nationals in commercial life.
Membership remained limited to a few thousands in each
country, distributed across the leading historic churches—the
Lutherans, Presbyterians, Methodists, Baptists, and Eisco-
palians. Missionaries came mostly from the United States,
and just as the early Colonial Franciscans had seen their
labours as a continuation of the crusade against the Moors in
Spain so the North Americans tended to regard the evangelization of Latin America as an extension of the American
Frontier at just about the time, in the last decades of the
nineteenth century, that the frontier was closing. Hence the
setting-up of unified Protestant congregations, with institutional apparatus originally fashioned for the civilizing of the
old west. As vehicles for social protest in Latin-American
towns, or on the remaining Latin-American frontiers—in
Southern Chile, for example—the historic Protestant denominations were not particularly satisfactory. They were
not the 'churches of the disinherited'; indeed, they were
the churches of new respectability, of thrift and hard work.
Occasionally the 'sect ideal' broke through, in moments
of revivalistic fervour which the North American missioners
found hard to handle. The Methodist temple in the Chilean
port of Valparaíso, for example, was subjected to the disintegrating impact of revivalism in 1909. There were *tomada de
espírito*, speaking in tongues, exultant and ecstatic weep-

ing and dancing. Some had visions. Similar manifestations occurred afterwards in the Methodist congregations of Santiago. The American missioners who controlled both groups regarded the events with distaste, condemned the excesses, and provoked schism. The resulting Pentecostal sect was a classic 'church of the disinherited'. It is, in fact, the twentieth-century growth of the Protestant sects, rather than the Protestant denominations, that has most characteristically served as the means by which the social dislocations of the urban poor have found some religious reconciliation.

Protestantism in Latin America has, in general, served as a protest against the *Hispanidad* values of traditional society, and as a rejection of the influence of the Catholic Church. As such, the Protestant denomination has sometimes achieved a following with small sections of the educated classes, with the aspiring middle sectors. It is interesting that at the present time the characteristically élitist nature of the radical political theology—élitist because of its intellectual indebtedness to the prevalent values of the intelligentsia—has found itself as much at home among some of the leading theologians of the Protestant denominations in Latin America as it has among the Catholics. Both belong to a single world of educated opinion. Rubem Alves and José Míguez Bonino are Protestants. There is a sense in which it may be said that the Protestant denominations are the churches of a rising middle class. But the conclusion requires careful adjustment of perspective: most members of the aspiring middle sector remain Catholics, nominal or practising. Among those who do regard Catholicism as incompatible with their new social consciousness, however, a higher proportion join the Protestant churches than the over-all incidence of Protestantism would otherwise suggest. The historic denominations do also retain a lower-class membership, and they have not, as in North American experience, divided along race lines.

The immigrants from overseas have in some places acted as a stabilizing element in South American Protestantism. Foreign immigration to Argentina, Chile, and southern Brazil, in the later nineteenth and in the twentieth centuries, has assisted the growth of existing middle sectors in society. In the last century and half something like twelve millions arrived, the overwhelming majority from Spain, Italy, and Portugal. At the end of the nineteenth century a quarter of Argentina's population was immigrant, and 80 per cent of them were from Italy and Spain. As in Brazil and Chile, most were Catholics and remained so. But among the Italians, especially, there was a significant defection to Protestantism, and this was supplemented by the smaller immigrations of German Lutherans and English Protestants. There were also some planned immigrations, of groups whose sectarian identity had already been well established in their countries of origin. In 1927 5,000 Mennonites removed themselves from Canada to settle a large track of land, granted to them by the government, in the Gran Chaco of Paraguay. There were communities of Russian Old Believers in Brazil, and Welsh Methodists in Patagonia. Argentina was also the home for Baron Hirsch's colony of Russian Jews. These communities were not expansionist, however. They sought refuge and the preservation of their religious identities—they were not an influence for change in the countries which received them, nor did they become the vehicles of social or other protest by those seeking alternatives to the monopoly of Catholicism.

It was the historic denominations who most profited from the immigrations. But there was also a drawback. Protestantism appeared alien to many Latin Americans because of its early association with North American missions; the influx of Protestant immigants from overseas merely added to the foreign image. This, however, must be set against the increasingly foreign character of the Catholic priesthood in Latin America. As the enormous population growth of the twentieth century overtook the manpower resources of the Church, the ratio of priests to people has radically declined and the size of parishes has increased. Foreign priests have therefore been introduced in large numbers, and at all levels of the Church: some as parish priests, some in the specialized ministries. Many came early in the 1960s, in response to the appeals by Pope John XXIII and Pope Paul VI for more clergy to undertake work in the developing world. In some countries, Brazil for example, or Bolivia and Guatemala, up to a third of the clergy are foreign. This must have assisted the integration of Catholic immigrants but it has not helped to lessen the cultural dislocations associated with the much more important internal migrations of peoples. And in some places it may have aided Protestant conversions.

Of all the Protestant groups it is the Pentecostal churches that have, in the present century, shown the most successful and rapid increase in Latin America. Unlike the historic denominations, these are the true 'churches of the disinherited' for those seeking an alternative either to Catholicism or to the radical secular politics which sometimes serve as an alternative expression of individual disorientation. The label 'Pentecostal' is not a particularly helpful one, because it suggests an affinity with European or African experience of religious revivalism which does not accurately describe the peculiar mixture typical in the Latin-American churches. Certainly the Pentecostal groups reveal classic and familiar manifestations of a common rejection of institutionalized religion; they are egalitarian both in organization and in their interpretation of spirituality. Above all, they are true sects. 'The Pentecostal sects of Chile and Brazil are class organizations, the historical churches are not,' as Professor Willems has observed. 'The Pentecostal sects are protest movements against the exisitng class structure.'[18] Those churches most obviously at variance with the surrounding social structure, in their own organizational rules, are the ones which have flourished, in places where there is cultural change, in the *anomie* of the urban areas, and in the rural districts where economic change has resulted in disturbance to traditional relationships. Within the sects there are numerous local variations. In Chile they have a strong anti-intellectual element, as classic sects normally have elsewhere in Christian history. Formal education is disapproved of, for both ministers and people, and schisms have actually occurred when some members have tried to introduce schools. In Brazil, on the other hand, there has been much less resistance to formal education and the Pentecostal Churches have used both journalism and broadcasting extensively in their campaigns of conversion. Chilean Protestantism, and especially the sectarian variety, had for many years an aversion to political involvement. This began to change with the success of

[18] Willems, op. cit., p. 218.

the Christian Democrats in the 1960s, but it was the denominations rather than the sects which then underwent a degree
of politicization—parallel to that taking place at the same
time in the Catholic Church. Many sect followers still regard
political activity as a wrong from of compromise with the
world. In Brazil, again, there is a contrast. After early rejection of the idea of political action by 'preachers baptised with
the Spirit',[19] leading Pentecostals like Manoel de Melo, Levy
Tavares, and Geraldino dos Santos decided, in the 1960s, that
political and social justice was an important aspect of Christian
service. Theirs was a shift in correspondence with general
movements of radical opinion within the Churches at the
time, and is further evidence of the openness of Brazilian
Pentecostalism to educated opinion.

Let it again be emphasized, however, that the phenomenon
of the sects, and of Protestantism in general, is not extensive.
In Chile, which is exceptional, something over 10 per cent of
the population are active members of Protestant congregations. As many people attend Protestant worship on Sundays
as go to mass, at least in the urban areas. The Pentecostals are
the largest group in Chile, concentrated in the expanding poor
districts of Santiago, Valparaíso, and Conceptión. Brazil is
similar, with a particular concentration of Protestantism in the
southern cities of Rio and São Paulo. Argentina has a
sizeable Protestant element as a legacy of its particularly
heavy immigration. But elsewhere, in the countries to the
north of the temperate zone of the hemisphere, Protestantism
has not flourished. In Colombia, Protestants came under
attack between 1948 and 1952; over 40 churches were burned
and 110 Protestant schools were closed, at the instigation of
the Catholic nationalistic enthusiasm inspired by Laureano
Gómez and Rojas Pinilla. In that most orthodox country,
Catholicism has not been seriously challenged by a protestant
advance, among either the poor or the middle sectors. Reli-
giously disaffected members of the intelligentsia do not find in
Protestantism a reasoned alternative to the Catholic faith:
they lapse altogether into atheism. Recent Protestant advances
have been made among sections of the working population of
the lower strata—especially in areas or groups of marked

[19] Walter J. Hollenweger, *The Pentecostals*, London, 1972, p. 107.

social dislocation, where Pentecostalism appears as a 'lower-class solidarity movement'.[20] In Paraguay, where the Catholic Church is perhaps the weakest in South America, Protestantism is still only 2 per cent of the population. The Protestants have not gained very much in Uruguay, either, despite the reduced influence of Catholicism and the official policy of de-Christianization, in the Batlle tradition, which has weakened it more than its potential rivals. Mexico saw a considerable growth of Protestant conversions in the 1950s and 1960s, and it was the sects which were the most effective. Yet the Protestant population of Mexico is still only 2 per cent.

Considered, then, from the wide perspectives of several centuries, the religious development of Latin America yields examples both of classic millenarianism and apocalyptic mysticism—though the tradition of these phenomena has been discontinuous—and of 'churches of the disinherited', though this tradition, until the modern rise of the Protestant sects, has largely resided within the institutional framework of Catholicism. *Religiosidad Popular* has been a spiritual phenomenon of quite amazing vitality. The key to the stability of the Catholic Church—of the ability to retain, in fact, two quite different religions within itself—has been, paradoxically, its weakness. Dominated for three centuries by the Crowns of Spain and Portugal, and then subjected to the ideological hostility of liberal secularism in the years following Independence, the Church has been institutionally inadequate through most of its existence. It has not been centralized or effectively authoritative. It has failed to retain intellectual respect. Bishops in their dioceses have, with the protection of local officials, exercised their functions with little reference to other ecclesiastical officers until comparatively recent times. Priests in the vast rural areas have been dominated by the *hacendados*, to whom they have owed greater loyalty than to episcopal authority. The religious orders have acted independently of both; their more substantial wealth giving them even greater measures of autonomy. It is only in the last century that Rome has acquired an effective over-all voice in the Latin-

[20] Cornelia Butler Flora, *Pentecostalism in Colombia. Baptism by Fire and Spirit*, Associated University Presses, 1976, p. 93.

American Church, and only in 1955 that, with the foundation of the *Conferencia del Episcopado Latinoamericano* (CELAM), the different national churches had a common forum for discussion of pan-hemispheric religious issues. The integration of folk religion with Iberian Catholicism thrived in these conditions. Ecclesiastical authority had neither the means nor the will to disturb an arangement of things which was externally uniform and which, it supposed, was suited to the limited intellectual and moral capacity of the Indian subculture. Latin-American Catholicism has remained, in consequence, almost entirely untouched by formal heresy or schism.

4

Christianity and Social Issues

In seeking to define and to act upon its relationship to society the Catholic Church in Latin America has encountered in an exaggerated form a problem found elsewhere in societies with a European inheritance. It is a problem created by the competition of alternative social ideologies and by the growth of a state interest in social welfare during the past century and a half. The difficulty is one of defining the relationship of church and state in an area whose boundaries are inevitably unclear and where there are almost no agreed guidelines from the past to help both churchmen and politicians in arriving at a demarcation of roles. The history of Catholic social action in Latin America divides around the middle years of the nineteenth century. Before then, the Church fulfilled a social purpose and maintained a network of welfare institutions in complete harmony with the civil authorities; after that time, the growth of liberal anti-clericalism, the secular idealism of Positivism and later of socialism, and the new paternalism of expanding state structures whose lineage was partly Hispanic, partly socialist, and partly pragmatic, resulted in the exclusion of ecclesiastical involvement from many of its traditional areas of social concern. Towards the most recent times, the expectations of an expanding social role for the state have been made for increasingly ideological reasons, and the resulting politicization of moral concern has added yet more difficulties for the Church.

The problem has been variously expressed within Catholic thought. Some churchmen have sought to re-define a traditional social function; to continue to regard the Church as most appropriately rendering its service through charitable institutions existing alongside the collectivist machinery of the state. Theirs is a conservative position, most at ease within traditionalist or military régimes of the political Right—whose social principles they have a tendency to sacralize. Some churchmen have sought to espouse the structures of collectivism, but within a Christian interpretation of social change whose content is largely derived, in fact, from prevailing liberal opinion. Theirs is the world of Christian Democracy: Catholicism and social pluralism are hand-in-hand. Some other churchmen—an even more recent development, which came to prominence in the 1960s— have frankly accepted the social diagnoses of secular political ideologies, especially those inspired by Marxist social analysis, and have declared the need for Christianity to surrender its former independent understanding of social dynamics and to support forces of change whose origins have lain outside Christianity. These are the progressive bishops and priests whose ideas have received considerable publicity in recent years, and whose clashes with the more conservative régimes are of precisely the same kind as the clashes which traditionalist clergy in the nineteenth century had with liberal politicians.

For nearly three hundred years—before the Independence period—the Latin-American Churches fulfilled traditional obligations in colonial society. Closely integrated with the structure of authority derived from the Iberian Crowns the social work of the Church was so much a part of the expected order of things that it usually went without remark and so has been largely unrecorded. What is not questioned rarely needs articulate defence or explanation. Complaints were heard in the colonial period about the abuse of clerical privileges or concerning the moral frailty of the clergy, but few accused the Church of the neglect of its social obligations. These duties lay in two areas: social control and social welfare.

The Crown expected the clergy to instruct both the *criollos* and the Indians in the requirements of civil obedience as a matter of Christian conscience. A continuous stream of ecclesiastical discourse on behalf of monarchy was the consequence— a work of social control so familiar and so accepted that it only began to appear self-consciously ideological during the Independence movement, when the structure of authority the clergy had upheld came under political attack. Then the Church divided. The episcopal hierarchy and the senior clergy remained loyal to monarchical institutions, the parochial clergy tended to support the local autonomy demanded by the *criollos*. From that point the traditional function of the Church as an instrument of social harmony ran increasingly into difficulty, and the nineteenth century was marked by an accumulating resistance to the idea that the clergy should be agents of social control at all. For nearly three hundred years the priests had taken their view of their social function from surrounding lay groups—from the *hacendados*, from the Crown officials, from the urban élites in the *cabildos*. The general weakness of any distinct sense of an ecclesiastical view of social organization was matched by the institutional weakness of the Church in relation to civil authority, and resulted in a very grave disorientation of the Church in the century following Independence. In the politically divided and often hostile world of the nineteenth century, the Church's social outlook itself became, through necessity, increasingly ideological as it came to defend itself against the competition of alternative ideologies. And lacking a tradition of autonomous social thinking, the leaders of Catholic opinion began to draw their social doctrines from whichever sections of lay opinion seemed most friendly. This, of course, in many places meant adhesion to traditionalist social values. But one result was quite clear: there continued to be no distinctly ecclesiastical view of social order—the Church took its agenda from developments in the lay and secular world of social values.

So much of the traditional Iberian social fabric survived into the new republican states that this fact was for long disguised. Unlike Europe and North America, the rise of middle sectors in the social hierarchy was not, in Latin America, so emphatically associated with a new social ethic or with a distinct class interest. The middle sectors regarded themselves as aspirants to the class values of the landed order. It is true that they furnished liberal reformers and secularists from amongst the *pensadores* and the *científicos;* but there was no general sense that middle-sector status involved, except very temporarily, distinct middle-class interests or values. The Latin-American Church, unlike the Church in Europe or North America, was not confronted with a bourgeois social outlook against which to test its own social attitudes and assumptions. Its choice of ideology, when that became necessary, lay between adhesion to the best it could discover of past traditionalism and espousal of the social changes promoted by those who hoped to avoid liberal secularization by timely adaptation. There were not too many of the latter.

The second of the social functions of the Church also required considerable adjustment after the Independence period: the performance of social welfare. In the colonial period, in both Spanish and Portuguese America, virtually all institutions of welfare were established and conducted by the religious orders, the cathedral chapters, the parish priests, or the lay brotherhoods. There were a number of royal foundations, but these were actually staffed by clergy. A very large part of the ecclesiastical property so frequently denounced in nineteenth-century anti-clerical polemicism was in fact devoted to welfare work, though some of this wealth, as in the case of Mexico after the secularizing reforms of the 1850s, was allowed to remain in Church hands precisely because the public authority was still unable to supply the services which would have been destroyed by confiscation.

The original vision of the missions, established at the time of the Conquest, had not survived the cooling of the first enthusiasms as the continent settled down into ordered Hispanic institutions, but the missionaries' combination of spiritual and civil vocations had endured. The *encomenderos* had been responsible for the conversion of the tributary Indians and they employed priests for the purpose. These were soon looked upon rather as domestic chaplains of the great families—but their social work continued, and established a pattern for future clerical involvement with welfare. In the colonial towns, too, the Church's social obligations were usually undertaken very impressively. On his visit to Lima, the Spanish Imperial capital, early in the seventeenth century, the Carmelite friar Antonio Vázquez de Espinosa described a flourishing network of charitable welfare agencies, with hospitals and schools, refuges for the destitute and orphaned, and homes for the care of the insane. In Mexico City he noted a comparable system of relief. On a lesser scale, appropriate to the less exalted urban centres, this sort of work was undertaken by the Church everywhere, with a continuous history right up to the secularizing reforms of the nineteenth century. In Brazil, the lay religious fraternities, the *irmandades*—of which the most celebrated were the Misericórdia of Bahia—carried out an enormous amount of social welfare work, especially for the sick. Crown and municipal financial assistance was negligible. The work was almost entirely supported by private and Christian charitable donations, for 'citizens of colonial Bahia regarded social philanthropy as part of the Catholic tradition and contributed generously'.[1] In the nineteenth century, extra-ecclesiastical philanthropic enterprises began to supplement this traditional work. Those who had been successful in commercial or industrial undertakings started to set up charitable institutions—just as their counterparts did in England and North America. But in Latin America the sense of paternalism, that seemingly indelible Iberian inheritance, was more clearly present in their motivation. Thus the Edwards family in Chile, who had made their wealth in the copper industry, promoted a number of philanthropic enterprises. In the 1870s they established refuges for the destitute, schools for poor children, hospitals and dispensaries for the sick, and a College to prepare poor boys for the priesthood. The clergy usually staffed these institutions. But indications of real change were at hand as well. In the area of medical care, Catholic charitable agencies were being supplemented by a state interest quite early in the nineteenth century. Chile, again, with its advanced welfare sense, provides the best example. In 1827, the Chilean government set up a Health Council. Interest in public health questions, as in Britain at the time, was just then beginning. A department for vaccination was established, and also the *Beneficencia Publica de Chile*, a co-ordinating body for public welfare services. The official put in charge of this was not a Catholic cleric but Dr Andrew Blest, an Irish Protestant minister who had arrived at Valparaíso in 1812 with a consignment of Protestant Scriptures supplied by the Bible Society in London. His appointment was a sign of a great shift in the provision of welfare. The Catholic Church, for so long the exclusive agent of social services, was about to progressively displaced.

It was, of course, education that witnessed the most obvious diminution of the Church's traditional social function. Here the change was accompanied by acute conflict, for the question was not merely about the improvement of men's social condition but about the formation of minds. It was therefore a conflict

---

[1] A. J. R. Russell-Wood, *Fidalgos and Philanthropists. The Santa Casa da Misericórdia of Bahia, 1500–1755*, London, 1968, p. 346.

rendered within deeply ideological terms of reference, where the ecclesiastics and the liberal secularists, and later the socialists, were clearly rivals. The Church's educational record was actually a very creditable one. Throughout the colonial period schools were being provided and maintained both for the sons of wealthy *criollos* and for the poorer whites and the *mestizos*. These were urban establishments. Rural schools before the nineteenth century were small parochial undertakings, for catechetical and practical instruction in manual crafts, set up at the initiative of individual priests. Before the Independece period there were some fifty schools giving primary education in Chile. Educational facilities existed in comparable numbers in Peru, Colombia, and Mexico. There were a few attempts at Indian education, like the Jesuit schools in Brazil, started soon after the arrival of the Order in 1549. These were mostly concerned with agricultural training rather than formal learning, however. In Chile, similarly, the Indians were not entirely neglected. In 1697 the Jesuits founded the *Colegio de Naturales* to teach the sons of Mapuche chiefs.

Universities were established in order to provide candidates for the Church's own ministry, but in the general sense that they encourage intellectual cultivation and a cultural élite they made a wider contribution to colonial society. The University of St Thomas Aquinas was founded at Santo Domingo in 1538, and the Universities of Mexico and Lima followed Crown assent in 1551. The University of San Felipe opened in Santiago de Chile in 1758 accoding to a plan originally devised by Bishop Antonio de San Miguel in 1738. Higher education was in part secularized after Independence, but it was the setting-up by the various republics of wholly secular institutions, inspired by anti-clericalism, which most clearly signalled the end of the Church's monopoly. The university reform movement, spreading from Córdoba in Argentina after 1918, was secular in inspiration.

The secularization of the schools had an erratic history in the nineteenth and twentieth centuries. In some countries the Church schools remained intact, and the state contented itself with the creation of its own schools; in others, attacks were made upon the Church schools themselves. In most of the state systems there was originally some provision for the teaching of religion, but this was removed after bitter trials of political stength between pro- and anti-clerical factions. The position was often unstable, with religion restored to the public schools during period of conservative political ascendancy. But behind the chronological diversity between the different republics, a coherent development may be discerned: the entry of the state into responsibility for education and its consequence in the reduction of the Church's sphere of influence. Although it is the controversy that is most obvious to the later observer—as often to contemporaries—this change as in fact dictated by necessity. The lines of conflict were established in the nineteenth century, before the rural education movement had begun. It was about urban schools. Already, however, the Church was finding its resources inadequate in many places to expand its system of education in proportion to the population growth—and with the massive urban expansion of the present century its situation became hopeless. Once the state had decided upon the need for an educated citizenry it had the choice either of financing schools run by the Church or establishing its own. In practice it at first did both. But given the stength of liberal anti-clericalism within the ruling élites, and the intellectual stength of Positivism in the second half of the century, it was inevitable that the scales would tip increasingly towards secular education. The secularists argued for a strong moral element in the formation of citizens, and this made them direct rivals to the influence of the Church. This attitude was seen clearly in the writings of the Chilean theorist Valentín Letelier, and his insistence that education be social in purpose, and directed towards 'social development'.[2] Juárez, in Mexico, had had a similar purpose. Begun under the inspiration of Gabino Barreda, another Positivist, the primary school system was enormously expanded, so that between 1857 and 1875 the number of schools increased by three times to eight thousand. Education was explicitly intended to produce citizens possessed of what the reformers regarded as rational rather than religious social attitudes. During the presidency of Diáz the number of schools doubled. In 1887 and 1888 the decisive battle about the nature of education took place in Mexico, with success going—against the deepest opposition of

---

[2] Valentín Letelier, *Filosofía de la educación*, Santiago, 1912, p. 51.

the clergy—to the secularists. Mexican rural education really began with the work of José Vasconcelos, the most celebrated of all Latin-American educationalists. His purpose, again, was highly ideological: to rescue the *campesinos* from the thrall of the clergy, to integrate them into the emergent Mexican socialist state. It was an aspiration much more idealistic than the Church's—whose rustic parochial instructors were infinitely less successful than their secularist opponents always supposed.

The most effective of the counter-offensives by the Church in the battle for rural education came with the Radio Schools movement of the 1950s. This *Acción Cultural Popular* was started in Colombia by Fr José Joaquin Salcedo, and was widely copied elsewhere in Latin America. In Brazil, before the 1964 *coup*, Catholic progressives increasingly used Church radio services to propagate advanced programmes for the socialist 'conscientization' of the rural masses. Since their message was in opposition to the intentions of the military government after the *coup*, Church and State were again drawn into conflict over the nature of education, but on this occasion in reversed roles.

Uruguay, like Mexico, offers another example of the ideological purpose behind the promotion of state education. In 1877 a system of secular schools was provided by legislation. They were the achievement of José Pedro Varela, who had been influenced both by Horace Mann, whom he had met on a visit to the United States in 1867, and by the prevailing anti-clericalism of the Uruguayan élite. The Church opposed the secular schools, without success. In Chile, the early governments after Independence encouraged the Catholic religious orders in their educational work, but Bernardo O'Higgins was also anxious to see a state interest in the expansion of education, despite his friendliness to the Church. In 1821 he invited the Revd James Thomson to Chile. This Protestant clergyman had helped to set up 300 schools using the Lancastrian system in Argentina after 1818. His stay in Chile lasted only a year—he then went on to Peru at the invitation of San Martín. It is an extraordinary testimony to the early determination of the Latin-American republics to foster state education that this Scottish Protestant should have been so influential—in the face of Catholic suspicions that he was a proselytizer. Foreign influence in the development of Chilean education, in fact, considerably weakened the hold of the Catholic Church in the schools, and assisted the state in its subsequent moves towards secularization.

In the educational controversies, therefore, ideological considerations in the states' reduction of Catholic social work may be seen with great clarity. But the same elements were present in all other fields of social action in the nineteenth and twentieth centuries, combining with the inexorable pressures of population growth to enlarge the area of state activity. The immense contrast between town and country in Latin America was evident in the degree to which change was effective. In rural areas in every country—with the exception of Uruguay, parts of Argentina, and, at times, Mexico—clerical participation in social welfare has remained at a high level until very recent times. In the least developed and less secularized nations, like Peru and Colombia, the clergy are still the main agents of relief, their welfare institutions receiving direct financial assistance from the state. Catholic opposition to the growth of welfare collectivism has itself had ideological associations. It has in some measure reflected Catholic teachings against the omni-competence of the State—teachings laid out in the social encyclical letters of the Popes. But it is also true that Catholic opposition to collectivism has been due to the accident that in Latin America the political forces favouring government growth have often been led by secularists. There was enough of the paternalist tradition of the Iberian inheritance to enable the Church to find state welfare service satisfactory enough if carried out by sympathetic political forces. The eleven-year presidency of Augusto Leguía in Peru, after 1919, saw a programme of paternalistic state welfare, principally aimed at giving workers security, with an expanding state bureaucracy. It had the full support of the Church, who supplemented it with Catholic Action programmes. But at almost exactly the same time, in Uruguay, the social welfare bureaucracy being created by the reforms of José Batlle y Ordóñez, between 1911 and 1915, met considerable clerical opposition. The reason is that Batlle was an advanced seclarist, and his intention was indeed to set up a secular state. The Church tended to formulate its attitudes to collectivism around local conditions, rather than in correspondence to any distinct body of Catholic teaching.

This conclusion at first appears to be at variance with the influence many have attributed to the Papal encyclicals on social themes: *Rerum Novarum* in 1891, *Quadragesimo Anno* in 1931, *Mater et Magistra* in 1961, and *Populorum Progressio* in 1967. It is certainly true that these have all in turn inspired pastoral letters from Latin-American bishops. But it is also instructive to notice that it was traditionalist Catholics, and not the progressive elements in the Church, who were the first to take up the social idealism of *Rerum Novarum*. Thus it was Miguel Antonio Caro, a conservative politician and *pensador*, who most vigorously propagated the social message of the Pope in Colombia. And in Mexico the hierarchy's campaign to put the encyclical into effect through Catholic social action was done in express opposition to Madero, who represented the progressive social ideas of the time. These instances suggest a different interpretation of the influence of the encyclicals. Far from bearing witness to a distinct Catholic social ideology at work in the Latin-American churches, they in fact point to the use made of them by Catholic activists to confirm their existing acceptance of whatever social values, derived from surrounding practice, they already found conducive. In very many instances the Papal encyclicals have served to reinforce Catholic adhesion to traditional paternalism. As Professor Frederick C. Turner has wisely remarked, 'The degree of respect for papal authority remains so low and so circumscribed by other forces in its attempt to influence the actual behaviour of citizens, that the impact of the encyclicals is far more limited than their champions have proclaimed.'[3] And that may be taken to apply not merely to the laity, but to have operated among the clergy themselves. In nineteenth-century Brazil many priests were Freemasons, despite the clear condemnation of Freemasonry in several Papel encyclicals. Contemporary Colombia, despite the attempts of the clergy to instruct the laity in the prohibition of artificial birth control, repeated in the encyclical *Humanae Vitae* in 1968, is the world's fourth-largest market for contraceptive pills. It is also one of the most Catholic nations in Latin America. As evidence of the ideological origin of Latin-American Catholic social thought the Papal encyclicals have clearly to be treated with reserve.

[3] Frederick C. Turner, *Catholicism and Political Development in Latin America*, Chapel Hill, 1971, p. 210.

It is surely in this perspective also that the twentieth-century Catholic Action programmes are to be viewed. They were obviously stimulated by the Papal encyclicals, but the social practices and reforms for which they actually worked disclosed considerable diversity across Latin America. This did not indicate pragmatic adaptation to differing circumstances of a single body of teaching, however, but that local balances of thought and tradition had themselves furnished the content of Catholic social idealism. In some countries individual Catholic thinkers were able to exercise a considerable influence on behalf of their own social ideas. Thus Carlos Alberto Siri of El Salvador helped mould the attitudes of an entire generation, early in the present century, with his vision of a neo-Thomist social order. The reception of the ideas of Jacques Maritain in Latin America, in the 1930s, was an important ingredient of the universal social explanation which Frei and others swept into Christian Democracy. Also in Chile, the social outlook of progressive ecclesiastics like Manuel Larraín and Alberto Hurtado were, at about the same time, indebted to neo-Thomist thought as well as to the social pluralism favoured by other sections of the Catholic intelligentsia. But in each of these cases the distinctly Catholic elements were soon absorbed into the general influence of prevailing secular ideology—almost as a condition of effectiveness. Dom Helder Camara, Archbishop of Recife in Brazil, now well-known for his association of Catholicism with socialist causes, has described how in his own life the earlier appeal of the corporate state was closely linked to his sense of Christian social concern. He became a supporter of the Integralist manifesto, published in 1933 by Plínio Salgado. 'In my opinion', he has said, 'the masses were so hungry and thirsty for a word of hope and love, that the doctrine of Integralism seemed to answer their needs.' [4] In his case the atmosphere of the Papal encyclicals had found its expression in a version of fascism; in a universal explanation of social phenomena which appealed to Catholic and secular opinion alike.

The association of Catholicism and socialism in the 1960s was not dissimilar. At that time the Catholic universities began to establish courses in the social sciences which fell at

[4] Dom Helder Câmara, *The Conversations of a Bishop. An interview with José de Broucher*, London, 1979, p. 68.

once under the direction of priests who were committed social activists—men like Roger Vekemans in Chile and Camilo Torres in Colombia. Foreign priests, especially those trained in the social sciences faculty at Louvain, also contributed to the accumulating pool of progressive thinking. A large number of the thousands of priests and religious from the United States who served in Latin America in the 1960s and 1970s were converted to radical politics. 'In Lima, a missionary has to be in politics,' as the Maryknoll Father Tom Burns put it; 'Here it's a culture of struggle.' [5] At the same time, the Catholic Action groups in several countries were being drawn towards socialism. In Brazil a section of the militants founded *Ação Poplar* in 1962—an organization whose social analysis quite openly favoured revolutionary social change. In Colombia, socialist priests René García and Manuel Alzate Restrepo espoused social beliefs which to the hierarchy were indistinguishable from Marxism. Indeed, the whole ferment of progressive idealism that marked important and influential sections of the Catholic leadership in Latin America in the 1960s and subsequently, and which was characterized by internal divisions over social doctrine and application, was almost entirely derived from external, non-Catholic ideologies: from Marxism, Castroism, reformist socialism, and liberalism. Attempts were made, expecially at the time of the Medellín Conference of 1968, to identify the new social ideas with papal teaching, and especially with *Populorum Progressio*. But this cannot bear critical examination. It is difficult to avoid the conclusion that the advanced social thinking of the 1960s was the adoption, by progressive élites within the Church, of the secular moral idealism of the Left—which was at the time strongly represented within the intelligentsia of the various republics. The result was surely the politicization of parts of the Church's leadership, not the Christianizing of secular political society. Most ordinary Catholics in South America see little connection between their religion and the wide issues of social or political reform. Any Church involvement with social change, therefore, which has any hope of convincing the mass of the Catholic people, requires to be closely associated with the political pro-

[5] Gerald M. Costello, *Mission to Latin America. The Successes and Failures of a Twentieth Century Crusade*. Maryknoll, NY, 1979, p. 188.

grammes to which they *do* look for improvement. With the possible exception of Chile, the progressive Church leaders of the 1960s probably went too far in their adoption of radical politics to carry the ordinary believers with them. There was, in consequence, a rift between sections of the leadership and the rank-and-file. It was evident throughout the continent, reinforcing the older rift between town and country in Latin-American Catholicism, for the progressive thinking of the Catholic leadership is characteristically urban.

During its history of concern for social welfare, the Catholic Church in Latin America has generally reflected the same balances of opinion as have existed in political society generally. It has not been notably behind the times: a view so often assumed in modern historical commentary. 'The conformist hierarchy shunned all contact with workers, peasants, and the poor,' Hugo Latorre Cabal, the Colombian political theorist has written, as if in summary of this viewpoint: 'They labelled anyone communist who asked them to descend from their thrones, or, if the mercy of their cold charity softened them, labelled them a mere rebel without condemnatory epithets.' [6] At the local level of the rural parishes there have been surviving traces of the spirits of Hidalgo and Morelos, both of whom believed, at the start of the Mexican Independence movement in 1810, that widespread social change would follow the political upheaval—a belief in which they were largely mistaken. But the typical parish priest of the nineteenth century was scarcely sensitive to the remnants of that radical tradition. He worked within the existing social order and feared for the survival of Catholicism itself if it was disrupted. The bishops and ecclesiastical thinkers have been more responsive to shifts of opinion within the political élites. Their rejection of nineteenth-century liberalism, however, set them at variance with the most dynamic section of the intelligentsia throughout the century; yet the liberals, for all their anti-clericalism, were in general conservative in social outlook, at least in class terms. It also meant that the Church was cast in the role of enemy to all reform.

But this exaggerated a dilemma in which the Catholic leadership found itself. For the Church was stuck with the social

[6] H. Latorre Cabal, *The Revolution of the Latin American Church*, p. 121.

values of landed society virtually without a choice: it was the political representation of that society which was the most friendly to its survival. In the twentieth century, on the other hand, Catholic leaders have in some cases been quite ready to adopt social reform. Conservative prelates have been as liable to this as the more liberal. Thus Archbishop Rossell Arellan of Guatemala upheld the claims of the workers to just wages and conditions in 1946, and in 1954 he condemned the exploitation of the poor in a pointedly political manner. Cardinal José María Caro of Chile criticized the rich in 1938 for their neglect of the working classes. Cardinal Leme, in Brazil, was a consistent advocate of social improvements for the workers in the 1930s. Archbishop Víctor Manuel Sanabria y Martínez of Costa Rica used his influence on behalf of social reform in the 1940s. It was in fact a conservative prelate, Archbishop Casanova, who declared in a Pastoral Letter that the Chilean earthquake of 1906 was a divine punishment for a society which had neglected the conditions of the poor. In these attitudes, of course, there is a large deposit of surviving traditional paternalism.

The pastoral letters of the various Latin-American hierarchies have, throughout the present century, faithfully reflected the social concern of the Catholic leadership. Some have contended for quite radical social change—like the Chilean collective episcopal letters of 1910, 1931, 1937, 1949, 1962 and the working document of 1971. This last statement is particularly notable for its close proximity to the social radicalism of the first years of the Allende administration. 'Es esa situación inhumana de marginación y de miseria en que viven miles de chilenos', the bishops observed, 'la que concede a la pregunta por el sistema socio-económico y por la opción política de los cristianos su carácter de dramática urgencia.'[7] Episcopal statements began to express a preparedness to see considerable social changes in Venezuela in the later 1950s—under the guidance of Archbishop Rafael Arias and Cardinal Humerto Quintero; in Boliva, at the same time, where the bishops supported the social reforms

[7] *Evangelio, Política y Socialismo. Documento de trabajo propuesto por los Obispos de Chile, 27 de mayo de 1971*, in *Documentos del Episcopado, Chile 1970–1973*, Santiago 1974, p. 67. (It is this inhuman situation of marginalization and of misery in which thousands of Chileans live, that gives to the question of the socio-economic system and the political option of Christians its character of dramatic urgency.)

of the *Movimento Nacionalista Revolutinario;* in Brazil, where the 1950s' growth of an ecclesiastical social consciousness was evident in the work of Bishop Eugenio de Araujo Salas in the under-developed north-east, and where the joint epicopal pastorals of 1960 and 1963 supported advanced programmes of social reform; in Peru, where in 1963 the bishops endorsed the need for changes in education, housing, land tenure, sanitation, and the conditions of labour. In Peru, the reforming spirit was symbolized, in 1970, when Cardinal Juan Landázuri Ricketts departed from his palace in Lima in order to live in a poor district of the city, thus giving a practical demonstration of the Church's solidarity with the working class.

In the sensitive question of agrarian reform, however, the Catholic Church has only in comparatively recent years shown any considerable preparedness to countenance change. Related closely to traditional patterns of tenure through its considerable stake in landed society the Church was, until almost the end of the nineteenth century, unable to separate its own means of support from the economic interests of landowning society in general. At the time of Independence, ecclesiastical wealth in most countries was enormous. Even had the financial needs of the new governments not impelled them to cast eyes upon Church wealth as a source of income, the degree of social and economic influence that their properties gave the ecclesiastics would certainly have anyway led to attempts at confiscation. The Church itself was unsympathetic about the reduction of its temporalities. There were a number of cases of Church leaders supporting land reform—quite a lot of them, in fact: but they expressed support for improvement in the conditions of tenure or obligation, not for redistribution of the land. There were a few exceptions even to that. Early in the nineteenth century Abad y Queipo, who became Bishop of Michoacán, in Mexico, had contended not only for quite radical changes in rural society but also for the actual redistribution of land to the Indian peasantry. This was, incidentally, the prelate who excommunicated the leaders of the 1810 rising and fled his diocese. Among the rebels, of course, was Hidalgo who, in his celebrated *grito de Dolores,* proposed the return of the land to the Indians. But the clergy in general were fairly solidly committed against basic agrarian changes in the nineteenth century.

In view of the campaigns of the secularist liberals against the landed wealth of the Church, this was hardly surprising. Conditions varied widely, however, and it is important to realize that the confiscations carried out in Mexico and Guatemala were not actually representative of a general pattern. Yet the terms upon which the Church held its property were in very many countries modified by state intervention in the nineteenth century, and that was enough to foster a sense of unfriendliness to the idea of all land reform in the minds of the bishops. The rural clergy had another reason to be suspicious of land reforms: their *urban* origin. Reform reflected the urban social ideals of the liberals and intellectuals whose schemes derived from doctrinaire social engineering rather than from acquaintance with the needs of the *campesinos*. Indeed, the liberals' concern was with the creation of a rural bourgeoisie; it was to encourage the over-all and drastic modernization of rural society. The clergy were a real impediment to this both because of their hold over the rural mind and because of their actual stake in the existing rural economy. The urban reformers' intentions were quite at variance with the aspirations of the *campesinos*, who sought only a modest legal readjustment of their conditions of labour, and who regarded the priesthood as a symbol of rural pride. The transfer of ecclesiastical property to secular owners, in the countries where it occurred, did not have the immediate effect of producing a radical change in rural society. The new owners rapidly acquired enough of the traditional values and manners of the *hacendados* to perpetuate much of their outlook into the twentieth century. The belief of the liberals that change in the pattern of landowning would itself operate to diminish the influence of the clergy did not prove well-founded either. There was no pool of rural anti-clericalism awaiting disturbance.

In the twentieth century, the position has changed. The expansion of the various economies has left the Church, in most countries, with an extremely marginal proportion of national wealth, and this has reduced its liability to appear as a hindrance to development, or even as a symbol of unreformed society. Once the political élites had replaced the secular progressivism of the older liberal tradition with less polemical social goals, churchmen began to adapt to ideas of agrarian reform, since these were not tainted with anti-clericalism. Even in Mexico, where the secularizers found an enhanced existence in the socialist idealism of Madero and his successors, the Church was able to show some measure of sympathy for land reform. This concern was, again, in contrast to the urban social analysis of the socialist revolutionaries. Following attempts at the foundation of rural co-operatives as part of the programme of Catholic Social Action, the Mexican hierarchy in 1920 turned to the organization of rural labour—an aspect of the labour movement the urban socialists had neglected. This led inevitably to confrontation with Luis Morones and the socialist unions and advanced the clash of Church and State. In Chile, on the other hand, the present century has seen an almost uninterrupted growth of Catholic involvement with rural reform. Archbishop Errázuriz included a call for improvements in the conditions of rural labour in his Pastoral Letter of 1910. Interest grew slowly, but by the 1950s, in some measure due to the pioneering work of rural Catholic Action, the Chilean Church had developed the most advanced attitude to agrarian questions in the whole of Latin America, as Oscar Dominguez has shown in his study of the work.[8] Manuel Larraín, when Bishop of Talca, began to transfer ecclesiastical lands to the tenants, and in 1961 the Chilean bishops collectively announced the sale of 13,000 acres of their properties to the occupiers. A Catholic Conference on Rural Life, held in Panama in 1955, and attended by representatives of nineteen Latin-American nations, endorsed the need for agrarian reform. In 1961, the Colombian bishops issued a Pastoral Letter with a similar message. The Peruvian bishops' Pastoral of 1963 followed the same line, and so did the Brazilian hierarchy in the same year—supporting land expropriation in the cause of social justice. Even in Cuba, Archbishop Enrique Pérez and Bishop Evelío Díaz supported Castro's land reforms on grounds of social justice. In 1966, a meeting of 200 bishops in Mar del Plata, Argentina, declared that social reform should have precedence over the rights of property. These sorts of declarations amounted, altogether, to a considerable shift in the thinking of the Catholic leadership of Latin America, which developments since the 1960s have certainly continued.

The Church's involvement with the organization of labour

[8] See Oscar Dominguez, *El Campesino Chileno y la Acción Católica Rural*, FERES, Fribourg, 1961.

has quite closely followed the development of unionism itself—
it has not noticeably lagged behind. The very earliest
trade unions contained elements which were plainly hostile to
Catholicism. Anarchists and revolutionary socialists stamped
the emergent labour groups with their views so that 'almost
without exception they were contrary to Church doctrine'.[9]
The bishops encouraged Catholic participation in order to
counter these influences. Leo XIII's encyclical, *Rerum Novarum*,
explicitly endorsed the idea of workers' associations, and this
legitimized the entry of the Church at the end of the nineteenth
century. But there was another reason why the organization of
labour appealed to Catholic leaders. Like the early union movement in Britain, the first associations in Latin America at the
end of the nineteenth century tended to be moral, educative,
and welfare combinations of skilled workers. They were more
concerned with social integration than with political action,
however much the doctrinaire activists sought to change that.
With the increasing migration of rural workers to the cities the
trade unions were confirmed in their role as social integrators.
It was a role that some churchmen clearly saw as corresponding
to their own pastoral mission. Church leaders came to promote
two courses. First, Catholic Social Action programmes encouraged the entry of the laity into existing trade unions. Second,
local leaders themselves began to set up distinct Catholic unions,
some as a development of their ordinary charitable associations.
In Chile, for example, the *patronatos*, founded from 1890 on-
wards, were mutual-aid and educative societies for workers,
under the direct control of the clergy. In 1905, at the Eucharistic
Congress, Archbishop Mariano Casanova appealed to the
workers to join Catholic labour organizations, and the parish
priests were enjoined to set them up. A similar development
took place in Argentina at about the same time. Mexico
was another country with Catholic unions early in the general
history of the labour movements. The first associations appeared
in 1913, and in 1920 the Catholic Labour Confederation was
formed in order to co-ordinate the work. Within two years it
had 80,000 members, concentrated heavily in the rural areas.
But in Mexico this early start was brought summarily to an end

    [9] Alexis U. Floridi and Annette E. Stiefold, *The Uncertain Alliance: The Catholic Church
and Labor in Latin America*, Miami, 1973, p. 21.

in 1926 when Calles enforced the anti-clerical articles of the 1917 constitution. In Guatemala, too, the Church was prohibited by law from involvement in labour organizations. This ban, in the Constitution of 1945, was removed after ten years.

The concentration of the Church on rural unionization was also characteristic of Brazil in the 1930s, and was especially associated with the establishment, in 1932, of *Círculos Operários*. This was the work of a Jesuit priest, Leopoldo Brentano. The entry of the Brazilian Church into urban labour organization in the 1960s was a symptom of its increasing politicization. Agencies set up by the bishops—themselves responding to progressive elements within the new corps of clerical bureaucrats—were frequently accused of political rather than social work. Thus the *Ação Católica Operária* and the *Juventude Operária Católica* found themselves under attack from the conservative press and from the military government after the 1964 *coup*. They had, anyway, not been particularly effective, at least in terms of their numerical appeal to the workers. They too faithfully reflected the ideals of a progressive bourgeois élite. The Catholic unions established by the hierarchy in Colombia, after 1944, on the other hand, have been most successful. But this was perhaps to have been expected in what is, after all, one of the least developed societies, and one in which the hold of the Church over some aspects of social life has been preserved. In 1954, the Latin-American Confederation of Christian Trade Unions (CLASC) was founded, and under the guidance of leaders like the Argentinian Emilio Máspero, the Catholic union movement has tended to ally itself with a strong Christian Democrat element. Individual members of the Catholic hierarchies of the various Latin-American countries have occasionally shown themselves to be rather in advance of political society in general in their preparedness to favour unions. This was the case in Venezuela in 1957, when Archbishop Rafael Arias asserted the right of labour to organize itself, in opposition to the policies of President Marcos Pérez Jiménez. Mostly, however, Catholic union organizers have pursued moderate objectives—they have been noticeably less radical in political outlook than the progressive activists within the priesthood in the past two decades.

Over the question of race, also, the Latin-American Church has followed a course in line with prevailing opinion. It is true that in the early colonial period a few churchmen, like Las Casas and Vieira, criticized the treatment of the subjugated Indians. And it is certainly the case that the debate, both in the colonies and in Spain and Portugal, about the moral nature of the newly discovered humanity and its status in the order of Creation, was almost entirely conducted by the clergy and within a distinctly religious frame of reference. It was a debate notable, in its day, for its enlightened attitude towards the Indians—whose depression into slavery as rejected on moral grounds. Studies of Indian society, customs, and religious beliefs were undertaken by the friars, both in the missions themselves, as they sought to understand the peoples they hoped to convert, and in academic institutions, prompting the learned and comprehensive writings of Toribio de Motolinía, Bernardino de Sahagún, Diego de Landa, and the Jesuit José de Acosta—whose *Historia Natural y Moral de los Indias,* published in 1590, became a classic.

There was a long history of clerical attempts to protect the Indians from exploitation by the white settlers. This was at its most enterprising in the ideal communities of Bishop Vasco de Quiroga at Sante Fé in Mexico, and of the Jesuits in Paraguay; it was evident, in less sytematic form, in the unrecorded labour of numerous priests in the parishes, and members of the religious orders in their missions. The work of Fr Luis de Valdiva on behalf of the Araucanian Indians of southern Chile, at the start of the seventeenth century, must be taken as the visible tip of a large hidden mass of concern by the local clergy everywhere. This Jesuit leader denounced the bad treatment of the Indians following their uprising at the end of the sixteenth century, and called for the abolition of the personal services to which they were subjected by the *encomenderos.* Bishop San Miguel also laboured for the improvement of the conditions of the Indians in Chile, founding hospitals and other charitable institutions for them. The exemption of the Indians from the jurisdiction of the Inquisition, on the grounds that they were not *gente de razón,* was further indication that the colonial Church regarded them as being in need of special and benign, if authoritative, treatment. This sort of concern gradually became less frequently articulated as colonial society settled down and the earlier hopes about the cultural assimilation of the Indians receded. The Araucanians of Chile were especially resistant to pacification, and the clergy may perhaps be excused for their growing belief in the inherent inferiority of that particular tribe of people when it is remembered that even Charles Darwin expressed the conviction, in the 1860s, that they were too low in the scale of life to be capable of civilization. Plans for the education of the sons of the Indian chiefs, and their preparation for the priesthood, were also abandoned at an early point; by the end of the sixteenth century a few *mestizos* were being received into holy orders, but no Indians. That the Church did not discriminate on race grounds over the reality of the Indians' capacity for religion, however, was witnessed by the recognition accorded the Virgin of Guadalupe— 'proclama la libertad de los indígenas' [10]— and in the devotions paid to Saint Martín de Porres, born at Lima in 1579, a mulatto who entered the Dominican Order and served the poor of the city until his death in 1639.

The belief of the nineteenth-century liberals that Indian society was culturally and morally inferior, and should be replaced with progressive enlightenment, came up against the paternalism of the priests. Writers and propagandists such as the Mexican, Francisco Bulnes, or the Argentinian, José Ingenieros, saw a danger in what they took to be the racial inferiority of the Indians, and proposed schemes of large-scale white immigration to guarantee the survival of civilized values. The Church, in contrast, tended to defend Indian traditional values against the secularizing ideals of progressive liberalism. But early in the twentieth century the Church found itself equally clearly ranged against the *Indigenismo* movement—because of its association with secularizing socialistic politics. This was especially evident in the ideas of the Peruvian intellectuals: Luis Valcárcel, Víctor Raúl Haya de la Torre, and, above all, José Carlos Mariátegui. Not only in the *Aprista* ideology, but also in the Mexican Revolution, *Indigenismo* had a strongly anti-Catholic element. It was the fanaticism of the Church, according to Mariátegui, that had destroyed the harmony of the pre-Conquest social order. Gustavo Adolfo Navarro, in Bolivia,

---

[10] *Una Gran Señal Aparecio en el Cielo*, Santa Cruz Altillo, Mexico, 1976, p. 40.

constructed a similar analysis of the blame ascribed to the Church for the depression of Indian culture. A powerful myth was created about the nature of pre-Conquest society; it was one in which Catholicism was represented as the spiritual arm of white exploitation. Catholic intellectuals were cautious of *Indigenismo* for another reason. Anthropological studies in Europe were already infusing a spirit of scepticism about the exclusive claims of Christianity, and the religious and moral relativism which they saw beginning to appear there warned Latin-American Catholic thinkers about the possibilities inherent in the rediscovery of Indian values. The attraction of Catholic intellectuals to the corporate state ideal, in the 1920s, 1930s, and 1940s, is not unrelated to these fears. They saw corporatism as a means of revivifying *Hispanidad* cultural values. Peruvian Fascism had a great attraction for the Catholic intellectuals: it was a direct reaction to the Marxism of the *Aprista* movement.

The institution of slavery was not one about which the Latin-American Church had a distinct view. Whereas the enslavement of the Indians was condemned, the blacks brought to South America, first by the Portuguese and then by the Spanish, were always regarded as racially suited to slavery. Neither the Papacy nor the local hierarchies condemned slavery as such. The Church, indeed, was itself a considerable owner of slaves. At the time of their expulsion from Chile, in 1767, for example, the Jesuits owned 1,300 black slaves in that country. In comparison with the legal position in British territories, the Spanish and Portuguese attitudes to the slaves was always enlightened. There was a detailed code of slave law, entitling the slaves to legal personality and other rights, including the right to give legal testimony. Slaves could become priests. But it was precisely because it was a relatively humane system that it proved so durable and attracted so little ecclesiastical censure. Throughout the history of slavery in Latin America there were always a few who spoke out against the slave trade, on humanitarian grounds. The best-known of these were Fernando Oliveira, Alonso de Montufar, and Bartolomé de Albornoz in the sixteenth century; Alonso de Sandoval and Saint Peter Claver in the seventeenth century; and Francisco Javier Alegre, Andrés de Guevara Basoazábal, and Pedro José Márquez in the eighteenth century. But the influence of these men was limited: they convinced some of the evils of the slave trade, but they did not create a general opinion opposed to slavery as an institution.

The Latin-American colonies had slave economies at the time of Independence. Yet the emancipation of the slaves followed soon afterwards in a climate of opinion partly derived from the contemporaneous movement against slavery among religious and moral propagandists in England, whose ideas, like the ideals of Political Economy, found considerable intellectual acceptance in Latin America. An examination of the cultivation of opinion in favour of emancipation, however, shows that the Church was merely part of the general movement of opinion— it was not a leader. The spearhead of reform was provided by groups of laymen whose motivation contained a strong religious moralism, and by groups of secular thinkers of the Englightenment, like Bolívar himself. In Brazil, the movement of opinion in favour of emancipation contained a number of ecclesiastics, but the abolition issue as such was not especially a Church one, despite the increasing moralism of the developing campaign. Emancipation was later in Brazil than elsewhere. Slave traffic was ended in 1850, yet by the 1870s, when the abolitionists moved into their most militant phase, there were still a million and a half slaves in the country. Emancipation came in 1888: but the moral case had been put by Joaquim Nabuco, a politician from the north-east, not by the ecclesiastical hierarchy, though it was in favour of the reform. Over the question of slavery, therefore, as over the race issue, the Church was not really separable from wider developments of opinion. In that, as in its other social attitudes, it was consistent with its general record in Latin-American history.

South Africa

1

Church and State

Until the most recent times, the relationship of Church and State has taken a curiously insubstantial form in the history of South Africa. Yet all the classic ingredients have been present: indeed, the double inheritance of the ecclesiastical institutions of both the Netherlands and Britain ought in theory to have heightened the prospects for a complicated and rich development of religious involvement in the political experience of the country. And in South Africa, in fact, there are familiar enough parallels to the histories of adjustment in Church and State relationships elsewhere in the modern world, but they exist on a modest scale, particularly surprising in view of the declaredly Christian purposes of so many of South Africa's political leaders. There has been no tradition of anti-clericalism in South Africa: a sure sign of the reluctance of the churches to participate in direct political management.

The relatively quiet history of Church and State relations may in part be explained by the nature of the churches themselves. But there is one feature in the political development of South Africa which also accounts for it: there was, throughout the nineteenth century, no clearly defined state structure with which the churches were liable to come into conflict. The machinery and authority of government was small in scale, reluctant to expand, and divided into a number of separate areas. Many of the social functions—like education—which caused enormous complications in the relations of Church and State elsewhere, because of the expansion of government into direct social responsibilities, were in South Africa left in the hands of the churches during most of the nineteenth century— the period in which the seeds of discord were sidely scattered elsewhere in the Christian world. Under the administration of the Vereenighde Oost-Indische Compagne, until the end of the eighteenth century, Cape society was anyway so small in size and so undeveloped politically that there was little possibility of church and state relations developing beyond the most basic practices. The British administration of the nineteenth century did see an emerging pattern of adjustments between the spheres of religion and government; but this failed to become a determining feature of other main developments because the century saw also the removal (to the territories beyond the Cape borders) of just those religious forces which might otherwise have contested the nature of the state's claims and actions. The creation of the Boer Republics in effect separated into distinct political units those whose mixture of religion and politics would otherwise have clashed with the British mixture at the Cape. The political pluralism of the last decades of the century, with the British–Dutch institutions of the Cape Province, and the institutions of the Boer States, was suddenly given a new significance by the discoveries of diamonds and gold, at Kimberley and the Witwatersrand, with an accompanying economic transformation which moved the future development of South Africa away from the Cape. The Sand River Convention, in 1852, may be said to have determined a pattern of political diversity for South Africa at just the time when European institutions elsewhere were coalescing into centralized administrative forms. By the time of the Union in 1910, South African society inherited a series of decisions about the position of Church and State that had already been made in relation to separate and different political experiences. The absence of a common set of definitions about the function of religion in political society thereafter divided first the English-speaking from the Afrikaans churches and then the Dutch Reformed churches themselves, as a legacy of their own different attitudes to government acquired separately in either the Cape Province or the Transvaal.

Just as there was, in the formative period, no coherent single state structure, so there was, on the side of the churches, a growing pluralism. There lacked, that is to say, a clearly defined ecclesiastical structure to which government could relate itself. It was not that the churches were themselves institutionally weak, but that cultural and ethnic conditions had established a pattern of Christian variation that was little calculated to allow the acceptance of an agreed religious basis for political society. The English 'civil religion' which members of the Anglican Church disclosed at the time of the Union was plainly impossible as a national expression of Christianity since it was rejected by Afrikaner society. And the tendnecy by some in the Dutch Reformed churches, and even more by Afrikaner political leaders, to regard the religion of the Afrikaners as an essential political cohesive, though powerful, was never allowed to go so far as the establishment of a formal connection between Church and State after the Union. This was for practical, not ideological, reasons: the existence of a religious pluralism in South African society. The Boer Republics had set up state churches, but even there religious pluralism also established itself—the Dutch Reformed faith split up, through schism, into three separate denominations.

The first signs of religious pluralism had been evident at an early point.' In 1780 the Lutherans, who had resisted efforts by the Cape authorities to integrate them with the Dutch Reformed congregations, got permission to build their own church and appoint their own pastor. That was rather an isolated acheivement. In 1700 the French Huguenots, who had arrived at the Cape in 1688 and 1689, were obliged by the Dutch officials to conform to both the language and the worship of the Dutch Reformed Church. Even under the British occupation of the Cape, in 1795 and again after 1806, attempts were made to enforce by law the unitary nature of religion by preventing churches other than the Dutch Reformed from setting up congregations. But de Mist's Ordinance of 1804, with its doctrine of official religious toleration, and the arrival in 1820 of 5,000 British settlers, themselves of mixed denominational allegiance, were irresistible steps towards the recognition of a practical religious pluralism which nineteenth-century developments in British liberalism converted into state guardianship of ecclesiastical diversity. South Africa then produced a luxuriant growth of denominationalism, the more complicated because the vertical divisions of confessional allegiance ere intersected horizontally by the creation of separate churches for the different ethnic groups. By the middle years of the twentieth century there were around eighty recognized denominations and mission societies in South Africa.

The history of the established church, the Dutch Reformed Church, really only became sigificant at the end of the eighteenth century. Although the Church had served the religious needs of the settlers and the garrison ever since van Riebeeck landed at the Cape in 1652, the scale of its activity was so small that by 1800 its organization was still residual. There were, at that date, only seven congregations in the entire area. The history of the Church really begins with its enormous nineteenth-century expansion, and almost at once, it was a divided history. The Church of the Cape Colony—and especially of the western Cape—evolved in greater openness to external influence: to British Constitutional ideas about the impropriety of attaching civil disabilities to religious profession, to the liberal theology of the churches in Holland, to a partial acceptance of racial diversity as provided in the franchise for Coloured people. The Dutch Reformed churches of the *diaspora,* however, were quite different in their basic responses to just those influences, and although the degree of their difference resulted in schisms it should not be forgotten that even the Cape Church, once it came to be founded within the Boer Republics, began to share the stricter confessional and national outlook of the Hervormde Kerk and the Gereformeerde Kerk. The external sign of this divergent experience was the setting up of state churches in the Boer Republics at exactly the time when the official recognition of Established Churches was being withdrawn elsewhere in European societies, in the second half of the nineteenth century. Internally, also, the churches that followed the Great Trek were unlike the established ecclesiastical polity of the Cape. The ideology of the Trek itself at first suggested an exclusive quality, a self-consciousness of divine calling and purpose. As the political and national centre of Afrikaner society moved beyond the Orange River, religious developments within the Dutch Reformed faith became more sectarian. The Churches began to assume more of the classic characteristics of sects than of denominations or religious establishments. The Church in the Cape Province was isolated from these changes yet in some measure influenced by them through the diffusion of Afrikaner national self-consciousness. In the Boer heartlands, however, religious exclusiveness became very advanced within the settled wilderness of the new nation.

There then occurred a further change. Just as the three Dutch Reformed churches were settling down and beginning to institutionalize into parallel denominational roles, the drift of the population to the mining cities once again placed a large number of people outside the parochial ministrations of the ecclesiastical structures. In the twentieth century, with increasing industrialization, a majority of the Afrikaners found themselves as a 'poor white' element within an urban society dominated by English-speaking entrepreneurs. The Dutch Reformed churches, which had followed them to the cities, operated within a wholly new situation. The same conditions, of course, affected the English-speaking churches. The white members absorbed the changes: their culture was already very much more urban-orientated and secularized than that of the Boers from the *platteland*. Their black members, on the other hand, often revealed sectarian religious characteristics—seen in the rise of the Independent black sects. The Dutch Reformed churches responded with a still more profound sectarianism: the *anomie* of the poor whites elicited a strong mixture of religious and political exclusiveness, which combined in race-consciousness. The churches bridged the two worlds of experience. In becoming, for the first time, and extremely rapidly, an urban institution, the Dutch Reformed churches of the Transvaal and the Orange Free State provided the moral and spiritual cohesion for a people whose aspirations required a sectarian identity in order to preserve cultural purity from the competition of the English and the blacks. The phenomenon was not stable; by the second half of the twentieth century the new urban church was showing signs of institutionalizing, of surrendering its sectarian insistence upon an exclusive national mission. The rearrangement of South African political society by the National Party after 1948 placed the Dutch Reformed churches within a friendly world of temporal reference: they started to shed the mantle of the urban wilderness. It may also be thought that the partial sacralization of Afrikaner politics, accomplished by churchmen both in the structure of the church and in the machinery of the state, has delayed the secularization of values so that even now Afrikaners are among the least secularized white people on earth, though change is becoming quite rapid.

The Dutch Reformed churches were, therefore, in effect, reconstituted around three distinct historical changes: at the Cape after 1800, in the new world of religious pluralism; in the Boer Republics of the later nineteenth century, in response to *trekker* ideals of a rural order free from British influence; and in the urban industrialization of the twentieth-century Transvaal, as symbols of the spiritual authority of Afrikaner cultural purity. The historical experience of the English-speaking churches was quite different. Like the Dutch Reformed Church they initially had some relationship to government. They received some state financial support in the first half of the nineteenth century, and their educational work got public assistance for very much longer. The disappearance of these elements of establishmentarianism was largely the result of movements of opinion within the churches themselves—as they came to reflect the notions of voluntary association and ecclesiastical autonomy that they encountered in British developments. The rise of Nonconformity, and the growth of liberal ideas about the neutral basis of the state's recognition of religious diversity, were quickly conveyed to the colony. The association of the English-speaking churches with British imperial-nationalism grew towards the end of the century—in correspondence with the development of ideals like those of Rhodes—and then declined. As the political initiative fell increasingly to Afrikaner nationalism, the political involvement of the English-speaking churches, in a national sense, slipped away as well. The race issue moved the churches into political opposition to the National Party government after 1948, but by then the secularization of white English-speaking society had advanced to the point where a national religious element in white politics was no longer a possibility. The leadership of the churches detached itself from the laity over the politics of race: a clear sign that no fusion of religious and political objectives was likely again on a mass scale within white society. As the English-speaking churches began to move away from the centre of national life they began to acquire sectarian characteristics. Their rejection of the social values of modern South Africa came to be expressed in a rhetoric of absolutes which has decidedly sectarian overtones. They are the new churches of the gathered: the leaders appeal, often in vain, to their own white flocks to join them in a call to righteousness over the race issue. The matter is one of tone, however, and is not to be exaggerated. It is a tendency only, at least as far as the mainstream denominations are concerned. Their external links, with churches and opinion overseas, modify their sense that they are isolated prophets in a land of unrighteousness.

Both the Dutch Reformed and the English-speaking churches
have one experience in common: the impact on religion of the
rise of the modern state. The growth of collectivism has,
as elsewhere in the world, diminished the social role of the
churches by removing most of their welfare functions. British
administrators had begun the expansion of the machinery of the
state in their government of the Cape and Natal, and the Union
government after 1910 continued this. It was, in general, a
pragmatic and non-ideological matter—the state advanced
into greater responsibility for the social and economic life of the
nation without any clear doctrine of state power. This paralleled
the development of the state in Britain and North America. But
the political success of Afrikaner nationalism introduced a
new feature: an ideological basis for collectivism. Apartheid
required, by its very nature, a much more rigorous collectivism
than South Africa had experienced before. It came on top of
'natural' growths to fashion a centralized, secular, powerful
machinery of state. For the churches, of course, this development presaged their own further marginalization. Even the
Dutch Reformed churches, for all their proximity to National
Party politicians, have found their social role in practice
diminished by the machinery of the state. The 'sacred' character
of Afrikaner political thinking, furthermore, despite the language
of religious epic in which it has been rendered, tended to replace
the churches with a quasi-secular alternative national moralism.
'It is not wholly correct to say that the Dutch Reformed Church
was (or became) the "National Party at Prayer" ', as de Kerk
has put it: 'It is more correct to say that the National Party was
itself becoming, if not a church, then a party imbued with
religion—a secular religion—at its very roots.'[1] When the
Dutch Reformed churches aspired to act independently of
National Party ideology, in however tentative a manner, they
discovered the realities of their residual role in the modern state.
Representations made to the government by the Federal Council
of the Church over the Native Laws Amendment Bill in 1957 no
doubt helped to secure the adjustments made to the offending
clause 29, but their main point—that it was the exclusive right

[1] W. A. de Klerk, *The Puritans in Africa: A History of Afrikanerdom*, London, 1976 edn,
p. 199.

of the Church to determine the circumstances of its mission—was ignored. The rejection by the government of the position taken by the Dutch Reformed delegates at the Cottesloe consultation, in 1960, was a further indication of how little the church actually set the terms of its association with public life. These were not evidences of a sort of erastianism, but a real separation of church and state.

One immediate difficulty in any survey of the relations of church and state, therefore, is the different experience of the Afrikaans and the English-speaking religious bodies. Despite that, it is possible to divide the history of Church and State relations into two distinct sequences: the nineteenth-century movement of the constitutional separation of religion and government, and the nineteenth- and twentieth-century acceptance by the churches, of both language groups, of a mission to political society—an identification with national ideology in the one case, and a criticism of it in the other.

The separation of Church and State in the Cape Province and Natal closely parallels British colonial experience in general during the nineteenth century. Both the ideas and the stages by which the separation became effective have their counterparts in Canada, Australia, the West Indies, and elsewhere. Events were related to the development of opinion in Britain itself, and, as there, the work of separation was carried out by Christian agencies themselves, concerned about the attainment of equality between the denominations and about the freedom of religion from government control. This was unlike the historical experience of Europe or South America, where separation was in general carried out by forces hostile to the churches. In South Africa, first the Vereenighde Ooste-Indische Compagne, and then the early British colonial administration, protected the principle of state religion. This gave the Cape, indeed, a religious uniformity not found in Holland itself. In the seventeenth and eighteenth centuries no opposition to the Dutch Reformed Church was permitted. Thus when, in 1737, the Moravian George Schmidt arrived, he was forbidden to perform ministerial functions in the settled areas and had to move on to a mission station. Whereas the provision of religion was scarcely the first obligation of the Company, in practice it appointed 900 *predikante* in the period of its rule at the Cape. Strict government control operated. 'By hul annkoms in die Kaap het die predikante onder die gesag van die goewerneur en die Politieke Raad gekom en die owerheidseggenskap is onderstreep deurdat hierdie aankomende leraars nie deur 'n Kerkraad na 'n bepaalde gemeente beroep is nie, maar na goeddunke deur die goewerneur geplaas is,' as Professor van der Watt has written.[2] In fact, this sort of control had a strongly erastian character. Moorrees remarked: 'Die Kerk word dus geheel beskou as 'n departement van die Staat, en sy dienaars met die burgerlike amptenare op gelyke voet gestel.'[3] The government named half the members of the *kerkraad*—first set up in 1665. But in return for control the Church was guaranteed in the purity of its teachings (in the decrees of the Synod of Dort), was supported finacially, and was entrusted with educational work in the colony.

When the British occupied the Cape in 1795, the articles of capitulation provided that the Dutch Reformed Church should continue as the official religion, and, again, in 1806, the British undertook to preserve the religious establishment. In fact the British governor, Sir David Baird, refused to allow the Church of England chaplain to the garrison to exercise religious functions among the civilian population; and when, in 1813, the Methodist Conference in England dispatched John McKenry to work at the Cape, the government would not allow him, either, to minister, and he departed for Ceylon. In 1820 Lord Somerset, when governor, took the initiative in bringing a band of Presbyterian ministers from Scotland to reinforce the Dutch Reformed Church. He had, however, the secondary motive of seeking to assimilate the Dutch Reformed Church to the English language: in 1828 English became the official language of the Colony. But his action did recognize a state obligation towards the maintenance of the existing religious establishment. The Scots pastors, as it happened, assimilated to the Afrikaner culture.

Despite the first British desire to sustain a unitary religious

[2] P. B van der Watt, *Die Nederduitse Gereformeerde Kerk*, Pretoria, 1976, i. 24. (At their arrival at the Cape the predikants came before the governor and the political council who took charge of them because they had not been sent by an ecclesiastical council to an accredited congregation but were placed under the control of the governor.)

[3] A. Moorrees, *Die Nederduitse Gereformeerde Kerk in Suid-Afrika, 1652–1872*, Cape Town, 1937, p. 478. (The Church is therefore wholly seen as a department of the state, and the ministers of the church are put on the same footing as the civil officials.)

establishment, in practice the state began—as it did elsehere in British Colonial experience—to give financial assistance to other denominations. A pragmatic concurrent endowment of the larger churches resulted: of the ministers who arrived in the wake of the British settlers of 1820. In the 1830s the Cape Dutch Reformed Church received over £4,000 in payments for the maintenance of its clergy, the Church of England got nearly £2,000, and the Roman Catholics and Presbyterians received £200 each. By the 1860s the allocation to the Dutch Reformed Church had risen to nearly £9,000. In Natal, similarly, state payments were made to the clergy. The government also gave substantial financial subsidies to the churches to conduct education, especially in the missionary districts. It was not until after 1841 that the state began to undertake direct educational work and even then it was restricted to the white populations. Practical acceptance of religious pluralism, therefore, had led to a widening of the basis of the establishment principle. State control of the official establishment also continued for well into the nineteenth century. Indeed, it had been reinforced by de Mist's Ordinance of 1804.

Between 1804 and 1806 the Cape was returned to the government of the Batavian Republic. The Commander-General, J. A. de Mist, representing the notions of administrative and legal codification which were part of the inheritance of the Eurepean Englightenment, introduced a programme of systematic governmental reform to the Cape. His Church Ordinance proclaimed official religious toleration, but it also subjected religion to even more systematic controls than had previously existed: a curious erastianism in view of the fact that the old relationship of Church and State had been dissolved in Holland in 1795. The Dutch Reformed Church was, in the Ordinance, organically divorced from the jurisdiction of the Classis of Amsterdam, decisions of Church Courts were subject to the approval of the Cape government, state permission was required for the establishment of new congregations, for the appointment of ministers, and for the assembly of all church meetings, consistories, presbyteries, and synods, and at these meetings the attendance of 'Political Commissioners', appointed by the state, was required by Article 46 of the Ordinance. It was also quite clear that, despite the toleration of other churches, the Dutch Reformed faith was to remain the official church. As a sign of this, de Mist insisted that the agents of the London Missionary Society should retrict their ministrations to the native population, on the explicit grounds that otherwise they would encroach upon the recognized church of the country. When the British resumed control of the Cape, in 1806, they continued to enforce de Mist's code. It operated, therefore, to perpetuate the principle of established religion into the nineteenth century. The appointment of two *Kommissarisse Politiek* to sit in the Consistories (until 1828) and the Synods (until 1852) was the symbol of this. Their powers, in fact, were rather more than merely symbolic. The Commissioners who sat in the first synod at Cape Town, in 1824, kept a close control of the proceedings and afterwards sent a report of the resolutions to London to receive the royal assent. The British government evidently found this inappropriate—perhaps not wishing to create so direct a relationship between the Crown and colonial ecclesiastical administration—for 'nothing further was heard of the matter'.[4]

By the middle years of the nineteenth century it was becoming plain to many that the principle of established religion, even in the broadened form then practised at the Cape, was anomalous. In 1842 one of the Political Commissioners secured the rejection of a decision of the Dutch Reformed synod, and this elicited from that body a resolution hostile to state interference in ecclesiastical matters. The governor, Sir George Napier, announced his preparedness 'to free the Church from the trammels of secular interference in all spiritual or purely ecclesiastical matters',[5] and the result was Ordinance No. 7 of 1843. Section 8 recognized the voluntary nature of religious associations, and Section 9 the independent spiritual jurisdiction of the Church. In practice this established the autonomy of the Dutch Reformed Church and repealed most of de Mist's regulations. It was a measure of disestablishment without raising ultimate principles of constitutional theory. 'Met dit in gedagte moet opgemerk word dat die Ned. Geref. Kerk veel by hierdie ordonnansie gebaat het: die kerk was nou vry in die bestuur van sy huishoudelike aangeleenthede soos blyk uit bepaling drie

[4] J. du Plessis, *A History of the Christian Missions in South Africa*, London, 1911, p. 253.
[5] John McCarter, *The Dutch Reformed Church in South Africa*, Edinburgh, 1869, p. 37.

van die maatreël dat die Sinode die bevoegdheid besit om sy eie
inwendige sake te reël.' Disestablishment, however, was not
complete—'Tog was daar nie volkome vryheid vir die Kerk
nie, want die staat het nog steeds 'n algehele toesig oor baie
dinge bly behou.'[6]
Once the relationship of the State to the Church had been
clarified by the Ordinance of 1843, other practical steps to
separation became possible. At the Cape after 1851, and in
Natal after 1866, no new grants were made to pay the stipends
of the clergy of the different denominations, although existing
arrangements were respected, and appointments to ecclesiastical
posts to which state financial aid was still attached continued
to require the formal assent of the government. Some eighty
clergymen continued to be paid by the state. These payments
were particularly offensive to the stricter nationalist element
within the Dutch Reformed faith, and it was in fact his receipt of
a British government stipend which made Dr Andrew Murray
so disliked among the sectarian *trekker* groups whom he visited
in 1849: 'Iemand wat van die Engelese regering betaling ontvang
het, deel aan sy sonde; en om die rede kon Ds. Murray geen
ware dienskneg van Jesus wees nie.'[7]
    The next stage of separation came in the momentous events
associated with the Dutch Reformed Synod of 1862. The stimulus
then given to the further separation of Church and State was
actually a by-product of an attempt by the liberals within the
Cape clergy to exclude members from the Transgariep—who
were more conservative in both theological and ecclesiastical
outlook. Many of the liberals were ideologically opposed to a
connection of Church and State. Articles in favour of complete
disestablishment appeared often in their journal *De Onderzoeker*.
The conflict with the Transgariep ministers revealed how different the two sections of the Dutch Reformed faith had become:
the *trekker* church on the one hand, and the settled church of the
Cape on the other, more open to external influences, more
relaxed in its understanding of the applications of Calvinism.

---

[6] van der Watt, op. cit., ii. 105. (Even so there was not complete freedom for the
Church because the State still had a complete right to look over and to maintain many
things.)
    [7] Moorrees, op. cit., p. 748. (Anyone who has received payment from the English
Government, for his sins does so, and for this reason Doctor Murray could be no true
servant of Jesus.)

After the 1862 Synod had declined to accept their protest against the presence of the ministers from beyond the Orange River, the liberals took their case to the civil courts. The result was a ruling that the decision of the 1852 Synod to admit clergy from outside the Cape Province was beyond the Synod's competence. This removed all the clergy of the Transgariep, eventually obliging them to set up their own synods and so recognize their own disestablishment. But the effect upon the constitutional position of the Cape Church was even more far-reaching. For in the Cape Province the civil courts had overruled the spiritual autonomy of the Church, as defined in the Ordinance of 1843. The Synod was then brought into direct collision with the law when their expulsion of J. J. Kotzé and T. F. Burgers (who was later President of the Transvaal) was ruled illegal by the Supreme Court. In 1866 the Synod committee appealed to the Judicial Committee of the Privy Council in London over the Burgers case; but they were not successful. Here, then, was a classic confrontation of the civil and ecclesiastical jurisdictions. It made the vestiges of the Church's established status appear particularly anomalous and convinced many, even of the most conservative opinion, that a complete separation was to be desired. In the Anglican Church, the Colenso case of 1865 had had a similar consequence.

The constitutional position of the Church of England in South Africa—the state church of the imperial power—had never been very precisely defined. It had received state financial aid, but so had the other leading denominations. For many years, and at least until the appointment of the first bishop—Robert Gray, in 1848—the governors of the province technically exercised ecclesiastical jurisdiction. In the middle decades of the nineteenth century, furthermore, nine churches were set up by the government, with state financial aid and legal incorporation, each separately related to the Church of England. But this situation was not really constitutional: the Church of England never enjoyed the legal privileges of the Dutch Reformed Church. By the second half of the century the Anglicans, too, were prepared to countenance a complete end of state financial aid to religion. The Scottish Disruption, a schism caused by the application of erastian principles, was reproduced among the Presbyterians of the Cape, who had their own schism in 1844, and this (although it did not last more than three years) acted as another stimulus in favour of complete voluntarism in religion.

The accomplishment of institutional autonomy by the churches—their separation from parent bodies in Europe— also assisted their disconnection from the state, since it strengthened their governing capacities and gave them a coherent existence independent of state protection or favour. The Dutch Reformed Church was finally separated from Dutch control by the convening of the 1824 Synod. The foundation of the Stellenbosch seminary in 1859 gave it the means to train its own ministers instead of sending them to Holland. The Church of England's independence was expressed by the assembly of the first Cape Synod in 1856 and the first Provincial Synod in 1870. The Colenso judgement in 1865 had established the principle that the Crown could not administer ecclesiastical jurisdiction in colonies which had their own legislatures. The Catholics received their independence from the Vicar Apostolic of Mauritius in 1827, the year in which Bishop Patrick Raymund Griffith was named as Vicar Apostolic of the Cape.

It was Saul Solomon, a Congregationalist, who promoted legislation for complete disestablishment in the Cape parliament. Eventually, in 1875, his Voluntary Bill passed, with the general approval of both the Dutch Reformed and the Anglican churches. All state payments to religious bodies were to cease, although existing life-interests were preserved: a pattern of disestablishment very similar to that adopted in 1869 by the Imperial parliament in relation to Ireland. Only the Catholics were divided in their attitude to the legislation. Bishop Thomas Grimley supported the principle of the Bill; Bishop Patrick Moran was against—because of its adverse consequences for church finance. In a characteristically British manner the debate about the disconnection of Church and State in South Africa was pragmatic and declined to go into theoretical implications about the moral basis of political society. Very few appeared to imagine that secularization of public life would follow.

The second sequence of church and state relations in South Africa was quite different. Developments within the Dutch Reformed churches beyond the Orange River were clearly ideological rather than pragmatic, 'sectarian' rather than 'denominational'. For the *trekkers* cultivated exclusivist religious ideals, and set up their own state churches in the new territories they settled. They were churches of a gathered people, seeing themselves as related by a special covenant with God. The Blood River Oath of 1838, indeed, was an expression of this ideal in directly covenantal language. In June 1837, the organic law of the first Voortrekker State—the Constitution of Winburg— established the Dutch Reformed faith as the national church. Piet Retief, in the oath administerd to him by Erasmus Smit, undertook to 'protect and defend the Christian Creed' according to 'the Catechism and liturgies of the Dutch Reformed Church'. The government of the new state would 'not permit any official to act as such in the administration of Church and Civil Goverment, except such as are members of the aforesaid Reformed Church'.[8] Just as the practice of established religion was being progressively removed in the Cape Province, as indeed in most European societies, in the Boer republics it was about to have an extended existence. In this, as in some other features, the political independence of the Afrikaners preserved aspects of public life which were fast disappearing elsewhere. In Natal, in 1846, it was declared that financial aid and legal recognition would be given only to the Dutch Reformed Church—'Dat door het Publiek of uit de Publiek kas niets tot eenige andere godsdienstige stigting zal worden toegedaan dan alleen tot de waare Gereformeerde Kerk, en dat ook geen andere Godsdienst onder ons zal worden getollereerd dan alleen de zuivere gereformeerde leer.'[9] In 1850 it was decided that only members of the official church could join the *Volksraad*, and so take part in political life. In the Orange Free State, similarly, the Dutch Reformed Church was established by the Constitution of 1854. In the Transvaal the Church was made an official establishment in 1852.

The Transvaal situation was complicated by the two schisms which resulted in the setting-up, first at Potchefstroom in 1853,

---

[8] Johannes Meintjes, *The Voortrekkers. The Story of the Great Trek and the Making of South Africa*, London, 1973, p. 73.
[9] G. D. Scholtz, *Die Geskiedenis van die Nederduitse Hervormde of Gereformeerde Kerk van Suid-Afrika*, Cape Town, 1956, i. 48. (That the Republic shall give nothing to any other religious group, only to the true Reformed Church, and no other form of worship shall be tolerated but the pure reformed faith alone.)

of the Hervormde Kerk, and then, at Rustenburg in 1859, of the Gereformeerde Kerk. Both were attempts at purifying the Dutch Reformed faith of liberal and anglicizing elements. One of them, the Hervormde Kerk, became the State Church of the South African Republic from the constitition of 1858 until the Union of 1910—throughout all the various political vicissitudes of the Transvaal. The state provided the stipends of the clergy and directly undertook to protect the doctrines of the Synod of Dort (by Article 20 of the Constitution) to refuse to allow the existence of Roman Catholic or other Protestant churches in the Republic (Article 21), to permit only members of the Dutch Reformed congregations to take part in political life (Article 22), and to recognize only the ecclesiastical jurisdiction of the state church (Article 23). It was the very exclusivity of this state confessionalism which stood in such contrast to developments elsewhere. As Frans Lion Cachet remarked in 1867: 'Een Republiek met eene staatskerk is in de 19de eeuw reeds *a priori* een *contradictio in terminis*,'[10] It was the more remarkable for being established in the face of an existing religious pluralism, with the two products of the schisms existing alongside the Nederduitse Gereformeerde Kerk which Cachet helped to reintroduce to the Transvaal. As a dissenting denomination, it set up its own Synod in 1872.

Within a decade, the economic and social upheaval associated with the gold-mining industry then began to add a large population to the Transvaal whose religious affiliations lay entirely outside the Dutch Reformed tradition. Some practical adjustments were required to the strict confessionalism of the state. As early as 1870 the performance of the Catholic mass had ceased to be a legal offence; and at the start of the twentieth century, indeed, Kruger's government actually gave state financial aid to a Catholic educational establishment in Johannesburg. Liberalization of the confessional aspects of public life was limited, however, and proved not irreversible—as the history of education in the Transvaal showed. The secularizing tendencies of Burger's educational legislation in 1874, which was in line with general developments in the Cape Province, were reversed in the Education Act of 1882. This was the work

[10] Ibid., i. 243. (A Republic with a state church is in the nineteenth century already *a priori* a contradiction in terms.)

of the Revd S. J. du Toit, a leader of neo-Calvinist and nationalist revivalism. Under his influence 'the Church was to be the guiding factor in educational organization'.[11] In view of the central position of the controversies over religious education in the classic nineteenth-century conflicts of Church and State elsewhere in the world, du Toit's accomplishment had a symbolical as well as an educational importance.

It was the nationalist and sectarian characteristics of the Afrikaner political experience, rather than theological or institutional considerations, that provided the basis for the involvement of the Dutch Reformed churches with the state in the second half of the nineteenth century, and in the succeeding century. This fact is not immediately apparent. Historians have rightly emphasized the influence of Abraham Kuyper's neo-Calvinism in shaping the national and political outlook of the Reformed Churches in the Boer Republics, but the real nature of that influence was more secondary than is often supposed. Kuyper had developed van Prinsterer's universal explanation of the division of common grace into the various social institutions. His was a sort of Dutch Calvinist counterpart of the neo-Thomism of Europe and South America in the second half of the nineteenth century and the first decades of the twentieth: a reaction against secularization and liberalism. In South Africa, Kuyper's theology was adapted to circumstance; his belief in a separation of Church and State, well suited to the unsympathetic world of European liberal politics, was not emphasized, but his teaching about the need for both religion and civil government to incorporate a common divine function, expressed in national destiny, was easily and rapidly conflated with the existing cultural opposition to the dominance of British ideals. Inside the Church, this gave a systematic rationale to the *trekker* dislike of the Evangelicalism and liberalism which had become so influential in the Cape Church. In S. J. du Toit, who arrived in the Transvaal from the Cape in 1882 in order to become Superintendent of Education, Kuyper's style of neo-Calvinism found both a South African theoretician and a forceful and effective political activist. It was du Toit who had already propagated the national ideals which found their expression in the Afriker Bond—ideas which were deeply religious, even

---

[11] Ernst G. Malherbe, *Education in South Africa*, Cape Town, 1925, i, 258.

theocratic. But despite the enormous importance of Kuyperian neo-Calvinism it was not the cause of the close association of religion and developing Boer nationalism. It acted, on the contrary, as an aid to the theorizing of church involvement with political society. Neo-Calvinism was not the source of the new religious nationalism: that derived from the sectarian nature of the *trekker* churches themselves, from the sectarian identification of the gathered elect which had already laid the foundation of the schism churches before Kuyperian theology was brought in to intellectualize an existing departure from the compromising ideas and practices of the Cape church. Thus it was the 'Dopper church', the Gereformeerde Kerk of the Transvaal, which disclosed the most classic sectarian characteristics, as it sought with the greatest precision and singularity of purpose to cleanse the Dutch Reformed faith of worldly (that is to say, liberal and anglicized) errors in its conduct of worship and its attitude to the creation of a Christian society. The schism which produced the Hervormde Kerk, also, was a rejection of an alien society with its political impurities; its foundation was 'due less to religious than to political motives', as du Plessis has written,[12] or, as perhaps it is more accurately expressed, more to social than to theological motives. For it was the hostile world of nineteenth-century secularizing change, as apparently represented by British social institutions, that the schism churches tried to discard. They were true sects—the means by which men sought to render their social aspirations and peculiar calling in contrast to the corrupted order around them. In a less austere form, furthermore, this vision of things was increasingly evident inside the Nederduitse Gereformeerde Kerk also, both in the Boer republics and in the Cape Province. With the urbanization of the Reformed chuches in the Transvaal and the Orange Free State, from the end of the nineteenth century, their sectarian quality acquired a reinforced utility. For it helped to give cultural pride and personal identity to the poor white Afrikaners as they found themselves once again encompassed by the alien values of Anglio-Saxon society in the industrial cities of the Rand. Perpetuated once again, the sectarianism of the Reformed churches slowly began to institutionalize into denominationalism as the political culture around them came

[12] J. du Plessis, *The Life of Andrew Murray of South Africa*, London, 1920, p. 144.

under their own influence, and then came to dominate the alien
world and make it serve their own purposes. That was a development which finally became apparent after 1948. Until
then, 'the self-preservation of the nation could be regarded as a
task for which the church was responsible'.[13] After the national
Party's victory the unavoidable combination of Afrikaner political sentiment and state collectivism rendered the Dutch Reformed churches increasingly less necessary as guardians of
national purity. Their denominationalization then occurred
because they had become real denominations: their place in
society could now merge into the other institutions, though they
retained some special honours because of their personal and
historical proximity to the governing groups. But they had
ceased to have the function of national churches, since the state
itself had come to act as the moral purifier of the social order.

The practice of state religion in South Africa therefore had an
informal existence after the disappearance of the last consitu-
tional establishment in 1910. Informal connections of church
and state are common enough in societies where there is a
continued public religiosity and determination to preserve religious equality between the competing denominations — in the
United States for example. But the South African position has
been rather different, because of the religious and moral nature
of Nationalist political ideology and its obvious association with
the Dutch Reformed churches. 'The history of the Afrikaner
reveals a determination and definiteness of purpose which make
one feel that Afrikanerdom is not the work of man but a creation
of God,' as Malan put it. 'We have a divine right to be Afrikaners,
our history is the highest work of the architect of the centuries.'[14]
Nationalist politicians have made frequent reference to the
Christian character of national institutions, and the Constitution of the Republic, promulgated in 1961, describes South
Africa as a Christian country. That, too, is not unusual, and
even quite secularized modern states offer examples of surviving religious reference in their organic laws. The second sequence
of the South African history of Church and State relations — the

---

[13] W. Kistner, 'The 16th. of December in the context of Nationalistic thinking', in
Theo Sundermeier (ed.), *Church and Nationalism in South Africa*, Johannesburg, 1975,
p. 81.
[14] Ibid., p. 85.

sequence describing the Dutch Reformed churches' national role—for all its surviving traces, is ceasing to be a vital element in national development.

In their approach to government, in fact, the Dutch Reformed churches do not now differ substantially from the English-speaking churches. What they disagree about, of course, and that very deeply, is the actual policy of the existing government. Where they are comparable is in their belief that it is the office of the Christian church to have a mission towards the state—to have a political function in the sense of articulating Christian opinion about the collective conduct of the nation's affairs. In recent decades only the Baptist church and the Indpendent Black churches have in general declined to embrace a public role of this sort. The Anglicans and the Catholics declared on public issues long before the rise of racial issues to the centre of politics in the middle years of the present century. The Angicans did so because it was a part of their inheritance as a former state church; because their association with British nationalism in South African development was a close one; and because their progressive criticisms of social and institutional conditions, copied from their parent body in England, projected them into political debate. The involvement of the Catholics resulted from—as W. E. Brown put it—'the Catholic tradition that a bishop should accept, as far as justice allows, the temporal outlook of his people';[15] from co-operation and conflict with the state over education; and from the political interests of Catholic journalism, especially *The Cape Colonist*, founded by Bishop Aiden Devereux in 1850—and which established an early tradition of Catholic commentary on public issues. In both these churches, of course, it is the race question which has, especially since 1948, drawn them further into the area of political discourse. The Methodist church has also acquired a mission to the state in consequence of the priority of race issues. The controversy over the so-called 'church clause' (Clause 29c) in the Native Laws Amendment Bill of 1957, saw most of the denominations in direct conflict with government policy. A major clash of Church and State resulted. The original clause, which empowered the government to restrict the attendance

[15] W. E. Brown, *The Catholic Church in South Africa. From its Origins to the Present Day*, London, 1960, p. 37.

of blacks at public worship in white-designated areas, was regarded as a clear state infringement of the churches' freedom of worship. The clause was modified, passed in parliament, but never implemented. The protest drawn up by Archbishop Geoffrey Clayton and the Anglican bishops had classic tones: 'We believe that obedience to secular authority, even in matters about which we differ in opinion, is a command laid upon us by God,' the bishops wrote to the Prime Minister. 'But we are commanded to render unto Caesar the things which be Caesar's and to God the things that are God's . . . we feel bound to state that if the Bill were to become law in its present form we should oursleves be unable to obey it or to counsel our clergy and people to do so.'[16] Opposition to apartheid also determined the circumstances in which other Anglican leaders defined a political role for their church. Trevor Huddleston observed in 1956 that 'Prophecy is still a function of the church,' and added, 'in short—in politics.'[17] Ambrose Reeves, Bishop of Johannesburg (until he fled to Swaziland in 1960), advocated church co-operation with secular, radical politics in order to defeat government policies. Joost de Blank, Archbishop of Cape Town, wrote in 1958: 'Our Lord was crucified because He was accused of interfering in politics. Acquiescence in a policy is just as much a political activity as criticism.'[18]

The white churches were not the only ones to be in some measure politicized by the race question. The black Independent churches have, it is true, continued to eschew a political role, and the main black denominational churches have only just begun to adopt social and political interests. But the rise of Back Consciousness, expressed within the Black Theology ideology of a small but growing urban élite within the contemporary black churches, has very decidedly established a black view on the mission of Christianity to the ordering of society. Like other versions of the Theology of Liberation, it associates the faith with the pursit of fundamental changes in the nature of social and political institutions. 'Black Theology', as Dr Allan Boesak, a coloured minister of the Dutch Reformed Church has written,

[16] Alan Paton, *Apartheid and the Archbishop. The Life and Times of Geoffrey Clayton, Archbishop of Cape Town*, London, 1974, p. 280.
[17] Trevor Huddleston, *Naught For Your Comfort*, London, 1956, p. 239.
[18] Bertha de Blank, *Joost de Blank. A Personal Memoir*, Ipswich, 1977, p. 116.

'must mean a search for a totally new social order.' [19] Advocates of Black Theology point to its attempt to restore the 'tremendous sense of community' in traditional black culture;[20] Christianity will help to give a social expression to the emergent black political order they hope to see established.

Within the white Dutch Reformed churches, too, the prominence of racial questions has in recent decades directed attention to their relations with political society. As institutions close to the aspirations of the Afrikaner people, as early promoters of the language movement, whose ministers have themselves sometimes directly entered politics—like Malan himself—the Dutch Reformed churches have an inherent proximity to the existing state. That does not necessarily mean, however, that they are unthinkingly given to complete identification with the results of the political processes. Criticisms have sometimes been made of particular governmental measures, usually privately. It is thought 'that members of the Government frequently consult *dominees* on matters of state'.[21] The Dutch Reformed churches, in fact, behave as the English-speaking churches do: they believe that the Church should be involved in social and political questions and that their message should not be merely pietistic. After he had visited South Africa in 1952, the then General Secretary of the World Council of Churches, Visser't Hooft, remarked that the Dutch Reformed churches should not be criticized for involving themselves in politics, but for involvement with the wrong sort of politics. The Nederduitse Gereformeerde Kerk has itself taught that although the Church ought to be associated with the people, it ought not to be absorbed by their interests; that 'the Church may never become a political institution which forsakes its own spiritual calling by pronouncing for or against the power structure within the state or in favour of one or other political party'.[22] This position, as the Reformed Church is fully aware, is in accordance with its own

[19] Allan Boesak, *Farewell to Innocence. A Social-ethical study of black theology and black power*, Johannesburg, 1977, p. 118.
[20] Sabelo Ntwasa, 'The Concept of the Church in Black Theology', in *Black Theology. The South African Voice*, ed. Basil Moore, London, 1973, p. 117.
[21] Ivor Wilkins and Hans Strydom, *The Super-Afrikaners. Inside the Afrikaner Broederbond*, Johannesburg, 1978, p. 284.
[22] *Human Relations and the South African Scene in the Light of Scripture. Report approved by the General Synod of the D.R.C., 1974*, Cape Town, 1976, p. 45.

traditional teaching—teaching whose centrality in Calvinism is never far from the historical understanding of the Church in South Africa. Civil and spiritual government are believed to be interdependent. 'For that spiritual reign, even now upon earth', as Calvin wrote, 'commences within us some preludes of the heavenly kingdom, and in this mortal and transitory life affords us some prelibations of immortal and incorruptible blessedness; but this civil government is designed, as long as we live in this world, to cherish and support the external worship of God, to preserve the pure doctrine of religion, to defend the constitution of the Church, to regulate our lives in a manner requisite for the society of men, to form our manners to civil justice, to promote our concord with each other, and to establish general peace and tranquillity.'[23] The results, in South Africa, as elsewhere, have fallen rather short of this ideal.

---

[23] *A Compend of the Institutes of the Christian Religion by John Calvin*, ed. Hugh Thomson Kerr, Philadelphia, 1939, p. 203 (*Institutes*, IV. XX. 2).

2

The Churches and the Race Question

It has become conventional, among interpreters of South Africa's complicated history, to discern a clear consistency in the attitudes of the Dutch Reformed churches on the one hand, and of the English-speaking churches on the other, to racial issues. Their differences of attitude, that is to say, were implicit from the start. They evolved in a parallel manner, until the final hostility between them erupted over the race policies of the National Party government after 1948. The Dutch colonists— according to this interpretation—had degraded the indigenous peoples of the Cape; in the nineteenth century they formalized their antipathy to non-whites by conflict with black tribal groups on the eastern frontier, institutionalized notions of white racial supremacy in the Boer Republics, until, in the twentieth century, Nationalist ideology presented their experience in a systematic state structure. The English-speaking settlers, in contrast, are represented as having had an early respect for the native populations, as having opposed their exploitation by the Boer farmers, and then, over a century and a half, as having developed a series of enlightened attitudes which, though only gradually coming to recognize the subtle qualities of Bantu culture, at least provided the components of what ought to have coalesced into a multi-racial democratic state—in correspondence to Christian teachings about human equality.

In fact, the history of religious opinion in relation to race issues is more helpfully expressed in three stages. In the first half of the nineteenth century the English and the Dutch churches were indeed opposed to each other in their different (and often exaggerated) responses to the native populations— largely because of existing political and cultural, as well as religious, antipathies within their joint European inheritance. But attitudes at that time were really still fairly fluid on some race questions, and within the churches there was probably less difference of view than in general society. Between the mid-

nineteenth century and the middle of the succeeding one, however, the white population groups moved towards sharing a
common approach: separation of the races for both humanitarian and cultural reasons. Then, in a third development, they
diverged again, as the ideology of Nationalism externalized the
inherent social and economic insecurities of the urbanized
poor whites, and as the sectarianism of the Dutch Reformed
churches, in the areas of urban growth, drew the Afrikaner
element in one direction, and defeated English nationalism,
together with knowledge of overseas developments and ideas,
inside the English-speaking churches, drew them in another.
Mutually exclusive views on the basis of society and government then emerged. There were, of course, in those broad
developments, a number of chronological disparities and some
individual exceptions. But the general pattern of the evolution
of opinion can still be made reasonably clear for purposes of
analysis.

Before the start of the nineteenth century the Dutch settlers
at the Cape had actually shown themselves quite ready to
assimilate persons of non-Dutch origin. Nearly a third of the
population in the eighteenth century were Germans, and round
15 per cent were French—mostly Huguenots. The French were
obliged to adopt the Dutch Reformed faith, but the Germans
retained their Lutheranism, and it was not until early in the
twentieth century that Lutherans of ultimate German origin
began to identify themselves with the aspirations of Afrikaner
society. This acceptance of cultural pluralism, of course, was
very limited: restricted to variations within north European
national groups. There existed, in relation to the Hottentots at
the Cape, and to the growing 'Coloured' population, a considerable prejudice, more among the Boer farmers than within
the relatively sophisticated society of Cape Town. Its crude
ideology was represented by a belief in their inability to
attain the manners of European society; its practical basis was
economic. The non-whites were the source of cheap labour,
and, on the expanding eastern frontier of the colony, where the
whites were in direct competition with blacks for land, they
were actual economic competitors. The emancipation of the
Hottentots in 1828 and the abolition of slavery in 1833–4 had
the joint effects of threatening the Boer settlers' way of life. It

was 'not so much the loss of slaves as a form of property, as it was their loss as a source of labor that undermined the foundations of the farm economy of the eastern frontier.'[1] The British settlers had no slaves, yet it was British missionary opinion and British administation which forced the changes that hurt the Dutch financially. That, however, was only one aspect of the national gulf between the two white populations—a gulf which transferred itself easily enough to sharpen religious differences. Yet before opinions hardened, the Dutch had allowed mixed-race marriages: the source of the Cape Coloured population. It was the custom of some of the missionaires sent out by the English societies to marry native girls—an attempt to set an example and foster multi-racial attitudes—which helped to discredit mixed marriages in the eyes of the Dutch residents. Vanderkemp's marriage to a slave child was regarded as particularly scandalous. Despite his Dutch origin, Vanderkemp worked for the London Missionary Society from 1798 and almost equalled Philip in the antipathy he aroused among the Dutch colonists. The Dutch Reformed Church of this period was not segregated. In 1829 the Cape Synod ruled that Holy Communion was to be administered to all members equally, and at the same time, without any distinction of colour. It was not until the Synod of 1857 that separate services were provided for: after that time no more coloured congregations were affiliated, though a few remained within the old white structure until they joined the black and coloured 'daughter churches' early in the twentieth century.

The attitude of the Dutch Reformed Church, and of the settlers in general, towards the non-white population was acquired largely in relation to the Hottentot and Coloured peoples—whose cultural differences were not regarded as threatening. The Hottentots could be left alone or, as some missionaries of the Dutch Reformed Church hoped, Europeanized; and the Coloureds were, anyway, scaracely separated in cultural terms from the whites. The eastward movement of the Cape frontier brought the settlers into contact with the Bantu, however. Their cultural integrity was much less assimil-

---

[1] S. Daniel Neumark, *Economic Influences on the South African Frontier, 1652–1836*, Stanford, 1957, p. 185.

able. This contact—which eighteenth-century administrators had vainly sought to prevent, in the edicts of 1727, 1789, and 1770—was a major reason for the hardening attitudes on race questions in the first half of the nineteenth century. The church of the eastern frontier, and the church of the Great Trek, shared the race-attitudes of their laity much more faithfully than the church in the Western Cape.

It was, of course, the influence of the British missionaries which did most to harden opinion within the Dutch Reformed Church. The missionaries were, in the first half of the nine-teenth century, only a small band, but colonial society was itself very small-scale, and their influence was for that reason—and because they had the ear both of the colonial administration and of parliamentary opinion in England—enormous. Their propaganda assaults upon the Boer farmers (and sometimes on their religion) for oppressive treatment of the native population proved to be the greatest trauma in Afrikaner history. The first Constitution of the *Voortrekker* state, the Constitution of Win-burg, adopted in 1837, contained an explicit condemnation of all English missionary societies. The effect of the Black Circuit of 1812 on Boer opinion was enduring. The missionaries had called upon the use of state power for social ends—racial equality—in a manner which provided much of the justifica-tion for the Great Trek. As a sister of Retief declared, the British policy was 'contrary to the laws of God and the difference in descent and religion'. [2] Dr John Philip, most influential of all the missionaries, because of his connections with Evangelical and Philanthropical reformers and government officials in London, has entered the demonology of Afrikaner historical writing. As Dr M. W. Retief said in 1953, when he was Acting Secretary of the Federal Missionary Council of the Dutch Re-formed Churches, Philip 'always sided with the barbarians against the whites'. [3]

Philip arrived at the Cape in 1819 to become Superintendent of the London Missionary Society's work there. To the Colony, only recently established as a British possession, he brought the

[2] Johannes Meintjes, *The Voortekkers. The Story of the Great Trek and the Making of South Africa*, p. 38.
[3] *Christian Principles in Multi-Racial South Africa. A Report on the Dutch Reformed Conference of Church Leaders, 1953*, Johannesburg, 1954, p. 71.

Evangelical moralism of the anti-slavery movement in Britain, and also a set of economic and social attitudes which the Dutch inhabitants found equally unsympathetic. Philip represented the alien world of Political Economy. He was, it is true, critical of some aspects of Malthusian doctrine, and he rejected John Bird Sumner's belief that the Hottentots were incapable of civilization—a notion expressed in Sumner's *Treatise on the Records of the Creation* (1816), a major work linking Christianity and Political Economy. Yet Philip accepted and propagated popularized versions of *laissez-faire* social and economic teachings in a fashion which was, since he related it directly to his understanding of Christianity, particularly offensive to the old-fashioned, isolated, paternalistic values of the Boer farmers. Once at the Cape, Philip heightened an existing antipathy between the English and the Dutch over attitudes to the racial mixture of the Colony by his appeals to the Governor and to the Crown to interfere in the relationship between whites and the native population, and by the publication, in 1828, of his *Researches in South Africa*. This large work, which has ever since provided source materials for English-speaking historians who have been concerned with the Boers' treatment of the natives, was a piece of highly polemical writing. Philip's use of evidence was notably selective. But however limited its reliability as historical evidence, the book was enormously important as a catalyst in the polarizing of race attitudes among the two white language groups. Religious opinion divided along the same lines.

Philip acknowledged that the Dutch Reformed Church had attempted missionary work among the native groups. To some Boer farmers, indeed, these missionaries were known dismissively as 'Hottentot predikants'. As the labour shortage worsened, owing to the government's philanthropic reforms, the farmers began to attack the mission stations set up by the English societies. Beneath the economic causes, however, Philip discerned racial attitudes at the centre of the Boers' relations with the natives. 'In the course of about a century and a half', he wrote, 'the Hottentots had been despoiled of their lands, robbed or cajoled out of their flocks and herds and, with a few exceptions, reduced to personal servitude, under circumstances which rendered them more wretched and more helpless than the slaves with whom they were now associated.'[4] The English missionaries, in contrast, had treated the Hottentots 'like rational beings' and had taught them 'the value of their labour'.[5] There was nothing inherently barbarous about the Hottentots. They were degraded by circumstance and needed to improve their situation by self-help— 'the vices of the Hottentots are the vices of their condition'.[6] This link between environment and moral behaviour was precisely the one being made in England at the time, in relation to the condition of the industrial working classes, by churchmen influenced by Political Economy and by philanthropic writings. Philip's application of the outlook to South African society was vigorous. 'the civilization of that degraded people is not only practicable, but might be easily attained: while they are by no means deficient in intellect, they are susceptible of kindness; grateful for favours; faithful in the execution of trust committed to them; disposed to receive instruction; and, by the use of proper means, could easily be brought to exchange their barbarous manner of life for one that would afford more comfort.'[7] In just such language had Sumner described the prospects for improving the English 'labouring poor'.[8] Religion alone, Philip believed, was the means by which that natives could be civilized, since 'the speculations of science, and the pursuits of literature, are above the comprehension of the untutored savage.'[9] He placed the obligation to undertake this work in ascending levels of importance. It was Hottentots' right under British law to equal treatment; such treatment was also due because of natural law; 'Independent of printed statutes, there are certain rights which human beings possess, and of which they cannot be deprived but by manifest injustice.'[10] Equal treatment was further required because directly commanded by God, who had, as Scripture declares, 'made of one blood all nations of men'. Philip added that this included even 'the wretched victims

---

[4] John Philip, *Researches in South Africa. Illustrating the Civil, Moral, and Religious Condition of the Native Tribes*, London, 1828, i. 55.
[5] Ibid. 141.
[6] Ibid. 159.
[7] Ibid. ii. 9.
[8] See J., B. Summer, *A Treatise on the Records of the Creation*, London, 1816, ii. 92.
[9] Philip, op. cit. ii. 357.
[10] Ibid. i, p. xxvi.

of European avarice and cruelty'.[11] These three grounds for Christian involvement with the race question, singly or in combination, recur throughout the subsequent history of South Africa.

The need to associate religion with the civilizing of native peoples was reinforced by the conviction—a false one, as it happens, but one very widely held, even by those who had lived among the Bantu—that the indigenous cultures contained no distinctly religious ideas. Philip thought this; so did another London Missionary Society agent, Robert Moffat—who wrote, in consequence, of what he called 'the vacant mind of the savage'.[12] Bishop James Ricards, Catholic Vicar Apostolic of the Eastern District, had the same belief: 'They have no visible symbols, no idea of the existence and attributes of a Supreme Being, nor of a future state, or rewards and punishments arising out of the moral qualities of our actions in life.'[13] With such conclusions it was clear that the missionary legacy would involve not only a deepened enmity between the Dutch and the English populations but also a cultural insensitivity to the real nature of Bantu society. Their doctrine of racial equality, however, did lay down a tradition of moral reference to which the missionaries' successors added subsequent evidences. Yet it is important to notice that beneath the polemicism of missionary writing, the Dutch Reformed Church at the Cape also taught basic human equality. It was the frontiersmen and the *trekkers* who for a time departed from this doctrine—and even then not so completely or systematically as is sometimes imagined.

After the mid-century, and in the hundred years that followed, the attitudes of the English and the Dutch towards the question of race began to grow together. The English-speaking churches, though they never departed from their formal adhesion to the ideal of complete equality, in practice reflected the drift of opinion within white society. As the Revd L. A. Hewson, historian of South African Methodism, said in his contribution to the Rosettenville Conference in 1949: 'the Briton has been in South Africa long enough to have reached, even if not by precisely the same routes, the same conclusion as the Boer with regard to the

[11] Ibid., p. xxxii.
[12] Robert Moffat, *Missionary Labours and Scenes in South Africa*, London, 1842, p. 267.
[13] Rt. Revd Dr Ricards, *The Catholic Church and the Kaffir*, London, 1880, p. 29.

mixing of race.' [14] The impulsions were strong ones: the tenacity of Bantu cultures and languages, even among the urban blacks, and the increasing urbanization of both blacks and whites in the period after the 1880s, which brought the races into immediate contact, often in situations of actual economic rivalry. The early missionaries, both of the English and the Dutch Reformed churches, had always assumed that eventually the native peoples would assimilate to white society. By the later years of the nineteenth century this optimism—acquired in relation to the disintegrating values of the Hottentots and the half-European Coloureds—began to evaporate. The Bantu often did not want to assimilate. Among the Zulus especially, as Fr Barret and Fr Gerard discovered during their attempted mission in 1854, there was little admiration for white values. There was, in addition, the permanent dilemma of missionary experience, in South Africa as elsewhere, of whether to convey the message of the Gospel through the simultaneous dissemination of European culture, or whether to attempt to represent it with indigenous values. In the end, most Christian agencies opted for a combination: an interim separation of the races, in mission stations or reserved territories, where the Bantu could be protected from the immediately blighting effects of white culture upon native social conventions, but where they could evangelized and educated into preparation for eventual assimilation. Bishop Colenso became well known for his advocacy of preserving native custom. This was the burden of his notorious plea for the baptism of converted polygamists. It also provided the theoretical basis of his *Journal of a Ten Week Visitation of the Colony of Natal* (1855).' His ideas, in fact, became a matter of controversy as much because of their religious heterodoxy as because of their acceptance of native custom. In practice, many were already coming to accept the notion that Bantu tribal ways had to be penetrated very much more sensitively than the first missionaries had done. The implication of this sort of missionary strategy was racial segregation, envisaged as an expedient but formalized in a number of ways. Shepstone and the land reservations in Natal, the idea of Trusteeships and Protectorates, the Glen Grey Act of 1894, laid the foundations of a race separation.

---

[14] *The Christian in a Multi-Racial Society. A Report of the Rosettenville Conference, July 1949*, Johannesburg, 1949, p. 49.

Within the Churches came the separation of white ecclesiastical parishes from black missionary units, and the setting-up of separate white and black churches. The period from the mid-nineteenth to the mid-twentieth century saw the gradual and piecemeal acceptance of race segregation by the English-speaking as well as the Dutch Reformed churches. Where they differed it was not over practice so much as over the degree to which they translated their structural arrangements into theoretical explanations of racial difference.

The Catholic Church in South Africa was perhaps the least touched by this. As Bishop Jean-François Allard remarked in 1856, in upholding the idea of mixed-race marriages, 'Jesus Christ died for all without distinction'.[15] Though rather slow to develop an indigenous clergy, the Catholic Church formally treated black and white alike. Even so, however, practical segregations occurred in very many places, not in worship or in ecclesiastical organization—as among the Protestants—but in the sensitive matter of education. Catholic schools, by the end of the nineteenth century, were racially segregated, a fact justified in 1895 by Bishop Charles Jolivet of Natal on the grounds both that the whites who financed them demanded segregation and that language differences required it in practice. The debate about segregation, discreetly veiled within the Protestant churches by being discussed under the heading of 'mission policy', was not absent from the Catholic Church either. In 1906 the Catholic Association of Cape Town arranged a public discussion about the need to create separate states for the black population of South Africa. As early as 1850, indeed, Bishop Aiden Devereux's paper, *The Cape Colonist*, had recommended the separate development of the races in designated white and black territories. In 1957 the Catholic bishops, meeting in Pretoria, noticed that 'the practice of segregation, though officially not recognised in our churches, characterizes nevertheless many of our Church societies, our schools, seminaries, convents, hospitals, and the social life of our people.' They added: 'We are hypocrites if we condemn *apartheid* in South African society and condone it in our own institutions.'[16]

The Protestant churches were rather more advanced in the

15 W. .E. Brown, *The Catholic Church in South Africa*, p. 181.
16 Ibid., pp. 350–1.

practice of race segregation. Only the Hervormde Kerk of the Transvaal actually went so far as to establish a theological formalization of segregation, restricting membership of the Church, at its foundation, to whites, and becoming the State Church of a Republic whose constitution (of 1858) declared that 'Het volk wil geene gelijkstelling van gekleurden met blanken ingezetenen toestaan, noch in Kerk noch in Staat.' It was the culmination of the *trekker* mixture of religious and cultural exclusivism.[17] The Nederduitse Gereformeerde Kerk never departed from theological assent to racial equality as a basic aspect of the Creation, holding that subsequent cultural divergences had produced a practical dissimilarity. Yet the Church developed separate ecclesiastical arrangements for the black and Coloured members in recognition of this secondary difference among men. In 1881 the first 'daughter Church' was constituted for blacks. The immediate motives were mixed: a reflection not only of a paternalistic desire to protect the culture of black society against the whites—at a time then the mining industry was beginning to draw an increasingly large number of blacks to urban centres—but as a concession to the fears expressed by ordinary white churchmen about the security of their identity. Racial feeling was clearly present in the second motive.

The English-speaking churches responded in exactly the same manner. Apart from the Catholics and the Anglicans, among whom the congregational element of the other churches was lacking (allowing less control from the popular prejudices of the ordinary membership), many of the churches had divided into black and white separate organizations by the end of the nineteenth century. They emphasized the practical and philantrophic purposes behind this, and retained formal adhesion to the idea of race equality. Beneath the altruistic professions about the 'mission churches', however, lay the fact of segregation. It is interesting to notice that this had been the policy of the London Missionary Society, and of Philip—whose churches were organized on separate race lines. At the end of the nineteenth century, the European missionary societies, and the

[17] See G. D. Scholtz, *Die Geskiedenis van die Nederduitse Hervormde of Gereformeerde Kerk van Suid-Afrika*, Cape Town, 1956, i. 142 ff. (This nation will not have any equality of blacks with whites, not in Church not in State.)

white churches in South Africa, devoted many conferences and meetings to discussing the separation of the races for ecclesiastical purposes: most agreed that it was necessary. But whatever the motives, the fact was that Christians were practising a separate development. Thus de Gruchy's observation, that the separation of the Dutch Reformed churches into white and black units provided 'an ecclesiological blueprint for the Nationalist policy of separate development',[18] should be enlarged to include most of the other churches in South Africa. The Congregational Union of 1883 was unusual in that it embraced some black members within its formal organization. But in practice, individual congregations still separated on race lines. In the Anglican Church, the Provincial Missionary Conference of 1892 separated the white parishes from the black missions; care was taken to establish that this was done for practical and not theological reasons. The subsequent history of Anglicanism in South Africa, however, discloses an enduring institutionalization of race segregation which went rather further than practical considerations required. Black clergy were given lower stipends than white ones (except in the diocese of Cape Town where there were, anyway, only a few Coloured clergy). The white priest, as John Kumalo said to the *umfundisi* in *Cry, The Beloved Country*, 'gets four, five, six times what you get, my brother'.[19] Geoffrey Clayton, in his first Charge as Bishop of Johannesburg in 1934, was very explicit about the need for segregation, describing the idea that black and white should worship together as 'disastrous to the spiritual development of Africa'.[20] The reasons, again, were paternalistic; the consequences were a continuing segregation of congregations. When Anglicans became such leading opponents of the government's race policies, in the 1950s, the Church was sometimes accused by opponents of double standards, particlarly because of educational segregation. The bishops were actually trying to end segregation by then, but the laity were often hostile—sharing, increasingly, the general racial attitudes of the rest of white society. In 1958 Clayton, then Archbishop of Cape Town,

[18] John W. de Gruchy, *The Church Struggle in South Africa*, Cape Town, 1979, p. 9.

[19] Alan Paton, *Cry, The Beloved Country*, London, 1958 edn, p. 35.

[20] Alan Paton, *Apartheid and the Archbishop. The Life and Times of Geoffrey Clayton, Archbishop of Cape Town*, p. 51.

urged Anglicans to remove apartheid practices from their schools. Many were critical of his position. 'As in the case of the Methodist Church, one has to face the stange phenomenon that in spite of the battle against discriminatory legislation the Anglican Church seems to have fewer adherents in both the white and the coloured community, from the second decade of the twentieth century,' Elfriede Strassberger has written; noting also that some of the white laity 'have not accepted the theological thinking involved in the persistent racial statements of their church and have seen these actions as "political involvement"'.[21]

The Methodists, the largest of the English-speaking denominations, have retained a unified ecclesiastical structure at the top, but the races actually belong to separate circuits and worship in separate buildings. Since the beginnings of National Party rule, however, the Methodist leadership has consistently declared against racial segregation, despite its own practices. The Presbyterian Church, like the Dutch Reformed Church, divided into separate institutions on a racial basis. Attempts in 1934, 1964, and 1971 to reunite the two groups—the Presbyterian Church of South Africa and the Bantu Presbyterian Church—were unsuccessful. One of the reasons for the establishment of Independent black churches and sects (a phenomenon which has grown enormously in the present century) was hositility to the white leadership and segregationist practices of the historic denominations. As Sundkler remarked, 'I have listened to scores of Independent Church leaders who have related instances of how they have been turned away from white church services because of their black skin.'[22] The success of the Indpendents has reinforced segregation in religion—from the black side. Sectarianism among the whites has had a similar effect: in 1961 the Apostolic Faith Mission, the leading (and mainly Afrikaner) Pentecostal Church, declared in its constitution that there should be separate churches for the different racial groups. Racial segregation does not necessarily, however, lead to dissatisfaction among the black members. By the middle of the 1970s the black Dutch Reformed churches had a member-

---

[21] Elfriede Strassberger, *Ecumenism in South Africa*, Johannesburg, 1974, p. 27.
[22] Bengt G. M. Sundkler, *Bantu Prophets in South Africa*, second edn, Oxford, 1961, p. 37.

ship of over one and a half million—rather more than belonged to the white Reformed churches.

It can therefore be said that by the mid-twentieth century the practice of racial segregation had made considerable advances in the South African churches of both the major language groups. But by the same period, political developments drew the leadership of the English and the Afrikaans-speaking churches once more into opposed attitudes to race. It was not only the advent of the National Party to power in 1948 that determined the change. The volume of legislation on race issues had already been increasing before then—as an aspect, in fact, of a generally heightened level of state intervention in social and economic relationships. The growth of collectivism during Herzog's government after 1924 operated to protect white economic interests. Before then, even, in 1911, the Mines and Works Act had legalized the 'colour bar'; land legislation, especially the measures of 1913 and 1936, had a similar effect. In 1936 the Cape franchise (for non-whites) had been virtually destroyed by removing Coloured voters to a separate register. In 1927 legislation had prohibited sexual relations between whites and blacks. These measures, and many others, are not to be judged as an indication of the rise of political race-consciousness solely within Afrikanerdom. They reflected more popularly based fears and convictions within the white populations of both language groups. Afrikaner nationalism, however, provided the ideology of race separation in political terms.

Beneath the hardening attitudes lay a changed demographic map. The Afrikaner people became urbanized in the first half of the twentieth century, with most profound consequences. The traditional society of the Boers drained away from the rural *platteland* to which the original *trekkers* had conveyed their almost apocalyptic hopes of a purified social order. 'The cities were still citadels of Anglo-Saxon culture and British economic power,' as de Klerk has written, in a famous passage: 'the new immigrant Afrikaners were, in fact, strangers in their own country.'[23] In the urban centres the poor whites found themselves to be economic and social rivals of an enormous black proletariat—also attracted to the city by the allure of raised living standards

[23] W. A. de Klerk, *The Puritans in Africa: A History of Afrikanerdom*, p. 110.

and the prospect of employment. In their self-conscious reliance upon the language and the religion of their fathers, the new urban whites overcame disorientation and *anomie* by cultural and racial pride. It is an over-simplification, but only a slight one, to observe that the policy of apartheid was the result of the conflation of the existing cultural National movement of the intellectuals (of men like Diederichs, Malan, Meyer, and Cronjé) with the aspirations of the urbanized poor whites. The Dutch Reformed churches were unavoidably involved. First, because they were anyway churches of the people, traditionally close to the feelings of the ordinary membership; secondly, because so many of the new National leaders were officials or ministers of the church—'In the normal order of life there are so many points of contact between church and nation that influencing is unavoidable,' as the General Synod of the Nederduitse Gereformeerde Kerk declared in 1966;[24] and thirdly, because of the ideological link of religion and nationality made by the intellectual formulators of the National Party. Virtually refounded anew, amidst the *anomie* and uprootedness of the teeming cities, the Reformed churches rapidly acquired markedly sectarian characteristics and a reawakened sense of the Scriptural nature of God's calling to the Afrikaner people. 'We are standing like Luther at the time of the Reformation, with the back against the wall,' Verwoerd said in 1958: 'We do not fight for money or possessions. We fight for the life of the poeple.'[25]

It would be unwarranted to assume, however, that the teaching of the Dutch Reformed churches on the race issue as merely a sacralizing of National Party ideology. Between the churches and public life there was a sort of dialectic: an examination of the development of opinion after 1948 makes it clear that considerable diversities of view have existed over the race question, both in Church and State. Nor were opinions easily formulated. The Nederduitse Gereformeerde Kerk and the Federal Missionary Council of the Dutch Reformed Churches arranged a number of conferences and discussions on the Christian principles which

[24] *Human Relations in South Africa. Report of the committee on current affairs adopted by the General Synod of the Nederduitse Gereformeerde Kerk, October 1966*, Cape Town, 1966, p. 44.
[25] W. Kistner, 'The 16th. of December in the context of Nationalistic thinking', in Theo Sundermeier (ed.), *Church and Nationalism in South Africa*, p. 86.

should guide consideration of race. There were five between 1950 and 1953 alone—in the years of the greatest controversy over the National Party's apartheid legislation. It became clear, also, that the Dutch Reformed churches advocated a policy of total racial separation, on a fully territorial basis—with its consequence that white would have to underake the unskilled and service work done by blacks in the areas designated for exclusive white residence. The Bloemfontein conference, in 1950, spelt out this policy, and declared that it was in accordance with God's will as revealed in Scripture. At the 1956 conference (also held in Bloemfontein)—a gathering which accepted the segregationist policies of the 1954 Tomlinson Report—the delegates resolved that 'there is no possibility of the peaceful evolutionary development of White and Bantu in South Africa into an integrated society.'[26] The participation of the Dutch Reformed churches in this conference, which was convened by the joint action of themselves, the South African Bureau of Racial Affairs, and the Federation of Afrikaans Cultural Societies, allied them to a strict segregationism. The position of the Coloured population and the Indians—much more assimilated to white culture, and lacking 'homeland' territories—remained a difficulty for the policy which was left unresolved. Both in this conference, and in other definitions of the Dutch Reformed position on the race issue, the grounds of separation were not held to be racist. Hewson conceded at the Rosettenville Conference—an interdenominational gathering—in 1949, that there was 'an element of idealism in the policy of apartheid, and no attempt to assess its signicance is adequate which fails to give due regard to this idealism'.[27]

In fact between apartheid, as understood by National Party leaders, and the Reformed churches' policy of territorial *separate development*, there were some important differences—differences which led Malan, after the 1950 conference, explicitly to reject the churches' policy on the grounds of its impracticability. The government, it may be felt, had a more realistic assessment of the position of the urban black population: their existence, de-tribalized yet not fully assimilated to white society, at the

[26] L. E. Neame, *The History of Apartheid. The Story of the Colour War in South Africa*, London, 1962, p. 126.

[27] *The Christian Citizen in a Multi-Racial Society*, p. 60.

centre of the growing industrial life of the white nation, could not, in the thinking of the National Party leaders, be accommodated within a fully territorial separation programme. The churches, for their part, had emphasized humanitarian and cultural considerations over economic ones in their thinking. Liberal opinion condemned existing segregation because of white economic superiority: many church leaders were determined to see that their notion of racial separation was not conceived in a manner economically disadvantageous to black society. 'The time had come', Dr J. A. van Wyk told the Pretoria Conference in 1953, 'for the Church to speak in favour of change as regards the economic *baasskap* (supremacy) of the European.' [29] The Church upheld the view that all people and all races are equal—'All people being created in the image of God are of the same status before Him,' as the General Synod of the Nederduitse Gereformeerde Kerk reported in 1966.[29] But 'the diversity of peoples implies a distinction in development and cultural maturity, and in this the concept of Christian trusteeship becomes relevant', the Synod continued. 'By this we understand the calling of a Christian people to instruct in true neighbourly love the undeveloped peoples with whom they come into contact . . . to lead them towards full cultural development in agreement with their own character, and towards political independence.' [30] Ethnic differences, therefore, were held to be the will of God. Some Dutch Reformed theologians argued, further, that the continuation of diversified ethnic social organization was a providential scheme sanctioned by Scripture: but this has proved to be a controversial position about which full agreement has never been attained. In view of the persistence of cultural and material differences between the racial groups in South Africa—it has seemed to Church leaders—the most Christian course appeared to be the separate development of each in accordance with its own prior experience. In 1974 the General Synod declared:

From the fact that the existence of a diversity of peoples is accepted as a relative, but nevertheless, real, premise, one may infer that the New Testament allows for the possibility that a given country may

[28] *Christian Principles in Multi-Racial South Africa. A Report on the Dutch Reformed Conference of Church Leaders, 1953*, p. 164.
[29] *Human Relations in South Africa*, p. 5.
[30] Ibid., p. 6.

decide to regulate its inter-people relationship on the basis of separate development—considering its own peculiar circumstances, with due respect for the basic norms which the Bible prescribes for the regulation of social relations . . .When such a country honestly comes to the conclusion that the ethical norms for ordering social relationships, i.e. love of one's neighbour and social justice, can best be realized on the basis of parallel development, and if such a conviction is based on factual reasoning, the choice of parallel development can be justified in the light of what the Bible teaches.[31]

The emphasis on cultural difference is important in this argument—as it had been in the attempts of the missionaires in the nineteenth century to protect the Bantu against the disintegrating effects of contact with European culture. Having fought to preserve their own identity against the British over a century and a half, the Afrikaners were fearful lest it was swamped by the numerical superiority of the black cultures. It was the cultural element, not the racial one, that the Church has tried to emphasize. But it was regarded as fundamental nevertheless. 'In speaking of the contact of the European and Bantu cultures we may justly speak of a clash,' remarked the Revd J. P. Jacobs, of the Synod of the Dutch Reformed Mission Church of the Orange Free State, in 1953; 'because these two represent essentially two different views of life and world views.'[32] On the same occasion Dr G. B. A. Gerdener, the distinguished church historian, said 'An ostrich policy of closing our eyes to our differences will take us nowhere.'[33] There must be, between the races, he concluded, mutual respect and co-operation, but not integration. Segregation, however, must be according to a scheme which genuinely allowed the non-white racial groups to develop according to their own cultural values.

The Dutch Reformed churches therefore taught that the peoples of the different races were equal but different. This was most clearly expressed by Eiselen in 1949: 'Apartheid is necessary not because the Native is of lesser potential value than the White, but because he is "anderssoortig".'[34] This word has both racial and cultural meaning: the black man is different, 'of

[31] *Human Relations and the South African Scene in the Light of Scripture. Official translation of the Report: 'Raas, Volk en Nasie en Volkereverhoudinge in die Lig van Skrit', 1974*, p. 32.

[32] *Christian Principles in Multi-Racial Sourth Africa*, p. 104.

[33] Ibid., p. 127.

[34] W. .W. M. Eiselen, 'Gedagtes oor Apartheid', in *Tydskrif vir Geesteswetenskappe*, Apr. 1949, p. 7.

another kind'. The Church's combination of this position with the teaching about basic human equality has involved some ambiguity because of the meaning of another concept—*gelyk-stelling*. The word, used in the 1858 Transvaal Constitution, does not mean 'equal' or 'equality' but 'treating as if the same'. The Churches developed the shades of meaning: there could be no realistic *gelykestelling* because of cultural diversity. The best course was a separate development in order to preserve and enhance the best qualities of each of the ethnic groups. In this sense, the Dutch Reformed policy of the mid-twentieth century was a continuation of the missionary strategy of the nineteenth. But the rise of Afrikaner political ideology, and its expression within the National Party government after 1948, made the position of the churches, however carefully defined, in prctice virtually inseparable from apartheid as understood generally in society. The vocabulary of nationalism, shared by many theologians with National Party politicians, reflected a mutual indebtedness to the ideology of the Afrikaner nation-state. 'In order to remain faithful to his divine calling', the Moderator of the Hervormde Kerk, C. B. Brink, said at Pretoria in 1953, 'the Afrikaner has to retain his identity. He had to love himself, that which he had become through the grace of God, in order to be able to love his neighbour. He had to separate himself in order to be a blessing to the millions of non-whites. Thence he derived his *apartheid* idea.'[35] M. W. Retief, of the Federal Missionary Council of the Dutch Reformed Church, outlined some basic Christian principles which ought to bear upon race relations. 'I do not include amongst those principles the view which is heard so often that all people, irrespective of race or colour, are entitled to equal rights and privileges,' he said. 'This is a concept which owes its origin to the humanism and liberalism of our time, but which is not taught in the Bible.'[36]

Many English-speaking Churchmen, in their criticism of apartheid, have been unaware of the difference between the National Party's view and the Dutch Reformed churches' policy of separate development—and of the general subtleties in the churches' enunciation of their position. Bishop Ambrose Reeves, one of the Anglican leaders most hostile to apartheid,

[35] *Christian Principles in Multi-Racial South Africa*, p. 32.
[36] Ibid., p. 70.

did acknowledge, however, in 1957, that the word was 'being used in so many different senses by different people, ranging from the idealistic form of the total separation of every ethnic group from each other to unblushing White domination.'[37] These different senses were certainly evident inside the Dutch Reformed churches. Whereas there can be little doubt that most of the ordinary membership espoused the principles of apartheid in a manner more approximate to the understanding of the National Party, it is also clear that the leadership of the churches contained a variation of interpretations. A small number—of whom the most celebrated was Beyers Naudé— left the Dutch Reformed Church altogether because they rejected separate development in any form. Naudé was deprived of his ministerial status by the Church in 1965, following his activities in the Christian Institute—a body he had used to oppose the apartheid policies of the State. Some church leaders supported separate development for practical reasons: as being the most realistic way of practising Christianity in the unideal and compromising circumstances of South Africa's ethnic mixture. Many of them denied that the policy should rest upon explicit Scriptural authority, since they could see no reason why cultural diversities needed to be frozen for all time according to patterns established in the flux of historical change. Two distinguished academics emerged as spokesmen for this position within the church. Ben Marais, the ecclesiastical historian, explained his support for separate development on pragmatic grounds in his *Kleurkrisis in die Weste* (1952); B. B. Keet, the Stellenbosch theologian, in his *Suid-Afrika-Waarheen?* (1956), attacked the Scriptural interpretations of many of the more conservative ministers in the Church. At the Pretoria Conference of church leaders in 1953, both men articulated their opposition to aspects of apartheid. Keet, in his opening address, said quite bluntly that those who wanted to maintain apartheid on biblical grounds 'were mistaken; they confuse *apartheid*, which is an attitude of life, with a diversity which includes unity'.[38] He went on to say that '*apartheid* cannot be unreservedly condemned', for 'its fruits, which can be seen so clearly in the growing independence and development of our coloured

[37] David M. Paton (ed.), *Church and Race in South Africa*, London, 1958, p. 46.
[38] *Christian Principles in Multi-Racial South Africa*, p. 17.

churches, are proof that God's blessing has rested upon it'—
adding, however, that this was 'no proof that it is the ideal or
that there is nothing better'.[39] This expression of opinion was
vigorously attacked as not being 'the declared policy of the
Dutch Reformed Missionary Churches', at the start of the
general debate, by D. G. van de Merwe.[40] Yet, as Marais
pointed out later in the discussion, 'some of the most heated
attacks on *apartheid* had come from Afrikaans-speaking delegates'.[41] Nor was it in general true that liberal opinion within
the Church was all totally opposed to separate development; R.
F. Hoernlé and H. J. Hofmeyr were prominent among those of
liberal outlook who defended the morality of the policy. 'For the
Native peoples of the Union', Hoernlé said in 1949, 'it should be
clear that there is no escape from White domination by way of
parallelism or Assimilation, but only by way of Total Separation,'[42] a view which he acknowledged to be impracticable in
some of its aspects. It was a view, paradoxically, later to be
adopted by Black Consciousness activists.

The Cottesloe Consultation, held in Johannesburg in 1960 by
the World Council of Churches, in the period of acute racial
tension following the Sharpville shootings revealed the differences of emphasis over the separate development policy within
the leadership of the Dutch Reformed churches. The conference
itself, conducted in an atmosphere of mutual trust between the
Afrikaans and the English-speaking churches, concluded with a
Statement that the delegates were, among other things, 'united
in rejecting unjust discrimination,' whilst acknowledging that
'widely divergent conviction have been expressed on the basic
issues of *apartheid*'.[43] Particular recommendations, in Part II of
the Statement, included declarations that no one should be
excluded from any church on racial grounds; and, on the abuses
associated with migrant labour, job reservation, wage variations
on race lines, that 'the right to own land wherever he is domi-
ciled, and to particpate in the government of his country, is part

[39] Ibid., p. 19.
[40] Ibid., p. 142.
[41] Ibid., p. 159.
[42] *The Christian Citizen in a Multi-Racial Society*, p. 61.
[43] *Cottesloe Consultation. The Report of the Consultation among South African Member Churches of the World Council of Churches, 1960* (ed. L. A. Hewson), Johannesburg, 1961, p. 73.

of the dignity of the adult man, and for this reason a policy which permanently denies to Non-White people the right of collaboration in the government of the country of which they are citizens cannot be justified.'[44] The delegation of the Hervormde Kerk afterwards issued a statement describing separate development as 'the only just solution of our racial problems',[45] and, in effect, rejected the Cottesloe formula. The Nederduitse Gereformeerde Kerk delegation, however, accepted it as compatible with their understanding of separate development: an interesting indication of how different some church leaders understood their policy to be from that of the National Party's one of apartheid—which the Cottesloe Consultation was plainly called in order to condemn. What then happened revealed the nature of divisions within the Church. The synods, both in the Transvaal and in the Cape Province, rejected the Cottesloe recommendations, and before long the Dutch Reformed churches withdrew from the World Council of Churches. It has been usual to describe the rejection as the rsult of pressure brought to bear by the government, the Broederbond, and by sections of the press. In fact, the rejection was an indication of how out of touch some of the more liberal leaders of the Church already were with the conservative attitudes of the congregations. The theologians had moved to a partial acceptance of external opinion, and they were abruptly halted at the first test of rank-and-file opinion. The Cottesloe débâcle did not witness to their complete eclipse, however divisions of view over the nature of the separate development policy have continued within the Dutch Reformed churches. They retain within themselves a much wider spread of opinion than outside observers imagine.

Many advocates of separate development within the Dutch Reformed churches had supposed that their differences from the English-speaking churches were over applications of Christianity, not basic principles. Their disagreements, as the 1974 report of the Nederduitse Gereformeerde Kerk put it, were 'not due to a different view of moral concepts and values or of Christian ethics, but to a different view of the situation in South

[44] Ibid., p. 75.
[45] Ibid., p. 79.

Africa'.[46] But most English-speaking church leaders came to deny it— as Bishop Cecil Anderson, the Anglican Bishop of Bloemfontein, said at the Pretoria conference in 1953, the principles of Biblical interpretation upon which the Dutch Reformed churches placed their arguments 'were different from those of other churches'.[47] Those differences, indeed, were growing. The English-speaking churches were in touch, through cultural affinity, and actual contact with their parent bodies in Europe and through the World Council of Churches, with the growing hostility to the practice of racial segregation in the years after the Second World War. The ideals of Afrikanerdom, which they believed they saw so faithfully reflected in the attitudes of the Dutch Reformed churches, appeared increasingly old-fashioned: the survival, at the tip of Africa, of social values which everywhere else in the societies of European peoples were being abandoned. It had looked, in the 1930s, as if the cultivation of liberal attitudes towards racial integration within some white élites in South Africa might be the start of a general move towards exactly the opinions which were being taken up in the wider world. This had not happened, and the leaders of the English-speaking churches laid some of the blame at the door of the Dutch Reformed faith. Some attributed the Dutch Reformed attitudes to qualities inherent in Calvinism itself. Huddleston wrote: 'The truth is that the Calvinistic doctrines upon which the faith of the Afrikaner is nourished contain within themselves—like all heresies and deviations from Catholic truth— exaggerations so distorting and so powerful that it is very hard indeed to recognize the Christian faith they are supposed to enshrine.'[48] English-speaking theologians had more readily adopted modern attitudes to Biblical criticism and exegesis than their Dutch Reformed counterparts; the historical sequences of the Old Testament, which formed some of the most familiar parallels to the Afrikaner vision of their own *volk* wanderings and peculiar history—not to speak of the idea that ethnic differences are providential—could not have for them the literal authority they appeared to have for the Dutch Reformed scholars. The departure of the English-speaking

[46] *Human Relations and the South African Scene*, p. 100.
[47] *Christian Principles in Multi-Racial South Africa*, p. 160.
[48] Trevor Huddleston, *Naught For Your Comfort*, p. 63.

churches from their former acquiescence in race segregation also lay in their political opposition to the politics of Afrikanerdom. If they saw the Dutch Reformed pastors as being too intimately related to the ideology of the National Party, the pastors, for their part, regarded the leaders of the English-speaking churches as too readily responsive to the secularized ideals of political liberalism. An element of frustrated English nationalism enterd the distaste of the non-Afrikaners for the religion of the ruling groups. 'We deprecate false concepts of nationalism by which any one section of the community, European or Non-European, claims the exclusive right to control national affairs,' the Rosettenville Conference declared in 1949. 'True nationalism will find its expression in the service of the community as a whole.'[49]

The leaders of the English-speaking churches came to regard the policy of separate development, as taught by the Dutch Reformed Church, as little more than a blinkered rationalization of racial self-interest. 'The most serious objection which may be raised against the *apartheid* policy', the Cottesloe report pointed out, 'is that it implies a concealed form of discrimination based on colour or race.'[50] Ambrose Reeves, while acknowledging the desire of exponents of apartheid 'to contribute to the welfare of racial groups other than the white one', also stressed that 'their main purpose is the preservation, at all costs, of white domination'.[51] There was, in their opposition to the policies of the National Party government after 1948, a great measure of agreement among the leaders of the English-speaking churches, both Catholic and Protestant. The liking of the Anglican Bishop Basil Peacey for apartheid was very untypical. 'Support for the Church's official view was not so wholehearted among the clergy and their congregations'[52] as among the leaders, however.

The English-speaking churches based their opposition to separate development on moral, theological, and practical grounds. Their abandonment of the former missionary strategy belonged to the last of these: the strategy had, by the middle

[49] *The Christian Church in a Multi-Racial Society*, p. 76.
[50] *Cottesloe Consultation. The Report*, p. 23.
[51] Paton, *Church and Race*, p. 27.
[52] Bertha de Blank, *Joost de Blank. A Personal Memoir*, p. 123.

decades of the twentieth century, been fulfilled. The separation of the races was no longer necessary because of the success of Christianization—not complete but very advanced—and because of the increasing assimilation of urban black society to at least the material conditions of white culture. Integration should accompany urbanization, they contended, although most leaders in the 1950s and 1960s still conceded that full integration lay some way off: the immediate concessions should be ones of political rights. 'We believe the rights to full citizenship in any country', as the Anglican bishops had declared as far back as 1930, 'are not dependent on race or colour, but on men's fitness to discharge the responsibilities which such citizenship involves.'[53] This was in the end a practical test, related to the levels of education or circumstances of employment. There were some slight differences of view between the churches as to the extent to which the conditions for racial integration were already present. The Catholic bishops, meeting in 1952, were cautious:

Were the attitude of the Europeans the sole reason for South Africa's reacial problem, it would be simple enough to condemn it as unjust and un-Christian, and, by a determined process of education, endeavour to modify it. However, the problem is far more complex than that. Its complexity arises out of the fact that the great majority of the non-Europeans, and particularly the Africans, have not reached a stage of development that would justify their integration into a homogeneous society with Europeans. . . . There must be gradual development and prudent adaptation. Nor must they be required to conform in every respect to European ways, for their own distinctive qualities are capable of rich development.[54]

The Cottesloe report, published in 1961, noticed that social integration between the races was 'desired by relatively small numbers of either race, and, because its extent must depend upon cultural parity, it is bound for some time to be fairly restricted'.[55] Whatever the continuing reservations, however, the leaders of the English-speaking churches had, by the 1950s, come to regard political parity between the races of a multiracial society as the only proper object of public policy for South Africa. By that time they had added moral and theological

[53] Joost de Blank, *Out of Africa*, London, 1964, p. 113.
[54] Brown, op. cit., p. 343.
[55] *Cottesloe Consultation. The Report*, p. 20.

reasons to the practical ones—reasons for which they had always contended, but which then seemed in need of urgent presentation. Their chief grounds of opposition to apartheid comprised, from that time, Scriptural statements about the fundamental human dignity of people of all races. As they have become so familiar there is little need to describe them here, but it is interesting to notice how they came increasingly to be rendered in Natural Law language—until, in the 1970s, they merged with the general liberal ideology of Human Rights. The Catholic bishops, in their 1952 statement, had referred to 'fundamental and individual rights' to which all races were entitled in civil society; and in 1957, although they declared 'immediate total integration' of the races to be impossible, they condemned apartheid precisely because it seemed to violate the basic existence 'in each human person by God's creation of a dignity inseparably connected with his quality of rational and free being'.[56] The Dutch Reformed churches would not actually have disagreed with this principle. But their contention was that the qualities of 'rational and free being' were most fully expressed within national and cultural developments of the separate ethnic groups. At no point has there been a real meeting of minds.

Some of the opposition to apartheid within the English-speaking churches was also an opposition to the growth of collectivism. Most of the churches, and especially the Anglican Church, with its progressive social attitudes in the 1920s and 1930s, had not been antipathetic to the growth of the machinery of the state when the political contol of government still seemed responsive to their influence. But, with the rise to political supremacy of the National Party, the growth of collectivism became identified with the power of Afrikanerdom. In the twenty years following 1948, there were 200 statutes dealing with race questions. In addition there were the unavoidable expansions of government social and eonomic machinery which all modern states have experienced. Opponents of apartheid within the English-speaking churches attacked the fabric of the state itself when they assailed the race policy which was at its centre. This was sometimes done consciously. 'Racial preju-

[56] Brown, op. cit., p. 349.

dices are increasingly being given legal sanction', Ambrose Reeves declared in a Charge of 1956, 'and tend more and more to exalt the state over the citizen.'[57] Opposition to the Bantu Education Act, similarly, had an anti-collectivist element. The Act had the effect of transferring large areas of public education from the control of the churches to the state. As Clayton said at the time, 'like other recent legislation it puts dangerously wide powers into the hands of an individual minister.'[58] There were, of course, other grounds of opposition to the Act—urged by those who believed in the principle of denominational religious education, and by those who believed the real purpose of the change was, as Huddleston put it, 'education for servitude'.[59]

A final contemporary note on the question of racial integration: here the new black militancy of the 1970s has added a vibrant opposition which has acquired some Christian support. The Christian element in independent black thinking in South Africa has been evident from the beginning—from the foundation of the African National Congress in 1912. Black leadership, as elsewhere in Africa, arose out of the mission schools, and Christianity has provided much of the motivation and reasoning for the rise of black nationalism in South Africa. Contemporary black society is less secularized than white society, and even though some leaders of Black Consciousness have not conflated their aims with those of the Christian faith, many others have. The Catholic bishops, in 1977, explicitly supported Black Consciousness as the vehicle of 'legitimate aspirations'. This statement, drawn up just after the Soweto riots, referred to the 'Social and political system of oppression' in South Africa, and affirmed that the Catholic Church was 'on the side of the oppressed'.[60] Most leaders of black Christian opinion who now express their indebtedness to the ideas of Black Consciousness, however, still favour some sort of racial integration. But the more militant do not. 'Perhaps the most significant factor which has made the emergence of Black Theology possible in South Africa', as Basil Moore has written, 'is the growing mood

[57] D. M. Paton, op. cit., p. 33.

[58] A. Paton, *Apartheid and the Archbishops*, p. 229.

[59] Huddleston, op. cit., p. 159.

[60] *Southern African Catholic Bishops' Statements* (Conference Plenary Session, Feb. 1977), Catholic Institute for International Relations, London, 1977.

among blacks against mult-racialism.'[61] Biko believed the policy of integration required closer scrutiny than it was receiving 'in white liberal circles', for it was 'white man's integration—an integration based on exploitative values'.[62] Professor Boshoff has written, 'Integrasie word verwerp omdat dit per implikasie veronderstel dat die Blanke iets het wat die swarte wil hê of behoort te wil hê, asof die oorname van die leefpatroon van die Blanke menswees die swarte sou vermeerder. Die liberalis word verwerp omdat hy reken en voorgee dat hy geen onderskeid weens huidkleur maak nie, maar in feite doen hulle dit wel.'[63] Developments of these sorts of ideas within Black Consciousness, and their reception within the churches, will unquestionably play a large part in the formulation of future Christian attitudes to racial issues in South Africa.

[61] Basil Moore (ed.), *Black Theology, The South African Voice*, p. 2.

[62] Ibid., 'Black Consciousness and the quest for a true humanity' by Steve Biko, p. 40.

[63] C. W. H. Boshoff, P. E. S. Smith and D. Crafford, *Swart Teologie?*, Pretoria, 1972, pp. 12–13. (Integration is rejected because it by implication suggests that the whites have something that the blacks ought to have, as though the taking-over of the life-style of the white people would enhance the blacks. The liberal is rejected because he calculates and puts forward the impression that he does not make any distinction of colour, but in truth he does.)

3

Frontier Religion and Sectarianism

Of the several features of South Africa's history which were favourable for the appearance of religious sectarianism, the existence of an expanding frontier was the most fruitful—as elsewhere in Christian history. The eastern advances along the old borders of the Cape Province, and then the northwards trek of the nineteenth century, were just the sort of population upheavals most conducive to apocalyptic and exclusive versions of religious phenomena. They duly appeared, both within the migrating denominations and in the form of classic sectarianism on the periphery of the advancing people. Among the black peoples, too, as they moved southwards into the area of modern South Africa, social dislocations—often on a dramatic scale—produced some comparable religious phenomena. As these fall outside the references of this analysis (at least until they were expressed within the religious attitudes of the black Christian converts) it is appropriate to point to only one, if the most famous, example: The Cattle-Killing of 1857 among the Xhosa was initially inspired by the millennial speculations of religious prophets. The pluralism of Christian organizations in South Africa provided an existing pattern of religious fragmentation, and this easily split up still further when urbanization, at the end of the nineteenth century, produced an extended experience of social dislocation among those who migrated to the industrial cities. Among both the black and the white urban populations sectarianism developed. In the case of the Dutch Reformed churches of the Transvaal it developed within institutional forms; among the Bantu of the cities classic 'churches of the disinherited' appeared as distinct and fissile sects.

Although sectarianism was most evident among those who migrated from the Cape Province in the Great Trek of 1836, the eastern frontier had, before then, produced clear signs of religious independency. The greater freedom and general lawlessness of the frontier, as in the experience of the United States in the same period, fostered a sort of religious democracy: small groups asserted their religious individuality against the distant authority of the Cape Town ecclesiastical authorities. As in the case of America, also, this took the form of Revivalism: and with the arrival of the British settlers of 1820, many of whom moved into the eastern frontier districts, the addition of denominational pluralism reinforced the existing sense of freedom from inherited ecclesiastical structures. The Revival of 1811 affected most Christian groups in the Cape Colony. It began, in classic style, with calls for respentance and personal conviction of faith—following an earth temor and an epidemic. Revivalism of this type remained latently within the mainstream denominations throughout the century, rarely spilling over into independent sects, but often producing religious excesses which the clergy were unable to prevent but which they were usually able, in the end, to contain. The small numbers of clergy available on the frontier, the enormous distances between the scattered settlements, and the consequent weakening of ecclesiastical order, all assisted the laicization of frontier religion—a feature most evident, of course, among the *trekkers*. Ordinary Revivalist phenomena occurred within the Namaqualand stations of the Rhenish Mission in the 1850s, and, more signficantly, in the Great Revival which occurred within the Dutch Reformed congregations, beginning at Worcester in 1860, and spreading throughout the Central Karroo. This was characterized by mass meetings, lengthy sessions of prayer and testimony, faintings and ecstatic trances, and other evidences of the sort of fervour familiar enough from contemporaneous examples in the United States. Indeed, a visitor to Worcester at the height of the Revival said: 'I have just come from America and this is precisely what I witnessed there.'[1] The effects lasted for a number of years, among both black and white religious groups. Fifty men came forward to offer themselves for the ministry. It was often Revivalism of this kind which found a particularly sympathetic expression among the recently converted black populations of the advancing frontier. The Revival of 1814 and 1815 at the Bethelsdorp mission station witnessed scenes of religious ecstasy and emotional meetings; some shook and danced. Com-

---

[1] J. du Plessis, *Life of Andrew Murray*, p. 196.

parable classic phenomena, combined with elements of tribal culture, occurred in the *Unzondelelo* Revival among the Zulus in 1866. The missionaries also reacted in the usual manner: they were initially hostile to the religious excesses, but by the middle of the next decade—when it had become apparent that the movement was not sliding into a syncretistic heterodoxy—they gave their approval.

Within the Revivalism of the white churches there was an absence of millennial speculation or apocalyptic mysticism. But some aspects of the mission stations suggested qualities normally associated with ideal communities, to some extent resembling the Jesuit Reductions of Paraquay. In the mid-century, in fact, Mgr Murphy of the Eastern Vicariate (Natal) actually suggested to Rome that the work of Zulu conversion should be organized explicitly on the Jesuits' Parguayan model. The main reason for assembling the native converts in village settlements was to protect them from the exploitation of the white farmers and from the disintegrating effects associated with the abandonment of tribal culture. Yet in the Moravian mission settlements—and in some of the enterprises set up in emulation of them by the other churches—a regimen of ordered living and disciplined labour developed which had some of the characteristics of an ideal community. Moravian work had begun with George Schmidt in 1737, among the Cape Hottentots. It had not been successful, and in 1792 three Moravians arrived from Germany to start the work again: Hedrik Masveld, Daniel Schwinn, and Johann Christian Kühnel. Their settlement at Baviaans Kloof (a name which means 'Valley of the Baboons', and was subsequently changed to Genadendal or 'Valley of Grace') developed rapidly into a self-supporting community which combined evangelistic intention with economic and cultural assimilation. By 1800 there were 1,200 Hottentots in the community, under the direction of ten white missionaries. There were 200 model cottages, a church, workshops, assembly rooms, and a mill. As du Plessis wrote, 'In growing numbers, visitors from far and near would journey to the station to satisfy themselves by personal inspection of the thoroughness with which the Brethren were doing their work, and of the eminent success which had crowned it.'[2] In 1805 Commissioner-General de

---

[2] J. du Plessis, *History of the Christian Missions*, p. 82.

Mist visited the community. In 1808 the Moravians began another settlement on the same *Hermhut* model at Groene Kloof, on land given by the British governor, the Earl of Caledon. A similar community was set up by Catholic Trappists from Germany in 1882. Under the inspiration of Prior Franz Pfanner they founded a model settlement for missionary purposes among the Zulus at Mariannhill in Natal, intending 'to draw the neighbouring tribesmen to the mission as tenants and voluntary labourers while their children were educated at the mission school'.[3] Soon there was a model village, a church, school, dormitories for the labourers, a refectory, workshops, and store-houses. New crops were introduced; external trade was organized for the marketing of the community produce. In 1886 a second community was started at Reichenau, and then others: by the end of the first decade of the twentieth century there were twenty-eight settlements on the original Mariannhill pattern. Though plainly intended as a practical means of combining Christianization with economic and cultural assimilation, the Trappists' work in Natal did have ideal characteristics. Pfanner himself was seeking to revive the purity of the medieval ideal of a social community with a religious purpose achieved through group living and common labour. In general, however, the settlements of the Moravians and the Trappists were isolated experiments. Features of their experience drawn on by other missionary agencies tended to be the practical rather than the ideal ones. The South African Missionary Society (Het Zuid Afrikaansche Genootschap ter bevordering van de Uitbreiding van Christus Koningrijk) began work among the Griquas early in the nineteenth century which perhaps came nearest to the ideal community model. When Lichtenstein visited the Klaarwater station in 1805 he described it as a 'Hottentot republic under the patriarchal government of the missionaires'.[4]

It was the Great Trek, starting in 1836 which provided the clearest example of the effect of the frontier on religious institutions. In addition to the political and economic reasons for the Trek, there were religious aspects of the movement which made it also an act of revolt against the authority of the established church. At its centre the Trek was sectarian; on the wings of the

---

[3] J. B. Brain, *Catholic Beginnings in Natal and Beyond*, Durban, 1975, p. 170.
[4] J. du Plessis, *History of the Christian Missions*, p. 109.

movement there were chiliastic and millennial characteristics. While a few ministers of the Dutch Reformed Church were sympathetic to the *trekkers*—G. W. A. van den Lingen at Paarl, for example—most were hostile. In 1837 the Cape Synod issued a statement critical of the movement which made it clear that the entire enterprise was to be regarded as an act of ecclesiastical disobedience; 'Die Sinode het nie net die geestelike veragtering van die Voortrekkers gevrees nie, maar het die hele beweging gesien as 'n daad van verset teen die owerheid.'[5] The minister at Cradock, preaching in March 1838, said of the prophet Jonah 'dat hy vlugte voor God, en bragt het over op diegenen, die nu staat Emigranten te worden'.[6] It was a common view among those who remained in the Cape Province, to bear the heat and burden of coping with the philanthropic intentions of the British administration.

The *trekkers* actually contained within themselves a variety of religious positions, from the Dopper purists to some who were already influenced by the Evangelicalism of the Cape Presbyterians. They were united in their opposition to the erastian practices of the Cape government. They were not, at first at any rate, opposed to the principle of erastianism as such—that sort of objection grew in the mid-century as the idea of religious Voluntarism spread within all the churches. It was a rejection of any connection between the British government and the appointment and payment of Dutch Reformed ministers which lay at the centre of their refusal to countenance existing erastian practices. Against the corrupting control of an alien political order the *trekkers* emphasized the notion of a gathered people, whose peculiar identity and special relationship to God transcended obligations to the worldly Cape Church—a Church, furthermore, happy enough with its state protection and incomes. In 1849 Andrew Murray (himself appointed minister of the Dutch Reformed parish of Bloemfontein by the Governor, and drawing his stipend from the state) travelled beyond the Vaal River with the declared purpose of seeking to overcome the *trekkers'* hostility to the Cape church. He had some success, but not with the Dopper element.

[5] P. B. van der Watt, *Die Nederduitse Gereformeerde Kerk*, ii. 13. (The Synod was not only scared of the spiritual scorn of the trekkers but saw the whole movement as an act of rebellion against the establishment.)

[6] Ibid., p. 11.

The Cape Synod periodically dispatched delegations of two ministers to travel among the *trekboers* and conduct services. But no regular or sustained ministry was possible. Erasmus Smit, a lay missionary who once worked with the London Missionary Society, and Daniel Lindley, a Presbyterian attached to the American Board of Commissioners for Foreign Missions, both provided such spiritual services as they could. The enormous distances and the dispersal of the *trekkers* made an effective ecclesiastical presence quite impossible in the early days. The Doppers, anyway, refused to accept Smit's ministrations. The result was the emergence of a lay religion based upon the patriarchal authority of the heads of families. It was Biblical, austere, puritanical even, but attached directly to the notion of a covenant between God and those who had gone into the wilderness. The Blood River Oath of 1838 was the formal expression of a covenant theology which had already evolved at the camp-fire Bible studies of the six thousand or so people who had joined the Trek. Just as the theology of Brigham Young developed through the experience of the wilderness in America, with Old Testament narratives coming alive in Mormon religiosity, so the *trekkers* of South Africa, in exactly the same years, discovered their own identity in the epics of Scriptural history. They, too, were on the way to the land of Canaan. The parallels were never far from their minds. When Gerhardus Maritz died in September 1838, on his way to Port Natal for supplies, he said, 'Like Moses I have seen the promised land but am not destined to live in it.'[7] They believed themselves to be the people of God, fulfilling a divine purpose—called to a destiny higher than the conventional obligations of the existing social order. The speeches of Paul Kruger were illuminated by references to salvation history. 'The history of the Transvaal Afrikaners to him had become a source of revelation', Dr Wolfram Kistner has written. 'He identified his people with the Isreal of the Old Testament.'[8]

Out of these developments there emerged a version of the Dutch Reformed faith which had several of the characteristics of a sect. The transformation was uneven; some professed to

[7] Johannes Meintjes, *The Voortrekkers*, p. 128.
[8] W. Kistner, 'The 16th of December in the context of Nationalistic thinking', in Theo Sundermeier (ed.), *Church and Nationalism in South Africa*, p. 80.

retain a measure of proximity to the Cape church and its settled ecclesiastical polity, others sought to embody the Dopper ideal of a gathered church. The result was that the Reformed faith of the Boer Republics represented a wide range of sectarian manifestations, with the Gereformeerde Kerk of 1859—the body which Kruger helped to set up—as the nearest in spirit to the Dopper ideal. The Hervormde Kerk had less advanced sectarian qualities, and when it became the state church of the Transvaal it began the series of adaptations which eventually turned it into a denomination. The congregations which remained loyal to the Cape church, the Nederduitse Gereformeerde Kerk, were obviously the least sectarian, but even among them the religious experience of the *volkswanderung* had left an enduring deposit of religious exclusiveness. The denominalization of all three branches of the Reformed faith took place in the rural circumstances and the small-town life of the early Boer Republics. With the secondary migration to the cities, early in the twentieth century, sectarianism reappeared again as the new urban dwellers found themselves once more cut off from the settled ecclesiastical authority of the rural areas. It should also be noticed, however, that not all the schismatic tendencies in South African church history have arisen as a result of social dislocation. Some reflected straightforward doctrinal or disciplinary issues. S. J. du Toit's Gereformeerde Kerke Onder die Kruis, of 1896, was like this; so were the Colensoite church and the other Anglican schisms of 1903, 1930, and 1938.

The Great Trek did produce some true sects in the most classic sense—among those whose enthusiasm for a Biblical identity transferred itself from the allegorical to the actual. 'We have never been able, even when willing', Andrew Murray wrote, 'to reach the real, stiff, Dopper mind.'[9] The Doppers wore distinctive dress and withdrew from social amusements. Most were merely ultra-orthodox Calvinists, but during the Trek some others disclosed millennial expectations. Led by John Adam Enslin, members of one group believed that they were fulfilling a course described by the prophet Joel, and were being drawn by God through a wilderness of plague and deso-

[9] J. du Plessis, *Life of Andrew Murray*, p. 175.

lution to the Holy City itself, set up in South Africa. These were known as the *Jerusalemgangers*. 'Hierdie mense het gemeen dat hulle die heilige volk van die Heer was, wat weens die verbastering van die Kerk in die woestyn gevulg het,' as Moorrees wrote; 'dat hulle spoedig geroepe sou word om na Jerusalem te tek, en dat hulle teenwordige verblyf in die woestyn slegs 'n rusplaas was op weg daarheen.' They were especially opposed to the Cape church, which they regarded as having been completely corrupted by its association with the government, and, through it, with England—'een van die tien horings van die bees is en derhalwe tot die ryk van die Antichrist behoor.'[10] Awaiting the return of Christ to the earth, and anticipating, still, the discovery of the Holy City, the *Jerusalemgangers* settled at Marico. In 1851 Enslin died of fever, together with some of his followers, and the numbers of the sect began to diminish. The remnants joined the Gereformeerde Kerk when it was founded in 1859.

The appearance of the most classic sectarianism in South African religious history came with black Independent churches. These first emerged at the end of the nineteenth century, and in the twentieth they have grown on a truly dramatic scale. In 1913 there 30 black separatist sects; by 1925 there were 130; in 1948 there were 800; and 1960 there were about 2,200; and in 1970 there were around 3,000 separate churches and sects. In the last ten years figures have stabilized; growth has stopped, but at a point where a quarter of all black Christians belong to the Independent churches. Many of these sects have perhaps twenty or even fewer adherents. A small number are extremely large—like the Zion Christian Church, with a quarter of a million members. The heaviest concentrations of the members are in the cities, and especially in Johannesburg. There are 900 Independent churches in Soweto alone.

The first to be founded was the Tembu National Church, set up in 1884 by Nehemiah Tile, a black Methodist minister. His secessionist body had strong tribal overtones and was supported by the Tembu paramount chief. Other early attempts at religious independency also had tribal and national characteristics, but already, by the 1890s, and especially with the foundation of the first 'Ethiopian' church on the Witwatersrand in 1892, seces-

[10] A. Moorrees, *Die Nederduitse Gereformeerde Kerk in Suid-Afrika*, p. 748.

sionism was taking on some classic sectarian characteristics. The independent groups of this period were not the first authentic expressions of black Christianity: from the start of the missions, African spirituality had appeared in varying degrees of syncretism within a prophetic tradition plainly influenced by Christianity. The Xhosa prophets Makana and Ntsikana, both of whom claimed a divine call, and began preaching around 1815, had been influenced by the missionaries. Their message, like that of some of the later Zionist sects, was strongly apocalyptic.

The emergent black religious groups of the twentieth century were originally divided for analysis, by Sundkler, in his pioneering study *Bantu Prophets in South Africa* (1948), into 'Ethiopian' and 'Zionist' types. The Ethiopian churches remained faithful to the organizational and doctrinal styles of the Protestant mission churches from which their members had seceded—sometimes for reasons that had more to do with dissatisfaction with the white leadership and racial segregation in the churches than with the actual presentation of Christianity. The Ethiopians were noted for their insistence on exact ecclesiastical forms and rules, and for the creation of committees and bureaucratic machinery, copied from the white churches, and revealing the extent to which their new church life was a substitute, as Sundkler put it, 'for the civic life which is denied to the Bantu in South Africa'.[11] Bishop Manas Buthelezi has observed that the Independent churches have 'supplied the social function of providing a cultural substitute in the form of a system of religious explanation, a substitute, that is, for social and economic emancipation'.[12] The Ethiopian churches, with their greater emphasis on education, and their enthusiasm for social clubs, are clearly better able to assist their members to a rising social status, even among the poorer levels of urban black society, than the Zionist churches. Part of the early Ethiopian movement was actually, for a time, linked to a denominational church. After the Pretoria conference of 1896, James M. Dwane visited the United States to seek affiliation to the African Methodist Episcopal Church. In 1899 he led some of his fol-

[11] Bengt G. M. Sundkler, *Bantu Prophets in South Africa*, p. 86.
[12] Ilse Tödt (ed.) *Theologie im Konfliktfeld Südafrika. Dialog mit Manas Buthelezi*, Stuttgart, 1976, p. 181 (*Studien zur Friedensforschung*, 15).

lowers into the Anglican Church—which, in 1900, formalized the Independents into the 'Order of Ethiopia'. But this was not a successful venture. It was, anyway, largely tribal: a Xhosa church. The impulse for separatism, even within the less extreme versions of Ethiopianism, could not be contained within conventional denominational structures.

This is even more the case with the Independent black churches of Sundkler's second category—the Zionists. The membership of these is drawn from even lower social groups; they are much less educated, and have much less respect for the bureaucratic structures of the white denominations. They are authentic sects, and their tendency to exhibit a syncretism of Christianity and traditional Bantu culture and practice— a feature much discussed, but which needs careful analysis— has appealed to those whose ascending social aspirations are less developed. Pauw has described the Zionists as 'a syncretism of Pentecostalism and Bantu tradition'.[13] The influence of American primitive sectarianism upon those who set up the first Zionist churches in South Africa indicates a direct link between black sectarianism and the sort of religious phenomena found elsewhere in Christian history where marginated groups feel impelled to assert their identity by claims to special divine revelation. In South Africa, the indigenous cultural element soon began to express itself strongly within the new sects. As Sundkler remarked of the Zionists' weekend services, 'Bantu emotional life, subdued and repressed during the week in the artificial world of the whites, is allowed to break through and find its outlet.'[14]

In his second study of Zionism, *Zulu Zion* (which he published in 1976), Sundkler added another category to his original typology of Independency. The 'Messianic' sects were, he then argued, a distinct group within the total spectrum of black churches: though perhaps 1 per cent of the total number, their membership is large and their influence very extensive. Into this category he put some of the most well known of the Zionist prophets—Shembe, Cekwane, Khambule, Nzuza, Lekganyane, and Limba. In his study of the Independent churches of Soweto,

---

[13] B. A. Pauw, 'The influence of Christianity', in W. D. Hammond-Tooke (ed.), *The Bantu-speaking Peoples of Southern Africa*, London, second edn, 1974, p. 435.
[14] Sundkler, op. cit., p. 85.

West rightly warned against oversimilifying classifications—in view of the enormous subdivisions to be found within the sects. He went on to distinguish between 'Apostolics' and 'Zionists'. He wrote: 'Broadly speaking, while Apostolics and Zionists have basically the same type of church, Apostolics would claim to be less "traditional" than Zionists, and although still fundamentalist, would place more emphasis on education and theological training for ministers.'[15]

These problems of definition should always to be kept in mind in any discussion of the Zionist churches. It is the Zionist groups, rather than the Ethiopians, which have been growing in numbers in recent decades. When examined closely the Zionist churches, despite the initial impression of huge diversity, have many similarities. In establishing their own claims to authority or special revelation, Zionist leaders themselves emphasize their differences, their peculiar gifts and spiritual characterstics. But general patterns are very clear. The churches and sects are, in the first place, concerned with life in the societies of present experience. Their very origin, in fact, lay in dissatisfaction with the pietism and individualism of the Protestant mission churches—in their attempt to re-enter the communal experience of the tribal life the members had lost amidst the circumstances of urban civilization. 'To these tribes with their communistic outlook came the missionaries to win individual souls for Christ', Eiselen has written. 'They came to teach a people, where individual personality counted for little and private interests were made subordinate to those of the group, that a man must leave father and mother and family in the pursuit of his own salvation.'[16] In the Zionist churches, on the other hand, communal loyalties could be re-restablished around the possession of spiritual mysteries. These could be employed to lighten the burdens of life here and now, not in the promises of eternity. Hence the central importance of the healing of sickness. In the Independent churches healing is once again directly associated with worship and with the everyday practice

[15] Martin West, *Bishops and Prophets in a Black City. African Independent Churches in Soweto*, Cape Town, 1975, p. 18.

[16] W. M. Eiselen, 'Christianity and the Religious Life of the Bantu', in I. Schapera (ed.), *Western Civilization and the Natives of South Africa*, London, 1967, p. 68.

of religious belief: a blend of traditional Bantu custom and the Christian doctrine of the Holy Spirit that the mission churches, as agents of westernization, had not allowed to develop. Despite their emphasis on the material conveyance of sprititual forces, however, the Zionist churches are not concerned with changes to the social arrangements of the material world. They are not politically conscious. There was, it is true, a link between Ethiopian preaching and the leaders of the Zulu rebellion of 1906, and suspicions that the entire Independent church movement was the preparation for an African political role led eventually to the setting-up, by the government, of the Native Churches Commission. But its report, in 1925, made clear that the churches were not likely to develop politically, and this has certainly proved to be the case. Although the churches are not in general organized on a tribal basis, the surviving sense within them of the traditional tribal life, in however shadowy a manner, weakens their capacity to be concerned with the national, secularized politics of a modern state whose issues are anyway defined by the structures of white society. As Christof Hanekom has observed, in his study of the Zion Christian Church, 'As gevolg van hulle stam- en tradisionele agterond is die lede van die Z.C.C. oor die algemeen nie geïnteresseerd in politiek nie.' [17] Part of the reason why the African Independent Churches' Association, founded in 1965, was unsuccessful in creating real links between the churches was the Association's connection with the Christian Institute—a highly politicized body, redolent of political opposition to the South African government. The Association also collapsed (in 1974) because of characteristic internal disputes over leadership.

The nature of leadership, indeed, has attracted the attention of anthropologists and sociologists: many observers, following Sundkler, have regarded the leadership patterns of the Inde-

---

[17] Christof Hanekom, *Krisis En Kultus. Geloofsopvattinge en seremonies binne 'n Swart Kerk*, Cape Town, 1975, p. 52. (As a result of their roots and traditional background, the members of the ZCC are, in general, not interested in politics.) Far from sympathizing with the political interests of emergent black political groups in South Africa, the ZCC, like the other Zionist churches, accepts existing political arrangements. On a visit to the headquarters of the ZCC at Moria, in Lebowa (in August 1979), I found that the audience room in which I met the bishop was decorated with photographs of successive National Party Prime Ministers of South Africa.

pendent churches and sects as partial restorations of the authority
structures of traditional society. Two types of leader have been
identified—the 'chief-type', suggested in the governmental
styles of the Ethiopian churches, and the 'prophets' of
the Zionists. The latter are regarded as adaptations from the
diviners of tribal custom. But, as West has pointed out in his
study of Soweto, the categorizations lose their accuracy when
applied to the highly urbanized areas, where the Independent
churches have most flourished, in fact. The leadership of the
Zionist churches is extremely hierarchical, with titles and ceremonial dress freely copied from the more ritualistic and authoritarian of the historic white churches; evidence more of western
than of tribal influence. As a result, there are over two hundred
bishops in Soweto alone. In some churches leadership is herditary. This is the case with the Zion Christian Church and the
Nazarites. Leaders are also expected to be married, for in
traditional society marriage imparts full adult status. In some
churches, where polygamy is practised, the marriage of the
leader has additional mystical qualities, linking him with a
divine family or with some other holy status. The place of
women in the Independent churches is an indication of their
heightened position since departure from traditional society.
Something like two-thirds of all the members of the Independent churches are women—a rather higher proportion in
the Zionist than in the Ethiopian groups—and although it is
unusual for them to assume exalted positions in the formal
structure of authority they often acquire enormous prestige as
prophets or diviners. The *manyanos* are associations of women,
and their influence on the general life of the Independent
churches is very great. The women members, in the white
uniforms of the Zionist churches, are a familiar sight in the
streets of Johannesburg. White, incidentally, is the usual colour
because black—the colour of the dress of the denominational
clergy of the western churches—signifies uncleanness in the
Zulu language. This fact must to some exent modify the contention of some writers that it was Europeans who created a racist
language 'whereby "white" symbolises that which is good, and
"black" that which is to be avoided or rejected'. As Fr Adrian
Hastings has written, 'Much of this was propagated not only by
Afrikaners in South Africa, but by Christian missionaries in

many other places, and the utter falsity of it has to be firmly analysed and refuted.'[18]

Like most Christian examples of sectarianism, the central beliefs of the Zionist churches are arranged around mystical experience and millennial speculation. Suggestions of syncretism with traditional culture are encountered here. Leaders are known by their symbolic dreams, and by their ability to discover holy stones, to commune with the divine, to identify holy mountains, to lead their people to promised sanctuaries of healing and purification. All these elements are found in classic white sectarianism, too. Indeed, in their account of the religious practices of the isolated community of Afrikaners who settled in the Kalahari at the end of the nineteenth century, Margo and Martin Russell have penetratingly observed, 'The parallels between these white sectarians and the independent black African churches of the next half century are striking.'[19] The search for Jerusalem passed, early in the twentieth century, from the Dopper purists to the Zionists. Its leading aspirations were the 'Messianic' black prophets, and in the Reserves, where the rivers and hills were given Biblical identities, they found their new Isreal. Most Zionist church members are urban, living in the conurbations of the Rand; the romantic appeal of the holy places in the countryside of their origins reinforced their existing inclination to seek the familiar in the half-remembered tribal customs. The cities became the new frontiers. The urban blacks lived once again through the revivalistic ecstasies which once occurred on the edge of the rural population advances. Isaiah Shembe, the founder in 1911 of the Nazarite Church, had wandered around Natal until, just north of Durban, he found his holy place, *Ekuphakameni*. His mystical powers were such that he is credited with having composed hymns after resurrection from the dead. Engenas Lekganyane travelled through the northern Transvaal. some time between 1910 and 1915, until led by God to a holy mountain quite near Pietersburg. There, in the Boyne Valley, he set up the new Moria, 'Volgens kerklidmate is die Zion City Moria die verkose

[18] Adrian Hastings, *Southern Africa and the Christian Conscience* (Justice Paper 3), Catholic Institute for International Relations, London [1975], p. 6.
[19] Margo and Martin Russell, *Afrikaners of the Kalahari. White Minority in a Black State*, Cambridge, 1979, p. 104.

stad van God, 'n heilige plek waar God Hom aan die mens geopenbaar het. Hier kom mense onder die indruk dat die heilige stad Jerusalem is, gesetel aan die voet van die berg Sion. Moria is nie slegs de truiste van die profect of "nuwe middlelaar" nie, maar word beskou as 'n sentrum van krag.'[20] George Khambule founded his church in 1919, after mystic dreams and a vision of Christ. His 'New Salem' Church was perhaps most famous for its 'Heavenly Telephone', installed in the vestry, through which the prophet received instructions from God. After legal difficulties he had to leave the Nqutu district of Natal, and then led a religious odyssey through the countryside, carrying a box of holy stones, and accompanied by numerous, mostly female, followers.

The appearance of Halley's Comet over South Africa, in 1910, was a major stimulus to Zionism. Prophetic utterance and the pursuit of the comet's course to find the holy places at its supposed end, gave birth to much permanent sectarianism. Enoch Mgijima's Israelite Church began with visions he had received after seeing the comet; so did Timothy Cekwane's 'Church of Light', set up upon the holy mountain of *Ekukhanyeni*. Cekwane received the stigmata on many occasions. Although it is true that classic signs of ordinary sectarianism are the main features of Zionist ecstasy and eschatology, there are in addition, of course, numerous specifically African characteristics. Most fundamental of these is the presence of *badimo*, the living-dead or the shades, assisting church members through the difficulties of daily life just as they did for their predecessors in traditional society. The Ethiopians acknowledge their help; the Zionists attach them more actively as essential guides, praying to them. Dreams and taboos are the means by which they are known or respected. Purification rites, following successful prophesying, link the information secured in this way to the divine. Everything is enveloped in complicated and exact ritual, whose externals are a mixture of Bantu custom and western ecclesiastical ceremonial, and whose inner meaning, too, is

---

[20] Hanekom, op. cit., p. 84. (According to members of the Church, the Zion City, Moria, is the chosen city of God, a holy place where God revealed himself to the people. People came here under the impression that the holy city is Jerusalem, situated at the foot of Mount Zion. Moria is not holy the home of the prophet or mediator, but is seen as a centre of power.)

similarly derived both from tribal witchcraft and from formalized representations of Old Testament practice.

The prophetic and mystic powers of the founders of the Independent churches raise problems of succession. In some cases this has been solved by the hereditary principle, but more typically the death of the first charismatic leader results in division and disintegration. Even the Zion Christian Church split in two over a leadership dispute on the founder's death in 1948: and this is a church with a herditary leadership. Secessions are also caused by disputes over finances and property, over the issue of polygamy, and by tribal dissensions. The Independent church movement, in fact, is in a permanent process of formation and re-formation; a steady-state in which only the really large and wealthy bodies remain truly stable. Members of the others drift from sect to sect.

It has become usual to attribute the extraordinary vitality and extent of the Independent Church movement to the race issue in South African society—to see these churches as a withdrawal into a world of their own values by those excluded from political life by the whites. That, certainly, was the view of Sundkler. Noticing that Independent churches were a feature of other African countries, he nevertheless concluded that the very much larger number of them in South Africa required special explanation. 'This root cause', he decided, 'is the colour line between White and Black.' The growth of the Independent churches was a reaction to separate development: 'The increase in the number of Bantu independent churches could be shown on a diagram as a parallel to the tightening squeeze of the Natives through land legislation.'[21] He instanced the 1913 Act excluding black persons from the purchase of land in white-designated areas. The Act of 1926, which restricted skilled mining work to whites, also, according to Sundkler, stimulated the growth of the Independent churches, many of whose leaders were unemployed skilled blacks. 'It is pertinent to our subject to observe', he wrote, 'that these restrictions were most strongly felt on the Witwatersrand, the most important centre of the Independent Church movement.'[22] Sundkler's explanation has found ready acceptance among writers most concerned to

[21] Sundkler, *Bantu Prophets*, pp. 32, 33.
[22] Ibid., p. 34.

point to the social consequences of apartheid. At the Cottesloe
Consultation, held by the South African members of the World
Council of Churches in 1960, one group looked into the growth
of the Independent churches, and in the report there was a
division of view, broadly between the Dutch Reformed church
members and the rest, over the causes of the movement:

The group considered how far the situation had changed
since Sundkler's investigation: and it was asked how far the present
racial policy of the Union government was a factor in the alarming
recent growth of the Separatist sects. Some denied that this was a
factor, citing cases of Japan and the United States where similar
phenomena could not be ascribed to racial policy. Others maintained
that the very policy of separation gave an incentive to groups to break
away from White-controlled churches; and Bantu members quoted
characteristic phrases constantly recurring in the sermons of sect
preachers, which showed that racial antagonism was being exploited.[23]

There can be little doubt that the hardening structures of
separate black and white churches, in the second half of the
nineteenth century, provided an incentive for separation, and
must, in any explanation of the causes of the Independent
church movement, have a place. It was an element which
remained constant. Thus when, in 1892, Mangena M. Mokone
resigned from the Wesleyan church and set up his black Ethiopian church, in Pretoria, because he objected to racial segregation in the Wesleyan body, and when, in 1950, Izak David
Morkel, a Coloured minister of the Dutch Reformed Church,
founded his Calvyn Protestantse Kerk in Suid-Afrika as a protest against race segregation, a common antipathy to racial
attitudes spanning half a century produced the same consequences. But, as Gerdener rightly noticed, however constant
the phenomenon, the scale of the increase in the separatist
bodies was out of all proportion to the original causes. 'Should
the colour bar have contributed to the causes of the separatist
tendency at the outset', he observed, 'the emphasis has certainly
shifted since.'[24] By the middle years of the twentieth century,
when the movement was entering its phase of most spectacular
expansion, it had become evident that the multiplication
of sects was the result of internal divisions within the black

[23] *Cottesloe Consulation. The Report*, ed. L. A. Hewson, p. 28.
[24] G. B. A. Gerdener, *Recent Developments in the South African Mission Field*, London, 1958, p. 190.

churches themselves. The impulsion to create a separate identity was as strongly felt between different black groups as it was between black secessionists and the white-dominated mission churches. The element of race protest has therefore to be set against other causes of the movement. Bishop C. J. Bengheza, President of the African Independent Churches' Movement, himself denied that the apartheid policy of the government was the cause of religious separatism. The movement, he pointed out, had originated too far back—'Dis 'n oorvereenvoudiging om so te sê! Apartheid het nou die dag maar eers gekom terwyl ons geskiedenis vér teruggaan. Die eerste inheemse kerk is al 1882 gestig!'[25] Secessions within the Independent church movement, furthermore, are not attributable to anti-white race protest at second remove: members do not exchange sects because they are looking for a more effective expression of race protest. The reason for the drift from the Ethiopian to the Zionist churches is to be found in sectarian and religious causes, not racial ones. There is a tribal element in a few of the secondary secessions; disputes over leadership, property, finance, and the question of polygamy, are more usual grounds; but even these are often rationalizations of more deeply felt pursuits of social identity through fundamental spiritual experience. There is some external evidence for this. Independent churches have flourished in the black countries of Africa during the period since their independence. Nearly everywhere they are an expanding phenomenon. 'Most independent churches have positive aims going beyond opposition to the "mission" churches,' Professor Ranger has written of the Independent churches of Tanzania; 'most offer solutions which they believe to be positively good instead of resting content with negative criticism of the missions.'[26] The reason for the strikingly greater expansion of the separatist churches South Africa is not to be found in the race policies of the state but in the enormously more advanced urbanization of the country. For although the Independent churches are both rural and urban in origin, it is in the vast city areas that they have multiplied and flourished.

[25] Piet Meiring, *Stemme Uit Die Swart Kerk. Gesprekke met detien geestelike leiers*, Cape Town, 1975, p. 134. (It is an oversimplification to say that! Apartheid has only recently arrived while our history stetches far back. The first independent church was already set up in 1882!)

[26] T. O. Ranger, *The African Churches of Tanzania*, Nariobi, 1972, p. 4.

The Independent church movement is to be seen as the South African version of a familiar enough religious phenomenon: the separatist congregations are 'churches of the disinherited'. They are a black response to the alien world of urban values by those seeking integration yet whose language and culture ill-prepare them for urban living. These conditions have been present since the start of urbanization—since the first drift of the black populations to the mining districts of Kimberley and the Rand, in the 1870s and 1880s. The Independent churches first began to spread among the disorientated and de-tribalized workers shortly after their migation. In the African styles of worship and healing, the black workers found some consolation for the loss of their traditional values. Their condition was described by the report of the South African Native Races Committee in 1901:

Very many natives have abandoned their tribal life, and have to take their place in the white communities. The transition is easily accomplished, but is full of peril for the native. He passes suddenly and without preparation from a life ordered by rigid custom and authority into a society based on individual freedom. The tribal morality of his people that guided his life in the kraal needs adaptation to the new conditions, and too often it is impaired or destroyed by the influences of town life.[27]

A higher proportion of the blacks who moved to the cities were Christians than of those who remained on the white farms or in the tribal areas. In his examination of Xhosa Christianty, Pauw found that this was because it was the more educated—those whose expectations had already been raised in the mission schools—who migrated. On the Witwatersrand, in particular, the loss of familiar custom and social cohesion was the most acutely felt; it was no coincidence that this was where the Independent churches underwent their earliest and most rapid expansion. The disruption of Bantu life during the Anglo-Boer War assisted the social dislocation in which religious sectarianism grew. The refugee camps were full of religious excitements. Similarly, the influenza epidemic of 1918 and 1919 helped the growth of the sects, by adding a further sense of apocalyptic catastrophe for those who were anyway disorientated by the urban conditions in which the illness had its worst

[27] *The Natives of South Africa. Their Economic and Social Condition*, edited by the South African Native Races Committee, London, 1901, p. 169.

effects. West's research has shown that ony 19 per cent of the Independent church members in Soweto in the period of his sample (early in the 1970s) were actually born in Johannesburg, and that 81 per cent came from the rural areas—mostly when they were young adults. 'With one exception,' they had all joined their present church in Johannesburg.' [28]

The Independent churches have appealed to the poorer, less-educated sections of the emergent black proletariat, uniting their members, even over tribal and linguistic barriers, in a new sense of personal significance; overcoming, for many, the *anomie* of existence in the cities. Leaders have been typically drawn from exactly the same class and type as the ordinary members: men who have experienced the common deprivations and dis-orientations of their followers, yet men marked out by the traditional Bantu gifts of prophecy and healing powers. The element of syncretism is important at precisely this juncture in overcoming the conditions of *anomie*. The separatist sects are characteristically small—a substitute for the community life of the rural past of the uprooted workers. Their ritual and formalism, their hierarchies of rank and spirtual gifts, impart superior status to those who are lowly in the estimation of the white culture around them. Not all of those who feel the disinte-grating effects of city life join the Independent churches by any means, nor do all those who seek to retain tribal and traditional observance within their practice of Christianity. Very many black members of the historic denominations—though no one knows how many—observe the ancestral rites in their homes, usually in the face of the disapproval of their own clergy.

The affinity between the South African Independent churches and the wider experience of sectarianism is not merely theoretical. The first Zionist churches were actually intro-duced to South Africa from the United States—and by white preachers. The *anomie* of the American cities, at the end of the nineteenth century, had furnished exactly the same conditions for religious sectarianism as in South Africa. There is, of coure, a history of the 'new frontier' religious phenomena of the American cities which contains some classic 'churches of the disinherited' among both white and black populations. The

---

[28] West, op. cit., p. 78.

parent of the South African Zionists was the 'Christian Apostolic Church in Zion' founded in Chicago by John Alexander Dowie in 1896. This apocalyptic sect placed miraculous healing and mystic power at the centre of its creed; it expected the imminent return of Christ to the earth to gather the elect, those who were purified. Alcohol, medicine, tobacco, and pork were all banned among the church members. These prohibitions, together with the practice of divine healing, passed directly into South African Zionism, imparting some of its most characteristic features.

In the first decade of the twentieth century, Dowie's ideas were spread in South Africa by P. L. Le Roux, Daniel Bryant, Edgar Mahon, and Johannes Bücher. 'The beginnings of Black Zion were not as exclusively African as one might presume or would like to believe,' as Sundkler conceded, in his second study of the Zionist churches. 'The movement had begun in a White Zion.'[29] Important as the syncretistic element in the South African Independent churches is, it is also helpful to notice that many of their practices—so easily attributable to tribal influence—are in fact directly contrary to traditional belief and custom. Their taboos over medicine and food are in general different from the tribal ones. Their views on the cause of illness, and on possession, are also unlike traditional Bantu ones. The actions performed in healing rites are modelled on the American Zionists and owe as much to Dowie as they do to remembered tribal ceremonial. They regard their divine healings as being in opposition to the practices of the tribal medicine men. Sundkler has himself become less persuaded of the syncretistic aspects of the Independent churches; he has modified his original supposition that they are a bridge to the past, a partial return to heathenism. 'To those in the movement', he has concluded, 'Zion meant newness of life, health, wholeness, a new identity.'[30] The Independent churches, that is to say, are nearer to main developments within the historical experience of Christianity, than a first judgement might allow. The South African 'churches of the disinherited' turn out to have a familiar enough pedigree.

[29] Bengt Sundkler, *Zulu Zion and some Swazi Zionists*, Oxford, 1976, p. 66.
[30] Ibid., p. 305.

4

Christianity and Social Issues

In social policy and action, as in so many other aspects of South
African church history, there were parallel developments between the churches of the two languages and between the ethnic
groups. The history of the churches' social work in relation to
black society is largely the history of the missions. It was not
until comparatively recent times—until the increase of state
activity after 1924 and 1948—that the paternalistic undertakings of the missions were at first substantially supplemented
and then, in some cases, almost entirely displaced. One of
the features of government legislation since 1948 has been an
enormous increase in state expenditure on social welfare for the
black population, both directly for the urban blacks, and in
development of the Homelands policy. It has sometimes been
this aspect of apartheid, the collectivist responsibility for work
previously done by the religious agencies, that has caused
disquiet among English-speaking church leaders—although
the main grounds of opposition have, of course, been to the
strategy of racial separation as such. The huge population
expansion itself determined the end of effective mission welfare
programmes; it outstripped the resources and man power capabilities of the churches, who had, anyway, been dependent on
state financial aid since the middle of the nineteenth century.
The ideology of the missions was also being destroyed: rejection
of the social paternalism implicit in the missionary approach
began to come from both white and black church members.
'Black Power's implications for the Church began with a re-
interpretation of church history and a reconsideration of the
role of missions and missionaries,' Boesak has written. 'Though
no one will deny the important and sometimes even liberating
role missionaries have played in the hisory of black people, one
shall have to discern very honestly precisely to what extent the
missionary movement had participated (and is participating)

in the oppression of black people.'[1] This is a point of view now often heard in discussions of mission work in such bodies as national councils of churches throughout the western world, but it has a particular significance in South Africa because of the vehemence of the rejection of racial separation by the contemporary leaders of the English-speaking churches. The missions had been early practitioners of separation, and their paternalistic intentions are now regarded, by white and black liberal opinion, as having prepared the ground for the policy of apartheid.

The most prominent feature of the familiar history of South African missionary labour is the early start made in the field: from the end of the eighteenth century the missionaries followed the expanding Cape frontier. The second feature was the association of Christianization with social welfare work from the very beginning. The earliest missions were to the Hottentots and the coloured population. For the century after van Riebeeck, missionary work of this sort was largely in the hands of individuals—the Cape settlement did not regard itself as potentially expansive since the policy of the Vereenighde Oost-Indische Compagne was itself opposed to further settlement, and the contact of the colonists with the indigenous people was not at first extensive. The first missionary work was not systematic. 'Hoe loflik hierdie pogings ook al was, is dit uit beskikbare getuienis egter baie duidelik dat hierdie eerste aksie met min sukses bekroon is,' van de Watt has noticed. 'Die kerk self moes eers ontwaak ten opsigte van sy sendigroeping én die besondere geleentheid aan die Kaap.'[2] This need was emphasized by the arrival of the British settlers of 1820: it helped to create a permanent religious pluralism and provided the conditions of rivalry within the mission field. The Dutch Reformed Synod of 1837, noting how little the church had so far achieved, set up a commission to stimulate mission work. From this point, the missionary undertakings of the Dutch Reformed Church began to pass from the control of individuals and into more centralized

[1] Allan Boesak, *Farewell to Innocence. A socio-ethical study of black theology and black power*, p. 55.
[2] P. B. van der Watt, *Die Nederduitse Gereformeerde Kerk*, i. 48. (However laudable these efforts were, it is clear from the available witnesses that these first actions were crowned with very little success. . . . The Church must itself awake as a response to its missionary work and the exceptional opportunities at the Cape.)

and authoritative directions. A missionary policy evolved. The schism churches which appeared after the Great Trek, in the Transvaal, took up to half a century to enter the mission field: the Gereformeerde Kerk in 1879, and the Hervormde Kerk in 1916. In both, and especially in the Hervormde Kerk, there was some hositility to the idea of evangelizing the heathen. The Nederduitse Gereformeerde Kerk had a Training School for missionaries from 1877, at Wellington; in 1903 it became an official church college. In all the Dutch Reformed churches the missionaries from the start envisaged their work as involving social welfare as well as religious conversion. The volume of their work has been impressive. 'The Dutch Reformed Church has the most extended mission programme of all the Christian Churches in South Africa,' as Elfriede Strassberger has written. 'Financially the DRC has contributed much more per member for missions than any other church in South Africa.'[3]

It was the Moravians who next began missionary work. The story is well known: George Schmidt's unsuccessful labours among the Hottentots from 1735 to 1743, and the arrival of the three Moravians in 1792 to commence what turned out to be a celebrated group of missionary settlements. The closing years of the eighteenth century also saw the pioneering work of Helperus Ritzema van Lier and Michael Christiaan Vos. It was within the climate of opinion favourable to missionary enterprise created by these men that from 1799 there began the operations of the South African Missionary Society. Work started at Klaarwater, among the Griquas, and by the time that Dr John Philip arrived in South Africa (1819) as Superintendent of the London Missionary Society's stations, there were already thirteen in existence, including the most famous, Bethelsdorp, founded in 1802, and Theopolis, founded in 1814. The first Methodist missionary also arrived in 1814: John McKenny. His work was restricted by the government, and so was that of the next to arrive, Barnabus Shaw, in 1816; sustained Methodist missionary activity only began with the settlers of 1820, and with William Shaw's work on the eastern frontier. The first Presbyterian mission began in 1820 with William Ritchie Thomson, John Bennie, and John Ross, in Kafraria. Isaac Bisseux inaugurated the work of the Paris Missionary Society

---

[3] Elfriede Strassberger, *Ecumenism in South Africa*, p. 20.

(Société Évangélique) near Wellington in 1829. In the year, also, the first agents of the Rhenish Missionary Society (Vereinigte Rheinische Missions Gesellschaft) arrived at Ceederbergen; they were followed in 1834 by another German mission, the Berlin Missionary Society (Die Gesellschaft zur Beförderung der Evangelischen Missionen unter den Heiden), whose work started on the Riet River in what later became the Orange Free State. They called their settlement Bethany. There had, of course, been Lutherans at the Cape since the early days of white settlement, and they had managed to preserve their religious identity. The German missions of the early nineteenth century reinforced this existing Lutheranism, just as in 1919, when South Africa was granted the mandate over German South-West Africa (Namibia), a further Lutheran population was added. The American Board of Commissioners for Foreign Missions began their work in South Africa, among the Zulus of Natal, in 1834.

No sooner had the first missions been established—in a burst of denominational competition, confirming South Africa's religious pluralism and conveying it to non-white society—than the frontier advances, associated particularly with the Great Trek, transformed the mission scene. Native peoples were now no longer encountered along a steady frontier line but were mixed up within the vast territories the white men had claimed for themselves. They were also a different people: the Bantu were less assimilable than the Hottentots and the Coloureds. They were nations in their own right, unwilling to see their cultures and institutions succumb to missionary endeavour.

This was the situation encountered by the first missions of the Church of England, as they came, rather later than the other churches, into the mission field. Church of England ministers at the Cape were suspicious of the London Missionary Society—because of its Disssenting Independency—and offered no co-operation in its work. But up to 1821 they had provided nothing themselves. In 1828 a missionary sent by the Society for the Propagation of the Gospel (William Wright) moved to the eastern frontier, but his work was not successful. Captain Allan Gardiner began Anglican missionary work in 1835, without the sponsorship of the Church, although he did manage to interest the Church Missionary Society in his labours among the Zulus of Natal. The CMS sent Francis Owen to Natal in 1837. The work of neither man was fruitful, however, and within a few years both had left—Gardiner moving on to South American missionary work, where he died in 1857. Formal Anglican missionary enterprise did not begin in South Africa until after 1848, the year in which Robert Gray, the first bishop, arrived. Until then, as du Plessis has written, 'it may be said that the Church of England was doing nothing for the spread of the Gospel'.[4] Gray's first notable missionary scheme, modelled on the Moravian pattern, was in 1858 at Abbotsdale in the Western Cape. Before that, in 1855, he had set up four mission stations with government grants. In the Boer Republics, Anglican missionary work at the end of the nineteenth century was dominated by the High Church religious communities sent out from England: the Community of the Resurrection, and the Wantage and East Grinstead Sisterhoods, were active in the Transvaal.

The Roman Catholic Church was also rather late into the South African mission field. This, however, was largely due to the hostility of the civil authorities. Catholicism was still illegal at the Cape until de Mist's Ordinance of 1804, and even after that date government officials of the resumed British administration (from 1806) refused to allow Catholic priests to function—in order to respect the established status of the Dutch Reformed Church. Catholic work among the Zulus of Natal commenced in 1857. In 1871 Bishop James Ricards urged Rome to establish a Natal vicariate in order to stimulate further missionary work; in 1882 the Trappists he had brought from Germany began their work at Mariannhill. The Jesuits started work around Grahamstown in 1880. These various undertakings were all directed towards the conversion of the Bantu; after the 1860s, first the Catholics, and then the Methodists and the Anglicans, began work among the Indian population of Natal, most of whom were Hindus.

During the first decades of the twentieth century most of the missionary labour passed into the hands of black and Coloured ministers—a consequence of the policy of racial separation adopted by most of the denominations in the second half of the century. There was an increasing number of ordinations of

[4] J. du Plessis, *History of the Christian Missions*, p. 241.

non-white clergy in the same period. By the first years of the twentieth century, also, there were some thirty separate bodies conducting missionary work in South Africa, in a diverse arrangement of denominationalism.

The association of Christian conversion with social welfare work produced some enduring difficulties as well as some immediate benefits. The first problem was the effect on the Dutch population of the Cape of the type of welfare work performed by the London Missionary Society. Dr John Philip did not separate his philanthropic activities from his assault upon the conduct of the Boer farmers towards the natives. This precipitated a fermenting mixture of social and economic, as well as religious incompatibilities whose leading characteristics were actually central to what the missionaries were trying to achieve in their welfare work. For against the old-fashioned, paternalistic, rural values of the Boers, Vanderkemp and Philip ranged the new science of the British Political Economists. The migration of the *trekkers* from the reach of British philanthropic and administrative reform was one of the consequences. Vanderkemp, though of Dutch origin, was an anglophile; he was better acquainted with the philanthropic outlook of the British Evangelicals than he was with the thought of the Political Economists, but his representation of their general attitudes at the Cape, from 1799, was enough to prepare the suspicions of the Boer farmers. When Philip arrived, in 1819, his frank advocacy of Political Economy thus fell uon an existing hostility. Philip belonged to the England of the new commerce and industrial enterprise. He was the son of a weaver, and had been the manager of Scottish mill. He believed that social advance was inseparable from industrial changes. 'We talk much, in the present day, of the light which philosophy has thrown upon all subjects connected with the progress of civil society and government,' he wrote, 'but, surely, things might have gone on in this way if Adam Smith, Fergusson, Malthus, Ricardo, etc., had never blotted paper.'[5] Yet he was fully indebted to their teachings in his attempts to raise the Hottentots of South Africa by individual enterprise and economic self-interest. Like the Political Economists in England, he was prepared to make exceptions to the

[5] John Philip, *Researches in South Africa*, i. 378.

normal operation of economic laws, in the interests of protecting those who were unable to enter into free contractual relationships. Hence his call for state intervention in the labour relations between the Boer farmers and their native labourers: he applied here exactly the sort of exceptional mechanisms that the English Political Economists allowed over the question of child work in factories. At the Bethelsdorp mission station, Philip attempted to get the Hottentots interested in commerce—'to get them', as he wrote, 'to desire the goods in the shop, and to see that by labour they could earn enough to buy them'.[6] Some were sent to collect aloe juice as part of the attempt to create a money economy at the mission: the juice was sold off to merchants. It was hoped that a market for British manufactures could be established among the converted Hottentots. Philip planned, but was never able to create, a savings bank, to stimulate thrift. The generation of a money economy was not as easy as he had hoped, however. The goods available for exchange were not sufficiently plentiful, in the small-scale Cape market, to encourage wage labour. But Philip worked hard to foster incentives. 'Man is naturally indolent,' he wrote, in the manner of classical Political Economy, 'and there are but two ways of overcoming his natural aversion to labour—fear, or hope; the first arises from the apprehension of punishment, and is the motive of the slave; the second is the more powerful, being most agreeable to nature, and cannot exist, except the labourer has a fair compensation secured to him, as a remuneration for his exertions.'[7] Not only were conditions unconducive to the application of Political Economy to the native population of the Cape, thus frustrating some of Philip's intentions, but the very articulation of his principles further alienated the Boer farmers amongst who Philip had to work. He appealed to the civil authorities, at various times, with success. The reforms which then flowed from the colonial administration— ultimately aimed at converting the native population from dependency to free agency within a competitive economy— offended the Boers still more. They regarded their world of familiar paternalism as preferable to the hard society of market forces. Yet the English missionaries were not the only agents of

[6] Ibid., p. 205.
[7] Ibid., p. 362.

social change with whom they had to contend. The reforms of de Mist, in 1805—and especially the educational reform—introduced the liberal and secular principles of the European Englightenment. But it was English Political Economy which proved the most destructive to the Boer farmers' traditional values. Administrative reform after 1806 plainly reflected the new influences: the success of the bullionists with the abolition of the Cape paper currency in 1825 symbolized the new society. Together with the alien social vision of the missionaries, this was enough to send some of the Boers into the wilderness. They began their Trek in 1836.

The question of slavery also showed how British social and religious thought combined with the work of the missionaries to provide a divisive element in South African devlopment in the early years of the nineteenth century. The first slaves had been imported to the Cape from other parts of Africa by van Riebeeck in 1658. From the beginning some attention was paid to their welfare by authorities in both Church and State. A slave school was established at once, and when the first permanent Dutch Reformed minister (John van Arkel) arrived in 1665 he set up a church for the slaves. In 1683 a government decree provided that slaves became free on their baptism. Social welfare work among the slave population was carried out from the earliest period by the *sieketroosters* (literally sick-comforters; lay religious officers of the Dutch Reformed Church). Michael Christiaan Vos, who began work among the slaves in 1778, believed their material condition was by then better than that of the lower orders in Europe: 'they are not maltreated, are troubled by no anxiety on the score of food and clothing, are carefully tended during illness, and even when married have no concern either for themselves or for their children.'[8] With the arrival of the British missionaries, however, the fervour of the English anti-slavery campaign was released upon the Cape, and in their writings the missionaries represented the material circumstances of slavery, as well as the absence of individual liberties, as equally oppressive. As the slaves were actually owned exclusively by the Boers, and not by the British, their emancipation in 1834 had, once again, the effect of dividing society along

[8]   du Plessis, *History of the Christian Missions*, 67.

national lines, with the social interests of the missionaries in the forefront of controversy. Retief said in his manifesto of 1837: 'We complain of the unjustifiable odium which has been cast upon us by interested and dishonest persons, under the name of religion, whose testimony is believed in England to the exclusion of all evidence in our favour.'[9] At the time of emancipation there were 29,000 slaves in the Cape Colony.

The other missionary legacy of those early years which laid down difficulties for the future was the association of Christianization with assimilation to the economic and social values and practices of white society. Both in the later nineteenth century, and at the present time, controversy and debate have attached to this development. Yet the first missionaries did not do it unthinkingly, as some have supposed, but with a profound conviction in the essential unity of the Christian religion and western material civilization. European society, they believed, had elevated the human personality and advanced individual liberty: Christianity had provided the motivation. 'Civilization bears to religion a relation similar to what foliage bears to a tree,' as Philip declared.[10] Vanderkemp, at the start of the missionary movement, had respected native custom. Indeed, he had adopted Hottentot dress and manners, and married a slave-girl. Colenso desired to Christianize Bantu society from within—without destroying its traditional structure. His contemporary in Natal, Sir Theophilus Shepstone, Secretary for Native Affairs (and the son of a Methodist missionary), sought to preserve tribal society after the conversion of the Zulus by insulating them on a territorial basis. The inevitable result of all attempts to spread Christianity while at the same time retaining Bantu custom was separate racial development. But even when the missions themselves practised this, from the middle years of the nineteenth century, assimilation to European culture still took place within the separated units. This, too, was inevitable. The missionaries found Bantu customs too oppressive of individual liberty—whose blessings they supposed Christianity to be centrally concerned with—and they failed to see that the communal nature of tribal loyalty was itself

---

[9] Johannes Meintjes, *The Voortrekkers*, p. 37.
[10] Philip, op. cit. i. 204.

intimately related to the customs they sought to destroy. Polygamy, especially, proved an issue of particular concern; converts
were generally obliged to conform to the western practice of
monogamy. The missionary assault upon *lobola* was similar. It
is important to realize, however, that in seeking these changes
the missionaries were appealing to what they conceived to be a
higher notion of human dignity. They were specially concerned
about the low estimation of women in tribal society, and worked
for their emancipation. 'Among all the savage tribes the women
are slaves', Philip wrote of Namaqualand; 'and one of the first
effects which attended the labours of the missionaries, among a
people of this description, has been the amelioration of their
condition.' [11] The Revd George Champion, who began work in
Natal in 1835, was so shocked by the sort of justice metered out
by the Zulu chiefs that he declared: 'I believe there is a cry
of oppression coming up from this land, long and loud, to
heaven.' [12] Such feelings led directly to the linking of conversion
with cultural assimilation. Government policy under Sir George
Grey, from 1854, supported the missionaries' social work precisely because of its civilizing effects. The *Umsunduze Rules*,
drawn up in 1879 for the Zulu church, symbolized the mission
policy: an exact demarcation between heathen customs and
Christian ethics was formulated in order to guide the work of
conversion. To the future, therefore, it can be seen that the
missionary enterprise of the nineteenth century bequeathed an
inherent hostility to black culture whose evidences are still
discernible. The work of conversion was actually achieved with
astonishing rapidity. By the time of the Union in 1910, a quarter
of the black population of South Africa was Christian; by 1858
this had risen to a half; today the proportion is around two-
thirds.

The South African churches, like Christian bodies elsewhere,
undertook social functions before the entry of the modern state
into welfare collectivism. Until the start of the twentieth century, most of the welfare and ecucational services of the country
were conducted by religious agencies, often with state financial
assistance. The history of this work, again, divides between

[11]   Ibid. ii. 206.
[12]   Alan R. Booth (ed.), *Journal of the Rev. George Champion, American Missionary in Zululand, 1835–9,* Cape Town, 1967, p. 82.

black and white, and between English and Afrikaans-speaking population groups.

The very earliest social welfare missionary work at the Cape was carried out by the *sieketroosters* of the Dutch Reformed Church. At the end of the eighteenth century this work passed to the multiplying missionary societies. These were concerned to provide for employment as well as for charitable works. The English apprenticeship system was introduced by the missionaries in the 1820s to provide training in trades for the native population. It is interesting to notice that child apprenticeships when practised by the Boer farmers was singled out for attack by the missionaries (who regarded it as a concealed form of slavery). In 1852, for example, two of Robert Moffat's missionaries were expelled from the Transvaal by General Pretorius for campainging against native apprenticeship. 'The Transvaal Boers', as the biographer of Moffat adds, 'were clearly determined to be free from the aggravating humanitarian-pressures they had endured for thirty years in the Colony.' [13] Throughout the century, and afterwards, missionaries opened workshops and mills, agricultural schools and mechanics' classes. The care of the sick also had an early start: in 1823 the Moravians were running a leper hospital, for example. Medical services, however, did not develop greatly among the missionaries until the start of the twentieth century. Bantu resistance to western medicine may be part of the reason. Gerdener's explanation should be treated with some reserve—'the climate of South Africa is one of the healthiest in the world, so that the ravages of diseases like sleeping-sickness, leprosy and even malaria never presented the Christian Mission with the same urgent challenge here, as for instance in the territories further north.' [14] By 1910 there were only three mission hospitals in South Africa; by the 1940s there were over fifty.

Missionary emphasis in welfare was stimulated by dislocations within Bantu society. The *Difaquane* resulted in the collapse of large parts of the social order; the Cattle-Killing among the Xhosa in 1857 had a comparable social effect. The missionaries found, in such conditions of disaster, that extraordinary relief measures were needed. As far as their resources allowed, they

[13] Cecil Northcott, *Robert Moffat: Pioneer in Africa, 1817–1870*, London, 1961, p. 204.
[14] G. B. A. Gerdener, *Recent Developments in the South African Mission Field*, p. 236.

tried to provide them, paying particular attention to food supply. Similarly, the urbanization of the blacks from the closing decades of the nineteenth century transferred the missionaries' social work, which had been framed in relation to rural settlements, to the cities. The challenge was enthusiastically met, and though the relief required far exceeded the churches' capabilities a great deal was achieved. Much overlapping also occurred between the various missionary agencies, especially on the Rand. From 1904 General Missionary Conferences were held every three years, attended by representatives of all the major organizations. Problems of social welfare were prominent in their deliberations. Reference to the list of those giving evidence to the South African Native Races Commission—an unofficial but prestigious body who published a report on the condition of black society in 1901—gives some indication of the investment of men and resources by the churches in social welfare: thirty-two of the correspondents were clergy, compared with twenty-four who were in lay occupations. After 1924, and the policies of Herzog's administration, the state increasingly assumed responsibility for many aspects of black social welfare—a movement to collectivism implied in the setting-up of the Native Development Account of 1925. By the time the Christian Council of South Africa was constituted, in 1936, religious agencies had come to accept the priority of the state in welfare. The reports of the various committees of the Council called upon the state to undertake the specific tasks they indicated: there was no longer any question that the churches could operate independently. This was especially evident in the Education and Social Welfare Reports, both published in 1937.

The work of the churches for social welfare in white society was much more institutionalized at the local level than the work of the missions. It existed as part of the normal parochial programme, financed by local subscription. Only in the Catholic and Anglican churches did the element of centralization assume any significance. Schools and orphanages, care of the sick and relief of the destitute: provisions were made by most of the denominations until, as with the missions, religious enterprise was succeeded by state responsibility in the twentieth century. As in black society, it was urbanization that created new problems for the white churches and prompted an extension of their social action. Related political developments, the growth of collectivism, and the huge increase of the urban population, led the churches into an acceptance of their diminished role in social welfare. This development was, of course, comparable to those which took place in Europe and the Americas, but there was a different chronology in South Africa because of the relation of the changes there to the evolution of National Party ideology. By the end of the 1930s nearly half the white population was resident in nine major cities; the appearance of the poor white element, concentrated in the cities, confronted the relief agencies of the churches with problems they at first sought to tackle with existing resources, but which they began to realize were so large that government intervention was inevitable. At the start of the century the churches had a dramatic experience of relief work within conditions of considerable social dislocation when the Anglo-Boer War of 1898–1902 disrupted large areas. The influenza epidemics of 1918 and 1919 further stimulated Christian social effort—seen in concern for urban housing and medical care. The Nederduitse Gereformeerde Kerk, which had in 1893 called a conference to consider the problems of rural poverty, established a tradition of special interest in the condition of the poor whites. In the 1920s this resulted in successful rural settlements, like the one at Kakamas in the north-west of the Cape Province. In the cities, the action of the Dutch Reformed churches began to merge with the social reformist element in Afrikaner Nationalism. The Herzog government of 1924, itself a coalition of Nationalist and Labour parties, further encouraged the social consciousness of the churches. 'From the composition of its electoral support,' as D. Hobart Houghton has written, 'the new government was under strong pressures to concern itself with three major issues: the plight of the farming community, the provision of jobs in towns for the poor whites, and the protection of the skilled white workers in mining and industry.'[15] The Dutch Reformed churches had been prominent advocates of action in at least the first two of these areas of concern. They generally welcomed the subsequent state intervention in social relationships, finding collectivism conducive enough when rendered within Afrikaner Nationalist ideology.

[15] D. Hobart Houghton, 'Economic Development, 1865–1965', in *The Oxford History of South Africa*, ed. Monica Wilson and Leonard Thompson, Oxford, 1971, vol. ii, p. 28.

Some, a small minority, sympathized with the idea of the corporate state—attracted by its social idealism as well as by its nationalist symbolism. Hence the appeal of the *Ossewabrandwag*, founded in 1938, for those who saw Christian civilization as best preserved by organic political concepts. But the popularity of corporatism was limited. After 1948 the identification of the Reformed churches with the heightened level of state activity required for the implementation of the Malan government's race policies, coming, as it did, at a time of enormous industrial expansion, gave the churches a friendly acceptance of the transfer of their social welfare functions to the state.

Within the English-speaking churches there was also an acceptance of collectivist practices in the twentieth century. Reservations about their actual nature, however, resulted because South African collectivism became inseparable from Nationalist ideology. The English-speaking churches in general reflected the views of the urban whites; British settlement had tended to be urban, in contrast to the rural life of the Boers until their drift to the cities in the twentieth century. Early acquaintance with urban problems gave these churches a disposition to call for state action to cope with the enormous scale of urban social need. The Catholic Church curiously failed to respond to the 'social encyclicals' of the Papacy—at least of the earlier period. *Rerum Novarum,* in 1891, with its teachings about the condition of the working classes, was promulgated at a time when the Catholic Church in South Africa was not sufficiently established to have an effective social voice. Catholic journals, nevertheless, welcomed the teaching. The Methodist church was also slow to acquire an attitude to collectivism; perhaps a reflection of its traditional caution, derived from English experience, towards a government involvement with social and religious issues. It was the Church of the Province of South Africa, the Anglicans, who were the first major religious advocates of a full programme of state social action. The reason for this lay in their proximity to English opinion. Most of the bishops and priests actually came from England, and with them they imported the Christian Socialism which was so influential in the English church, and especially within the Anglo-Catholic party to which many of them belonged, at the turn of the century and subsequently. The Pan-Anglican Congress of 1908, in London, had been convened to discuss missionary work; it also became what one historian has described as a 'socialist field-day'.[16] The idealism of social reform soon expressed itself within the writings and preaching of leading South African Anglicans: Bishop Talbot of Pretoria, Bishop Carey of Bloemfontein, Bishop Karney of Johannesburg. The ideas, and sometimes even the actual social programmes, of William Temple's social movements in England, and particularly his 1924 conference (COPEC) and his 1941 conference at Malvern, were faithfully reproduced in South Africa. In 1940 Geoffrey Clayton, at that time Bishop of Johannesburg, set up a commission to plan a new social order, with nine committees concerned with particular issues: education, industry, economics, social welfare, Native affairs, Coloured peoples, race relations, religious disunity, and the relations of Church and State. Many reforms were suggested—each one of which required an extension of state activity into social and economic relationships. The Report, published as *The Church and the Nation,* in 1943, failed to recognize the full implications of its endorsement of collectivist principles, however. State action was urged, but no clear ideology of a collectivist state merged in the commission's findings. No doubt, with Smuts's government in office at the time, the Anglicans hoped for pragmatic post-war political developments sympathetic to their social liberalism. In fact, of course, the success of Afrikaner Nationalism in 1948 meant that the next acceleration of collectivism was rendered within an ideology they found deeply antipathetic. One of the consequences, in modern South African history, has been the opposition of Anglican leaders to many aspects of the state machinery which have developed. Like the Anglicans, the Christian Council of South Africa was extremely attentive to social issues, with a number of committees of inquiry into proposed reforms in the years following its constitution in 1936. The Council—again like the Anglicans—reflected external opinion, especially the development of progressive social attitudes within international missionary conferences and, after its formation in 1938, within the World Council of Churches.

There can be no doubt that the most important social service

[16] P. d' A. Jones, *The Christian Socialist Revival, 1877–1914,* Princeton, 1968, p. 216.

the Churches have provided in South Africa has been education. There was, once more, a parallel history between the work of missionary education in black society and the provision of education in white parishes.

Philip wrote of the importance attached to their educational work by the London Missionary Society— 'The influence of the system of education adopted at our missionary stations diffuses itself over the whole mass of the population: the parents see and acknowledge the improvement of the children; and the progress made by the young is pushing forward their seniors.' [17] The enthusiasm for popular education, which led to the foundation of so many schools for poor children in England in the first decades of the nineteenth century, followed the missionaries to South Africa. All the missions set up schools, with the Methodists leading in the field by the end of the century. By 1900, in fact, virtually all the education for blacks was being provided by the churches. In the Cape Colony there were 585 mission schools, and a further 474 schools for aboriginals in the frontier districts; with 11 training schools for teachers, many of whom were black or Coloured. In Natal, native education was rather less advanced by 1900: there were 188 mission schools for blacks, and schools for Indians, mostly in Durban— 23 conducted by the Anglicans, 7 by the Methodists, 2 by the Catholics, and 1 each by the South African General Mission and the government. In Basutoland (Lesotho), the Paris Evangelical Missionary Society operated 153 schools, with some 50 others run by the other denominations. Perhaps the most famous of the educational institutions of the missions was Lovedale, set up in 1824 by the United Free Church of Scotland, in the eastern Cape. Instruction was non-denominational from the start; it was also unusual in that blacks and whites were educated together, and in its scope— education extended from infants to the training of ministers. There were 700 to 800 students at most times, drawn from several tribes. A very few went on to higher education, at Fort Hare Native College, after its foundation in 1916. By 1945 there were 4,360 mission schools in South Africa, and only 230 schools conducted by the government for non-whites. At the end of the 1940s, in fact, the priority of the churches in educational work

[17] Philip, op. cit., i. 203.

was shown by the report of the Bantu Education Commission: in the Cape Province 23 different religious bodies were running mission schools in receipt of state financial aid; in Natal 27; in the Orange Free State 6; in the Transvaal 26. State support for the educational work of the missionary societies and the churches had existed from the beginning, and was, indeed, an essential condition of their success. A large part of the costs were met directly by state subsidy, the rest coming from overseas charities and home donations. As the system of mission schools spread, state subvention increased. The schools in receipt of aid were subject to government inspection. At the time of the Bantu Education Act in 1953, the state element in financing the schools was large, and the salaries of teachers were entirely at state expense from 1841. The churches had themselves urged increased state aid. In 1937, for example, a deputation from the Education Committee of the Christian Council of South Africa had met the government and requested increased financial aid for black schools.

Resistance to native education by some sections of white opinion also made state aid essential: white enthusiasm, at least at the parish level, was not such that regular private financing could be relied upon. Feeling against black education had been strong among the Boer farmers in the Cape in the early days, but by the end of the nineteenth century it had conveyed itself to the English-speaking population as well. 'No one can travel a day's journey in any part of the frontier', Bishop James Ricards observed in his *Catholic Church and the Kaffir*, 'who will not hear, from the colonial farmers or others who employ native labour, a strong opinion in favour of the "raw" Kaffir, as he is called— the Kaffir who has never been a member of a missionary institution—as compared with the "converted".'[18] Congresses of the Afrikaner Bond, in the 1880s, frequently called for a reduction in the state grants made for native education. 'The truth is that the Kaffir does not yet require book-learning,' as a local official from Natal told the South African Native Races Commission in 1899.[19] In the face of such opposition the missions were increasingly dependent on state support. Relations between

[18] J. Ricards, *The Catholic Church and the Kaffir*, p. 9.
[19] *The Natives of Sourth Africa. Their Economic and Social Condition.* (Evidence of G. M. Davies, a Forest Ranger), p. 334.

Church and State over the education of blacks were stable all the time this arrangement continued. State attempts to centalize and systematize black education were successfully resisted by the churches—who feared the effect of such changes on the nature of religious teaching. In 1937, when the Transvaal Department of Education proposed to amalgamate all the black schools under its own control, with an agreed non-denominational syllabus, the Anglicans objected forcefully, as much to the subverting of confessional instruction as to the principle of state control. The clash of Church and State over black education came with the Bantu Education Act in 1953. The nationalization of educational responsibilities formerly undertaken by the churches has been a feature of the modern state in many parts of the world. It is the application of collectivism in the educational sphere, as much required by the inability of the religious bodies to finance the education of expanding populations as by the rise of ideologies about the social competence of the state. In the case of South Africa the state, which by 1953 was giving enormous subsidies to the mission schools, decided to withdraw the grants from 1955 and take direct control of black education. Only the Catholics tried to keep their black education going without state aid—and even they, by 1959, had had to close down some sixty schools, and three of the six Catholic colleges for the training of teachers. The churches opposed the Act because of the ideological purposes they believed it expressed: the government, they thought, wished to control black education in order to use it to prepare blacks for their place in an apartheid society.

Within white society, the work of education had been a traditional Christian responsibility from the start of the Cape colony. Left originally to the *sieketroosters*, education came, by the begining of the eighteenth century, under the authority of the *kerkeraad*, itself subject to the government through the Political Commissioners. The pattern of development remained fairly stable until the nineteenth century, when the churches' involvement with education became complicated by the variable balances between English and Dutch educational methods, policies, and languages. The Lancastrian System was introduced by the Revd John Campbell and was soon in use in both white and mission schools. At around the same time, in 1812, the goverment financed the so-called *Koster Scholen*, which linked Church and State in educational enterprise—but not to the satisfaction of the *kerkeraad*. State financial grants were also given to the schools of the various denominations. In 1838 there were 23 establishments in the Cape Colony in receipt of aid administered by the Bible and School Commission, a mixed committee of churchmen and government officials. Arrangements were not very effective, and in 1839 an Education Department was created, under an official charged with responsibility for all Cape schools: a development influenced by the growth of the educational interests of the government in Britain. In the same year the Education Committee of the Privy Council was set up in London. The Cape legislation of 1865 provided that state aid for church schools would be given to those in which there was non-denominational religious instruction, and that grants would be made at a level which would double the sums raised by the various denominational bodies themselves. The Catholic Church encountered serious difficulties over state aid—in trying to secure parity with the Protestants in the allocation of state funds. In 1863 there were negotiations between Bishop Thomas Grimley and Dr Langham Dale, Director of Education at the Cape, which stabilized grants to Catholic schools but at a lower level than the schools in which non-denominational instruction was given. This was recognized in the 1865 Act, but the issue remained one which disturbed relations between the Catholic Church and the state up to recent times. Catholic investment in education was very considerable. Bishop Grimley made a particular effort to get schools established; in Natal, also, effort increased towards the end of the century. During the period in which he was Vicar Apostolic of Natal (1875–1903), Bishop Charles Jolivet founded eighty-two schools.

The different political systems which operated in South Africa at just the time when education was undergoing its greatest expansion, in the later years of the nineteenth century, resulted in dissimilar educational policies. At the Cape, English administrative ideas dominated a system which was largely in the hands of local Dutch Reformed officials. Natal established grants-in-aid to church schools in 1852, and then developed a centralized educational system after 1878. Education in the Orange Free State was in part based upon Scottish practice. In

the Transvaal, education was declared to be a national obligation in the 1858 Constitution, and was explicitly linked to the
Dutch Reformed Church (Article 24)—which was, in 1859,
given the exclusive right to conduct the schools. The confessional
nature of education in the Transvaal was firmly entrenched in
the religious identity of the people. This was revealed by the
unpopularity of the Education Act of 1874, passed by President
Thomas Burgers—himself a minister of the Church. The Act
was regarded as secularizing in tendency; it provided only
non-denominational religious instruction. A reflection of
Burgers's own theological liberalism, yet establishing, in effect,
the Cape practice, the Act was replaced in 1882 as part of the
neo-Calvinist reaction of S. J. du Toit, who was by then Superintendent of Education. Thereafter Dutch Reformed confessional
instruction was given in the schools. During the Anglo-Boer
War these arrangements lapsed, and education in the period of
reconstruction was according to the non-denominational principles of Milner's anglicizing attitudes. By the terms of the
Union, in 1910, educational policy was devolved to the provinces,
as a practical way of avoiding further difficulties over the language
issue. It was this issue, indeed, which provided the greatest
clash in the relations of Church and State over educational
questions in South African history.

The preservation of the language had, of course, been central
to the development of Afrikaner nationalism in the later years of
the nineteenth century. This paralleled the language element in
the many other contemporaneous nationalist movements in
European societies. The Dutch Reformed churches were closely
associated both with language and nation—having a position
comparable, for example, to the relationship of the Catholic
Church to the emergent nationalism of Ireland in these years.
As far back as 1839, when the Cape government, anxious to
promote the spread of English, had given preference to schools
teaching in that language, in the allocation of state grants,
many clergy of the Dutch Reformed Church had encouraged
the foundation of private Dutch-language schools. The close
proximity of language and religion was reinforced by the late
nineteenth-century cultural revival. When, during and after the
Anglo-Boer War, Milner's policies broke that link in the new
school system provided for the Boer Republics, a confrontation

of Church and State became inevitable. The movement of *Christelik-Nationale Onderwys* was the outcome, especially after the Transvaal Synod of 1903. Much of the work for the setting up of the dependent Afrikaans schools was done by H. S. Bosman. Sowat 'n maand ná die verdaging van die Sinode het hy in 'n preek verklaar dat dit die taak van die kerk was om teen gevaarlike strominge te waarsku. 'Wij hebben veel geduld beoefend om met de Regering te onderhandelen over de Taal en over het school-onderwijs. Wij worden altijd vriendelik ontvangen doch ook altijd vriendelik afgewezen! Wij hebben de Regering gesmeekt: noodzaak ons toch niet om afzonderlijke scholen te gaan oprichten. Wij willen het niet gaarne doen.' [20] This strength of feeling against state policy was seen in the success of the new confessional schools. By the end of 1903, there were 151 Christian National Schools in the Transvaal, paid for by local donations and subscriptions organized by the Dutch Reformed churches. Some financial assistance came from Holland. Religious teaching was strictly according to the principles of the Synod of Dort. In the Orange Free State the movement was not successful, owing to the inability of local enthusiasts to provide adequate financing. The Smuts Act of 1907 eventually took over the Christian National Schools in the Transvaal; it was a compromise—allowing more Afrikaans instruction and local educational control but requiring non-denominational education. The ideal of the *Christelik-Natiionale Onderwys* did not disappear, however; it has remained within Afrikaner nationalism ever since, reappearing from time to time as a sort of standard of authenticity against which to test the educational intentions of successive governments. The clash of Church and State at the start of the century therefore cast a long shadow. When Smuts's wartime administation proposed educational reforms which would have retained both English and Afrikaans language groups in the same schools, the Nationalists under Malan urged segregation. The Revd William Nicol,

---

[20] G. D. Scholtz, *Die Geskiedenis van die Nederduitse Hervormde of Gereformeerde Kerk van Suid-Afrika*, ii. 148. (About a month after the adjournment of the Synod, he declared in a sermon that the task of the Church was to warn against dangerous currents. 'We have exercised a great deal of restraint in dealing with the government over language and school education. We were always cordially received and always bidden farewell in a friendly way! We have been conciliatory with the government: necessity will never force us to set up separate schools. We don't want anything to do with that.')

who became the leading clerical advocate of language segregation at the time, returned again to the contention that religion
and nationality went together. In May 1944, the Church declared: 'Our aim with the Afrikaans language, which is also the
language of the Church, is to preserve and develop it, thus
making sure of promoting the future interests of the Church,
since the mother tongue school serves to preserve future Church
members and their descendants for the Afrikaans Church.'[21]
As with so many other aspects of church history in South Africa,
therefore, the involvement of the churches with education shows
an acceptance of the pluralism of national and political ideologies.
Nor is this a feature restricted to the Dutch Reformed churches.
In contending for alternatives to the policies of Afrikaner
nationalism, the English-speaking churches derive their social
and political visions from developments of opinion within
western liberal ideology outside the country. Their policies, too,
are sectional. There is, in the end, no single church history of
South Africa, not even in educational and welfare questions.

[21] Ernst G. Malherbe, *Education in South Africa*, ii. 44.

Comparative Note

'Every society', as Plekhanov wrote, 'lives in its own particular historical environment, which may be, and very often is, in reality very similar to the historical environment surrounding other nations and peoples, but can never be, and never is, identical with it.'[1] It may at first seem as if the historical environments of Latin America and Southern Africa are too dissimilar to bear fruitful comparison. Latin America itself hardly has a unitary history, despite its shared Iberian inheritance and its common Catholic institutions. The force of individual nationalisms, since the period of Independence, has resulted in quite significant variations in the styles and chronologies of political change. South Africa's colonial mixture—the parallelism of Dutch and English political religious institutions—was internally divisive, producing two white sociieties whose incompatibilities very deeply affected the nature of national development. Yet, for all that, the larger common features have been important and make comparisons profitable. Catholicism and Protestantism were successfully transplanted by two European groups, of the south and of the north of Europe, and were both changed (as they came into contact with indigenous cultures) and preserved (as missionaries and political officials sought to protect their theological integrity and their civilizing capabilities) in ways which certainly reveal some common features.

There were, of course, some untidy variations—as in the case of the exported political institutions. Colonials sometimes asserted ecclesiastical rights or claims different from those of their parent bodies in Europe; indigenous peoples sometimes converted Christian orthodoxy into the currency of their existing religious practices; the political ideals accompanying the development of national self-consciousness were easily attached to obviously diverse understandings of Christian social order.

[1] G. Plekhanov, *The Development of the Monist View of History*, Moscow, 1956 edn, p. 224.

The centre of a useful comparative view must reside in the nature of the exported Christianity itself: despite all the adaptations, can it still be said that its religious message about the structure of human social organization demonstrates a stable content? This is a basic question, which the historical developments of South America and South Africa illustrate but do not satisfactorily answer. The information to be derived from these examples of Christian applications richly indicates the enormous difficulty religious associations encounter when they seek a view of their purposes independently of the relativism of historical and ideological change. A comparative assessment will have an immediate utility for one contemporary body of Christian opinion. The exponents of Liberation Theology—themselves, of course, convinced that Christianity does have a stable content which may be embodied in political and social institutions— have in recent years been seeking ways of uniting African and Latin-American Christianity around an analysis of the common exploitation of their continents. Initially they found their cultural and national diversities too great to bear much further examination. 'It was a new experience for the Latin Americans to enter into the world of African and Asian religions,' as the Chilean priest, Sergio Torres, wrote[2] about the first Conference of theologians from the Third World, which met in Dar es Salaam during August 1976. For many of this school, however, the content of Christian social action has now disclosed its universal validity in the Marxist understanding of *praxis*. The comparative observations which follow do not, in themselves, suggest a coherent conclusion; but they do confirm that very different historical environments may still produce effectively similar Christian responses where the non-religious influences present in that environment are comparable.

The relations of Church and State, both in Latin America and in South Africa, have followed the same transition as in Europe and North America—from exclusive interdependence either to complete separation or to the maintenance of more or less residual links. The crowns of Spain and Portugal, and the Dutch East India Company, enforced a strict religious uni-

[2] *The Emergent Gospel. Theology from the Underside of History*, ed. Sergio Torres and Virginia Fabella, Maryknoll, New York, 1978, p. xix.

formity in their overseas territories; both insisted upon a rigorous confessionalism by political institutions and gave the churches, in return, protection and favour. The Catholic Church in Latin America was in general weak, both politically and istitutionally, as a result of this control, and remained so after the independence of the colonies. The Dutch Reformed churches and the English-speaking churches in South Africa were strong socially and at times politically, but South Africa's double ecclesiastical inheritance—from Holland and Britain—created religious rivalries and pluralities which neutralized the potential advantages this gave them to act as really decisive influences upon secular developments. The absence of effective state structures with authority over both the main white population groups, in the most formative years of South Africa's national experience, limited still further the prospects for relations between Church and State. Within each of the Latin American states such prospects did exist and were at times fulfilled; but in the largest perspective it must be concluded that Latin-American political experience had clarity, if not stability, and that it was a clarity often achieved, during the advances of nineteenth-century liberal ideology, at the expense of the churches.

Adjustments in the relationship of Church and State were, in Latin America, characteristically accomplished as a result of direct attrition between the insitutional church and the political and intellectual forces of secularism. It was a bitter history, and it still continues, though the ideologies have changed hands—it is the social and political radicalism of the Catholic Church which today provokes the hostility of conservative political forces. This divisive legacy is not paralleled in South Africa. There the nineteenth-century adjustments of Church and State were according to the British pattern of ordered, pragmatic, legislative separation by gradual stages. Disestablishment was carried out by fiendly agencies, with the general agreement of the churches themselves. It was regarded as a measure of ordinary civil justice, required by the existence of an admitted religious and social pluralism. The creation of the Boer Republics in the mid-nineteenth century removed those elements making for conflict in the relations of Church and State at the Cape and in Natal, and this greatly assisted the relatively smooth transition to disestablishment. The Dutch Reformed congregations who did not go on the Trek—a large majority, of course—were already, as the *trekkers* complained, sufficiently open to anglicizing influences to adopt the same attitudes in relation to the political status of the church as the English-speaking Christians around them. The new State Churches of the Boer Republics, on the other hand, gave the practice of exclusive state confessionalism an extended existence in South Africa. In Latin America, too, many of the state establishments of the Catholic Church survived—in countries as different, for example, as Argentina and Peru—and with their survival went a large measure of state control. But state control was also often maintained in countries which secularized: the history of Mexico offers the most well-known example. The Catholic Church in most Latin-American countries has been the only institution with a fully national existence. This has not in general, however, assisted its political effectiveness since it has attracted the hostility of the civil authorities, unwilling to countenance a rival in the vast rural territories over which the urban élites, who have conducted political life, have at times exercised little control. The separate denominations South Africa have each enjoyed a national existence as well, but they have broken up on ethnic lines, between the two major white population groups, and between the black and Coloured racial sections. The absence of a tradition of anti-clericalism in South Africa's history, and its enormous importance in Latin America's, is a very accurate indication of the different levels of influence the clergy of the two areas have either sought to exercise in public life or have had imposed upon them by political forces seeking the adhesion of 'traditional' values. This is, indeed, one of the most notable differences in the experience of South America and South Africa. In the first case the liberals of the nineteenth century worked for the direct destruction of the influence of the Church in the furtherance of their rival view of man, of society, of progress, and of political capabilities. In the second, the proximity of the Dutch Reformed churches to the political aspirations of Afrikaner society did not encounter significant opposition within that society. It did, of course, from the English-speaking South Africans, but their political eclipse after the rise of modern Afrikaner nationalism, and the emergence of race as the central political issue dividing Christian leadership, absorbed any potential anti-clericalism which may have been directed against the ministers of the Dutch Reformed churches. Such feelings as did exist were overwhelmed by the larger national antipathies. Some anti-clericalism inspired by the conduct of the liberal leadership of the English-speaking churches has appeared among some Afrikaner political groups.

The issue of state control of ecclesiastical appointments occurred in both Latin America and South Africa as a further accompaniment of the re-definition of the relations of Church and State. In South Africa—where the Great Trek was in part a protest against the exercise of patronage within the Dutch Reformed Church by the British colonial authority—the state lacked the aggressive will to maintain control over the church after disestablishment. In Latin-American countries that was rarely the case. The ideology of liberal secularism, which had procured the separations explicitly in order to diminish the influence of the Church, regarded the continuance of state control over religion as an essential guarantee of liberty. This involvement with ecclesiastical appointments, though claimed as inseparably united to the exercise of national sovereignty, drew the governments into conflict with the Papacy. Only in the early years of the new republics, however, did this appear as a really formidable problem: thereafter positions were formalized and compromises were arranged. The truth was that the authority of the Papacy was anyway not strong in the Latin-American Church. Rome was never the decisive external force that the anti-clericals described in their polemical assaults upon Catholicism. There was no effective external control of the Churches in South Africa, either. During the nineteenth century the various denominations secured their autonomy from jurisdictions overseas—like the Classis of Amsterdam or the English religious establishment—and the ordinary civil courts thereafter guaranteed them in the possession of their property and the integrity of their institutional rules.

Despite the appearance in South African history of considerable political power initially exercised by the Dutch and the English churches and despite the similar appearances in Latin-American history (in relation to the Catholic Church), the realities suggest that in neither area did religious groups set the terms of their association with the state or with political parties.

The sacralization of Afrikaner political nationalism was a complicated phenomenon, in which the leaders of the Dutch Reformed churches were very prominent; but it was a laicized religious influence that resulted. Malan's refusal to accept the Church's interpretation of separate racial development in 1950, and the rejection of the Cottesloe formula by the National Party leaders in 1960, were clear enough indications that the official ecclesiastical leadership could not exercise independent political judgement. In Latin America, similarly, the Catholic leadership has frequently, since independence, endorsed *Hispanidad* social and political values, but it has never done so effectively as an independent influence—only when called upon to do so by political interests. The Church's political role in the national period has always tended to have this dependent quality, whatever the actual nature of the politics it has endorsed. In, for example, both the support at first given by the Church to Perón in Argentina in the 1940s, and in the very different support given to García Moreno in Ecuador in the 1860s, the Catholic hierarchies were not the initiators of political influence: they were the beneficiaries of political ideals whose fulfilment, for various reasons, were made easier with the sanction of religious opinion. There was no universally accepted concept of political sovereignty in Latin America once the authority of the Iberian crowns had been laid aside. Conservatives thereafter often needed the Church as a symbol of traditional social authority; liberals mistook the symbolical for the actual, and attacked the Church for the possession of powers it never really had.

The link of nationalism and religion was just as complicated, in both areas, as the political influence of the Church. In South Africa the churches of the two white-language groups have closely associated their understanding of Christianity with rival nationalisms. A developed nationalist ideology was no less evident in the English churches, at the time of Rhodes and Milner, than it was within the Dutch Reformed churches. The experience of the Trek, and the Biblical significance attached to the destiny of the Afrikaner people, made the national self-consciousness of the original Boer Republics, and later of the National Party in the Union and Republic of South Africa, one of the clearest examples of religious endorsement of nationalism in modern history The Church was very strongly represented in the intellectual élites who formulated the ideology of Afrikanerdom. In Latin America, on the other hand, nationalism divided the Catholic Church on national lines. Neither the universal nature of the Church, nor the external jurisdiction of Rome, was able to act as a unifying force. With the rise of national-cultural feelings founded upon a rejection of the Spanish inheritance—with the *indigenismo* of Peru and Mexico— nationalism was itself turned against Catholicism. The Church was not well represented within the intelligentsia, whose secularized ideals depicted the Church, indeed, as the anti-national agency of unprogressive rural stagnation. Latin-American Catholicism lacked a religious rival, of the sort the competing denominations of South Africa had. Its rival was secular; the battle was therefore more political, and the support of the Church for nationalist politics, when this occurred, was in direct opposition to other versions of nationalism. This became particularly evident in the present century, when Catholic support for the corporate state—Brazil in the 1930s, for example— must be assessed in the light of this sort of background of conflict rather than as straightforward emulations of the Fascist orders in Spain and Portugal. The appeal of the corporate state ideal in South Africa was to a small minority of Afrikaner purists. The Ossewabrandwag of 1938 was, unlike the Latin-American examples, much more obviously dependent upon European Fascism for its ideology. To most Afrikaner nationalists, however, Christian civilization did not require such structures for its salvation: the existing inheritance of Christian nationalism was enough, provided its cultural integrity could be safeguarded. At this point, race separation became essential to their vision, and at this point also, because of their different understanding of the most ethical means of effecting separate development, the leaders of the Dutch Reformed Church became less influential within the direction of Nationalist political idealism.

The impact of European social and political ideas upon the churches was felt in rather different ways in both the areas of this study. In part this indicated the different experience of political institutions, the varying chronologies of responsiveness to changes in the European ideologies, the inherent incompatibilities of Calvinism and Catholicism, and the fact that

South Africa remained, for obvious reasons, closely related to northern European developments and Latin America to southern European ones. The religious ideas upon which these external influences came to bear were orthodox, however. Each of the denominations in South Africa remained almost entirely free of heresy, and separatist movements (of which the Independent black sects are the most important)—though without doubt 'heretical' in the classic sense—have in rality been expressions of the unsuppressed beliefs of indigenous peoples outside the developments of the historic churches. Genuine heterodoxy, like the Colenso schism in the Anglican Church, has not been numerically significant. In Latin America, similarly, Catholicism has been preserved from heresy in spite of the pervasive syncretism characteristic of the rural folk Catholicism of the Indian peasantry. It is only in the last few decades that the internal controversies over Marxism and social radicalism within the Catholic Church have produced claims and counter-claims of orthodoxy and error that have echoed the styles of the great heretical movements of past European ecclesiastical experience. The Theology of Liberation, appearing first in Latin America, is now a force within South African Christianity as well. It shows in both areas, however, a common responsiveness not to some stable inheritance of the Christian past but to the seclarized ideologies of contemporary political radicalism. Its appeal in both areas has been to a minority, but in Latin America that minority has tended to comprise some of the most prestigious and influential sections of the religious leadership. The reason for the difference between the two regions in this particular is to be found in a more general phenomenon: the adoption by church leaders of the social, moral, and political attitudes and modes of thought to be found in the educated sections of the societies in which they are set. Theological rationalizations have followed the absorption of political ideologies. This has meant, in both places, that the civilizing mission of the Churches to the indigenous peoples has conveyed the European cultures and political ideologies in a Christian guise. Subsequent opponets of missionary practice—Black Consciousness in South Africa, or the *indigenismo* writers of Latin America—hae notice just how relative the notions of basic 'Christian' social order preached by the missionaries actually were. Educated opinion in Latin America has, in the last century and a half, been much less influenced by Christianity than it has in South Africa. Yet Christian opinion has retained a close proximity to the changing ideals of the intelligentsia: hence the spread of Marxism to those sections of the Latin-American church nearest to educated society today. Hence, also, the absence of a significant Marxist impact upon South African White Christianity—Marxism is not, in South Africa, part of the encompassing texture of intellectual attitudes.

Responsiveness to external opinion has actually varied a great deal between the churches of the two white-language groups in South Africa. The Dutch Reformed churches developed fairly independently of the changes in European thought long before the arrival of British ideas early in the nineteenth century. The general intellectual outlook of the European Enlightenment—which so shaped the Independence movement in Latin America—was largely ignored at the Cape. When de Mist first attempted to reform the Church according to its principles, his work was rejected by the Boer farmers as fundamentally alien: the Dutch settlers had for too long been out of touch with the social and political transformation of Europe. The continued theological conservatism of the Cape church (compared with the Church in Holland), and the Great Trek with its legacy of religious independency, perpetuated the separation of South African Dutch Reformed faith from external ideas. When theological novelties were introduced from outside some of them divided the Church—as the importation of theological liberalism did in the nineteenth century—but most, like the reception of Kuyper's ideas, were notable for serving as preservatives of existing traditionalism. The English-speaking churches of South Africa, in constrast, were always responsive to developments in Britain. It was English churchmen who introduced the progressive values of Political Economy early in the nineteenth century. This had the effect of offending the paternalistic social values of the Dutch citizens, just as in Latin America the introduction of the principles of Political Economy in the first half of the nineteenth century upset the paternalism of Catholic traditionalists. In both areas the advocates of Political Economy employed their science as a critique of the unprogressive outlook of the landed social order. In the case of South Africa these

exponents were British missionaries; in Latin America they
were liberal *pensadores*. The leaders of the South African English-
speaking churches have retained close links with English opinion.
It was this continued external reference which made them—
unlike most of their white congregations—opponents of
apartheid in the middle years of the twentieth century. Many of
the officers and parochial ministers have continued to be re-
cruited from the English churches, bringing liberal values with
them; a situation exactly comparable to the arrival of the
European and North American missionary priests in Latin
America in the 1960s and 1970s, carrying with them the radicalized Catholicism of the northern hemisphere. The Catholic
leaders of Latin America in the nineteenth century had not been
out of touch with European developments, however. Ultra-
montansim and neo-Thomism, and the Papal encyclicals, were
recieved and assimilated in an intellectual atmosphere of universalist thinking not dissimilar to their liberal adversaries'
indebtedness to the European ideas of Postivism, Krausism,
and so forth.

   The social function of religion was conceived and practised in
similar ways both in South Africa and in Latin America during
the pre-collectivist stages of their political developments. In
both places the churches fulfilled traditional obligations in
relation to charitable instititions, and in education. There were
some variations in the social position of the churches which
affected the degree to which they became identified with particular sectional interests, however. The Church was strong in
the urban areas, and rather weaker in the rural districts of
South Africa; in the Latin-American countries the reverse was
the case. The urban population expansion of the twentieth
century was more easily accommodated within South African
Christianity—despite, even so, some formidable problems—
than was the experience of Latin-American Catholicism. The
shortage of clergy in Latin America has anyway, in both urban
and rural areas, aggravated an already difficult situation. The
landed wealth of the Latin-American Catholic Church (before
the reforms of the last century and a half) had no counterpart in
South Africa, where the churches, accordingly, had no substantial stake in economic activity. This also helps to explain
the absence of anti-clericalism from reformist groups in South

African society. Yet in the nineteenth century the Dutch Reformed Church was associated with rural, landed values, just as the Catholic Church in Latin America was. Secularization, in both cases, was produced by urbanization, and more slowly in South Africa because the churches' relative strength in the expanding cities retained the traditional values of more of the immigrants from the countryside than proved to be possible in Latin America. The ideological element in secularization, though not the decisive cause of change, also operated more strongly in Latin-American society. In both places the growth of the social and administrative machinery of the modern state—starting rather earlier in South America, and especially in the southern part of the continent—diminished the social function of religion and hastened the marginalization of the Church and so assisted the secularization of public values. In both places, also, this was in large measure a 'natural' growth, forced forward by the inexorable pressures of population increase and economic changes. The modern collectivist state was, in Latin America, frequently advocated by progressive political groups for ideological reasons, in opposition to Catholic traditionalism, but the more basic forces making for a wider state activity were anyway irresistible. There are, in the twentieth-century history of Latin America, examples of corporate state collectivism promoted both by Church and State in the name of agreed Catholic principles. Where they have endured long enough to bear useful analysis their existence cannot be shown to have impeded the advance of secularization in public life. In South Africa collectivism was promoted for social welfare reasons by incontrovertibly Christian opinion in the churches of both the white-language groups. The rise of Afrikaner nationalism inspired a state structure so friendly to the social values of the Dutch Reformed Church that the addition of collectivist powers did not seem threatening. For the English-speaking churches, of course, the reverse seemed to be the case. The nationalization of Bantu education, in 1953, was a symbolical as well as a real advance of state power which particularly alarmed them—in some small measure because they feared the secularization of education, but mostly because the state had race and cultural objectives rather than religious or secular ones. Although the impulsions making for collectivism have come from demo-

graphic and economic changes, and were in that sense independent of political considerations, the means by which the
actual powers of the modern state have been directed have
proved just as 'ideological' as they have in Latin America.

Attitudes to race in both areas disclose a number of contrasts.
In Latin America the first white advances were accompanied
by an intensive and systematic programme of missionary action
by the Catholic Church. In South Africa the indigenous peoples
were not greatly affected by white influence for some time: the
Hottentots of the Cape were generally regarded as beyond the
possibility of civilization and Christianization, but the matter
was not a pressing one because for the first century and a half of
Dutch settlement there was no intention of allowing the Colony
to expand beyond the immediate area of the Cape itself. The
Bantu peoples had not yet begun their movement into the
adjacent territories. Among the Spanish and Portuguese in
South America the indigenous peoples were not reduced to
slavery, and a sophisticated body of Catholic and Natural Law
teaching was formulated which recognized certain rights
attaching to the newly discovered humanity, however inferior
the social role to which they were relegated. Yet the black
populations of both areas were deemed suited to slavery, until
the start of the nineteenth century. The timetable for the emancipation of the slaves was actually about the same in South
America (except for Brazil) and it was in South Africa. In the one
case it represented the principles of the European Enlightenment as understood by the men who broke with Spain; in the
other it was imposed by the British colonial power, as an
extension of the Evangelical and philanthropic idealism which
at that time characterized reforming agencies in England. In
South Africa the question of abolition divided opinion much
more sharply and with an enduring legacy of bitterness between
the English and the Dutch. Of neither area can it be said that
abolition was really spearheaded by the formal ecclesiastical
structures: the general picture was of an over-all cultivation of
opinion in favour of emancipation, often expressed in Christian
moral terms, but with the official churches inseparable from the
development of attitudes as a whole. Some notable Christian
propagandists on behalf of the rights of the native peoples had a
wide importance in their day—Philip's description of the con-

dition of the Hottentots in the early years of the nineteenth
century is clearly comparable with the strictures of Las Casas
about the state of the Indians of Spanish America two centuries
before.

Racial questions, of course, have come to dominate the social
thinking of the churches in South Africa, and although the issue
of separate development now divides the denominations along
linguistic and cultural lines, the history of the last century
shows that all the churches once saw advantages, to both white
and black peoples, in segregation. The churches then divided
into 'parishes' for the whites and 'missions' for the blacks.
Latin-American Catholicism, in contrast, has not been racially
segregated, even from the earliest times—just as it was not in
the Catholic Church of South Africa. In Latin America, the
Indian missionary stations were rapidly converted into ordinary
ecclesiastical parishes, and jurisdication passed from the religious orders to the episcopate. The Jesuit Reductions in Paraquay were cetaily an exception to this, since their object was to
separate the Indians from the whites. But the intention was not
racial; it was cultural and religious. It was an attempt to protect
the customs of the indigenous peoples, just as the Moravian
missions in South Africa contrived a similar missionary strategy
for the same sort of reasons. Intermarriage between the races in
Latin America began in the earliest period of settlement, with
no objection by the Church. In South Africa intermarriage,
while always theoretically allowed by the churches, has not
persuaded the laity: it was made illegal in 1940.

In practice, throughout the whole of its history, a degree of
racial separation has always existed within Latin-American
Catholicism in a number of recognized and accepted coventions.
The mestizos, Indians, blacks, and mulattos have belonged to
different religious fraternities from the whites. The different
racial groups maintain separate altars and chapels inside the
churches. Popular devotions have represented different racial
groups as well. The non-whites have adopted San Antonio de
Padua, patron of the poor, for example, for their special veneration; and also San Isidro, beloved of agricultural workers; San
Martín de Porres, the mulatto 'priest of the poor'; and the cult
of Nuestra Señora del Rosario. These and numerous local saints
have been converted by Indian spirituality into the main symbols

of *Religiosidad Popular*. The great shrines of Latin America have themselves tended to appeal to different ethnic categories. In Mexico it was mostly the Indians and mestizos who prayed to the Virgin of Guadalupe; the Spanish cultivated devotions to La Solidad of Oaxaca. In Peru, similarly, the Indian masses venerate the Señor de los Milagros in Lima's Nazarenas Church—a picture painted by a liberated slave; the Spanish prayed at the sanctuary of Santa Rosa de Lima. The divergence between *Hispanidad* values and *indigenismo* had always existed in the popular devotions of the different races.

Religious sectarianism has existed in the ecclesiastical histories of both Latin America and South Africa. The institutional and social developments of both areas took place at a time when the sacred and the secular were separating in European historical experience. Although the separation was to some extent slowed down among the settlers of the southern hemisphere—where the union of culture, politics, and religion retained some strength—European changes nevertheless filtered through in time. Yet Catholicism in Latin America, and Protestantism in South Africa, had been planted among societies whose cultures did not separate the sacred and the secular—and which persisted in not doing so. In Latin America this lead to the *Religiosidad Popular* of the Indian masses, whose strongly sectarian characterstics were nevertheless retained within the Catholic fold; and in South Africa it lead to the black Independent churches, which actually did represent a break from the historic denominations, for they are classic religious sects. The black religious cults of the South American and Caribbean coastal regions are also sects; they are not survivals of ancient African religions, imported by the slaves, but syncretisms of half-remembered African beliefs and Catholic devotional practices made during the last century or so, and indicating class as well as racial protest against the white domination of religion. Like the Pentecostal churches which have, during the present century, spread among the poor of the expanding urban areas of Latin America, these are true sects, very similar in the social levels they attract, and in the nature of their spiritual exclusivity, to the black Independents of South Africa. In Latin-American folk Catholicism religious values are not derived from the formal Church but from family practice and local custom.

This also compares with the renaissance of Bantu custom within the Independent sects of South Africa. Both religions phenomena were born of social deprivation or social disruption. They are typical 'churches of the disinherited', with strongly syncretistic elements linking them to preceding cultural values. Both are concerned with the application of religious practices as aids to daily life; they are reactions against the white men's separation of the sacred and the secular. The adherent of the black cults of Brazil, as Roger Bastide observed, 'visualized the saints and the Blessed Virgin of his black church exactly as he visualized his gods or his ancestors, not as bestowers of celestial grace but as protectors of his earthly life'.[3] With such daily spiritual sustenance, furthermore, members of sectarian religious groups, both in Latin America and in South Africa, have not been greatly interested in political participation. The sects have been notable for their refusal to associate Christianity with political action.

In both areas there has, of course, been a 'frontier history', as the advance of the settlers pushed further from the coasts. The major frontier expansion was ended in South America within half a century of the Conquest; in South Africa, too, in the nineteenth century, the area of the present modern state was occupied in a period of something like fifty years. In both places the churches were affected by the experience of the frontier, and in both it produced a laicization of religion—seen in the Biblical paternalism of the *trekker* heads of families in South Africa, and in the *Religiosidad Popular* of the Latin American *campesinos*. But the resilience of the institutional churches, and the enormous missionary efforts they made in both areas, acted to prevent excesses. Messianism, millennial speculation, and apocalyptic expectations occurred at various times, as they always have on the fringes of Christianity where social disruption has weakened the parochial structures. In neither of these two areas, however, did the appearance of these phenomena greatly affect the central development of the churches. The churches, in fact, demonstrated a remarkable degree of adaptation, in the extent to which they have employed native cultures to serve the purposes of evangelism, and in the ways in which they have still managed to preserve their traditional ecclesiastical structures. The achieve-

[3] Roger Bastide, *The African Religions of Brazil*, p. 141.

ment is astonishing; their thin line of advance demonstrating a confidence capable of transforming the religious beliefs of immense numbers of people. It is clear in the largest perspective, however, that the earlier interdependence of religious and non-religious forces has been replaced by a pattern of influence less advantageous to the churches: although the political and cultural environment has become more secularized, the leaders of Christianity have continued to reflect prevailing opinion. It may be that the future offers little prospect of a more effectively independent Christian voice, for the existing trends do not appear to be, in either area, especially ephemeral. But this situation cannot appear as formidable to contemporary churchmen as the task of Christian conversion must have seemed to the Catholic friars on the Altiplano, or to the Protestant missionaries on the Limpopo, as they regarded the entrenched paganism of the peoples to whom they felt they had been sent. 'No estás bajo mi sombra y protección?' as the Virgin of Guadalupe said to Juan Diego, 'necesitas alguna otra cosa?' — 'Are you not under my shadow and protection? Do you need anything more?'

Bibliography

I. Latin America

Alexander, Robert J., *The Perón Era*, New York, 1951.

Alonso, Isidoro, *La Iglesia en América Latina*, FERES, Fribourg, 1964.

Anderson, C. W., *Politics and Economic Changes in Latin America*, New York, 1967.

Arms, G. F., *El Origen del Metodismo y su Implantación en la Costa de Sud America*, Santiago, 1923.

Ayarragaray, Lucas, *La Iglesia en América y la Dominación Española*, Buenos Aires, 1920.

Azevedo, Thales de, *O catolicismo no Brazil*, Rio de Janeiro, 1955.

Badanelli, Pedro, *Perón, la Iglesia y un cura*, Buenos Aires, 1960.

Balderrama, Luis C., *El Clero y el Gobierno de México*, Mexico, 1927.

Bastide, Roger, *The African Relgions of Brazil, Towards a Sociology of the Interpretion of Civilizations* [*1960*], Baltimore, 1978.

Bazant, Jan, *Alienation of Church Wealth in Mexico. Social and Economic Aspects of the Liberal Revolution, 1856–1875*, Cambridge, 1971.

Bilbao, Franciso, *Obras completas* ed. Pedro Pablo Figueroa, Santiago, 1898.

Blanco Moheno, Robert, *Historia de dos curas revolucionarios: Hidalgo y Morelos*, Mexico, 1973.

Bolton, H. E. 'The mission as a frontier institution in the Spanish American colonies', in *American Historical Review*, 23, Oct. 1917.

Boxer, C. R., *The Church Militant and Iberian Expansion, 1440–1770*, Balitmore, 1978.

Braga, E., and Grubb, K. G., *The Republic of Brazil: A Survey of the Religious Situation*, New York, 1932.

Bruneau, Thomas C., *The Political Transformation of the Brazilian Catholic Church*, Cambridge, 1974.

Bruno, Cayetano, *El Derecho Público de la Iglesia en la Argentina*, Buenos Aires, 1956.

Cabal, Hugo Latorre, *The Revolution of the Latin American Church*, Oklahoma, 1978.

206   *Bibliography*

Cadavid, G., *Los fueros de la iglesia ante el liberalismo y el conervatismo en Colombia*, Medellín, 1955.
Callcott, W. M., *Church and State in Mexico, 1822–1857*, Durham, 1926.
——, *Liberalism in Mexico, 1857–1929*, Stanford, 1931.
Câmara, Dom Helder, *The Conversations of a Bishop. An Interview with José de Broucher*, London, 1979.
Camus, Carlos, *Testimonio Social de la Iglesia Chilena*, Santiago, 1976.
Caraman, P., *The Lost Paradise: an account of the Jesuits in Paraguay, 1607–1768*, London. 1975
Carneiro, J. Ferando, *Catolicismo, Revolução e Reação*, Rio de Janeiro, 1947.
Casiello, Juan, *Iglesia y Estado en la Argentina*, Buenos Aires, 1948.
Caycedo, Olga de, *El Padre Camilo Torres o la Crisis de Madurez de America*, Barcelona, 1972.
CELAM, *Iglesia y Religiosidad Popular en America Latina*, Buenos Aires, 1976.
Chávez, Héctor Cornejo, *Que se propone la democracia cristiana*, Lima, 1962.
Considine, J. J., ed., *The Church in the New Latin America*, Notre Dame, 1964.
——, *Social Revolution in the New Latin America: A Catholic Appraisal*, Notre Dame, 1965.
Costello, Gerald M., *Mission to Latin America. The Successes and Failures of a Twentieth Century Crusade*. Maryknoll, New York, 1979.
Costeloe, M. P., *Church Wealth in Mexico. A Study of the 'juzgado de capellanias' in the archbishopric of Mexico, 1800–1856*, Cambridge, 1967.
Cuevas, Mariano, *Historia de la Iglesia en México*, El Paso, 1921–8.
Cunninghame Graham, R. B., *A Vanished Arcadia: Being Some Account of the Jesuits in Paraguay*, New York, 1901.

Damboriena, Prudencio, *El Protestantismo en América Latina*, FERES, Bogotá, 1963.
D'Antonio, William, and Pike, Frederick B., *Religion, Revolution, and Reform. New Forces for Change in Latin America*, London, 1964.
Dellhora, Guillermo, *La Iglesia Católica ante la Crítica en el Pensamiento y en el Arte*, Mexico, 1929.
Dewart, Leslie, *Christianity and Revolution: The Lesson of Cuba*, New York, 1963.
Documentos del Episcopado, Chile 1970–73, Santiago, 1974.
Dominguez, Oscar, *El Campesino Chileno y la Acción Católica Rural*, FERES, Fribourg, 1961.

Egaña, Antonio de, *Historia de la Iglesia en la América Española-Hemisferio Sur*, Madrid, 1966.

Eyzaguirre, Jaime, *Historia de las instituciones políticas y sociales de Chile*, Santiago, 1967.

——, *Historia de Chile*, Santiago, new edn, 1973.

Farrell, Gerardo T. *et al.*, *Comentario A La Exhortacion Apostolica De Su Santidad Pablo VI 'Evangelii Nuntiandi'*, Buenos Aires, 1978.

Fichter, J. H., *Cambio social en Chile: Un estudio de actitudes*, Santiago, 1962.

Figuera, Guillermo, *La Formación del clero indigena en la Historia Eclesiastica de America, 1500–1810*, Caracas, 1965.

Flora, Cornelia Butler, *Pentecostalism in Colombia. Baptism by Fire and Spirit*, Associated University Presses, 1976.

Florêncio da Silveira Camargo, Paulo, *História Eclesiástica do Brazil*, Petrópolis, 1955.

Floridi, Alexis U., and Stiefold, Annette E., *The Uncertain Alliance: The Catholic Church and Labor in Latin America*, Miami, 1973.

Frei Montalva, Eduardo, *Sentido y forma de una política*, Santiago, 1951.

Gale, Laurence, *Education and Development in Latin-America*, London, 1969.

García, Genaro, *El Clero de México durante la Dominación Española*, Mexico, 1927.

——, *La Inquisición de México*, Mexico, 1906.

Gheerbrant, Alain, *The Rebel Church in Latin America*, London, 1974.

Gibbons, William J., *Basic Ecclesiastical Statistics for Latin America*, Maryknoll, New York, 1958.

Gómez Hoyos, Rafael, *La Iglesia de América en las Leyes de Indias*, Madrid, 1961.

Hennessy, Alistair, *The Frontier in Latin American History*, London, 1978.

Hernáez, Francisco Javier, *Colección de Bulas, Breves, y Otras Documentos relativos à la Iglesia de América y Filipanas*, Brussels, 1879.

Historia y Mision, Ponencias, aportes y experiences de II Encuentro Latinoamericano de Religiosidad Popular, celebrado en Santiago de Chile, mayo, 1977, Santiago, 1977.

Holleran, Mary, *Church and State in Guatemala*, New York, 1949.

Houtart, François, *La Iglesia Latinoamericana en la Hora del Concilio*, Bogotá, 1963.

—— and Pin, Émile, *The Church and the Latin American Revolution*, New York, 1965.

Hudspith, Margarita Allan, *Ripening Fruit, A History of the Bolivian Indian Mission*, Harrington, NJ, 1958.

Kadt, Emanuel de, *Catholic Radicals in Brazil*, London, 1970.
Kennedy, John, *Catholicism, Nationalism and Democracy in Argentina*, Notre Dame, 1958.

La verdadera y única solución de la cuestión social. Carta pastoral colectiva que la Episcopado chileno dirige a los sacerdotes y fieles de la Nación, Santiago, 1932.
Landsberger, Henry, ed., *The Church and Social Change in Latin America*, Notre Dame, 1970.
Larraín, Manuel E., *Redención proletaria*, Santiago, 1948.
——, *Escritos Sociales*, Santiago, 1963.
Larrea, Juan Ignacio, *La Iglesia y el estado en el Ecuador*, Sevilla, 1954.
Lea, H. C., *The Inquisition in the Spanish Dependencies*, New York, 1908.
Leite, Serafim, *Summa Histórica da Companhia de Jesus no Brazil, 1549–1760*, Lisbon, 1965.
Letelier, Valentín, *Filosofía de la eduación*, Santiago, 1912.

McLean, J. H., *História de la Iglesia Presbiteriana en Chile*, Santiago, 1954.
Mariátegui, José Carlos, *Seven interpretive essays on Peruvian Reality*, trans. Marjory Urguidi, Austin, 1974.
Marsal, S., Pablo, *Perón y la Iglesia*, Buenos Aires, 1955.
Mecham, J. Lloyd, *Church and State in Latin America*, revised edn, University of North Carolina Press, 1966.
Mesquita, A. N. de, *Historia dos Batistas do Brazil*, Rio de Janeiro, 1940.
Meyer, Jean A., *The Cristero Rebellion. The Mexican People between Church and State, 1926–1929*, Cambridge, 1976.
Miller, Herbert J., *La iglesia y el estado en tiempo de Justo Rufino Barrios*, trans. Jorge Luján Muñoz, Guatemala, 1976.
Mörner, Magnus, *The Political and Economic Activities of the Jesuits in the La Plata Region. The Habsburg Era*, Stockholm, 1953.
——, *The Expulsion of the Jesuits from Latin Ameria*, New York, 1965.
Mutchler, David, *The Church as a Political Factor in Latin America: with Particular Reference to Colombia and Chile*, New York, 1971.

Pérez Lugo, J., *La Cuestión Religiosa en México. Recopilación de Leyes Disposiciones Legales y Documentos para el Estudio de este Problema Político*, Mexico, 1927.
Peragallo, Roberto, *Iglesia y Estado*, Santiago, 1923.
Phelan, J., *The Millenial Kingdom of the Franciscans in the New World*, Berkeley, second edn, 1970.
Piaggio, Augustín, *Influencia del Clero en la Independencia Argentina*, Buenos Aires, 1912.
Picón-Salas, Mariano, *A Cultural History of Spanish America. From*

Conquest to Independence, trans. I. A. Leonard, Berkeley, 1962.

Pike, Frederick B., *The Conflict between Church and State in Latin America*, New York, 1964.

Pin, Émile, *Elementos para una Sociologia del Catolicismo Latinoamericano*, FERES, Bogotá, 1963.

Ramirez, Humerto Muñoz, *Sociologia Religiosa de Chile*, Santiago, 1957.

Read, William R., *New Patterns of Church Growth in Brazil*, Grand Rapids, 1965.

Restrepo, Juan Pablo, *La Iglesia y el Estado en Colombia*, London, 1881.

Ricard, R., 'Prophecy and Messianism in the works of Antonio Vierira', in *The Americas*, 17, April 1961.

Romero, José Luis, *El pensamiento político de la derecha latinoamericana*, Buenos Aires, 1970.

Rosales, Juan, *Los Cristianos, los Marxistas y la Revolución*, Buenos Aires, 1970.

Russell-Wood, A. J. R.,*Fidalgos and Philanthropists. The Santa Casa da Misericórdia of Bahia, 1550–1755*, London, 1968.

Sánchez Espejo, Carlos, *El Patronato en Venezuela*, Caracas, 1953.

Sariola, Sakari, *Power and Resistance. The Colonial Heritage in Latin America*, Ithaca, 1972.

Segunda Conferencia General del Episcopado Latinoamericano, Medellín, Setiembre de 1968. Documentos Finales, Buenos Aires, 1972.

Silveria Camargo and Paulo Floriencio, *Historia Eclesiastica do Brazil*, Petropolis, 1955.

Stepan, Alfred, *The State and Society. Peru in comparative perspective*, Princeton, 1978.

Taylor, C. W., and Coggins, W. T., *Protestant Missions in Latin America*, Washington DC, 1961.

Thornton, Mary C., *The Church and Freemasonry in Brazil, 1872–1875. A Study in Regalism*, Washington DC, 1948.

Tormo, Leandro, *La Historia de la Iglesia en América Latina*, FERES, Fribourg, 1962.

Toro, A., *La Iglesia y el Estado en México, estudio sobre los conflictos entre el clero católico y los gobiernos méxicanos desde la independencia hasta nuestros días*, Mexico City, 1927.

Torres, Camilo, *Cristianismo y revolución*, Prólogo, selección y notas de Óscar Maldonado, Guitemie Oliviéri y Germán Zabala. Mexico second ed., 1972.

Turner, Frederick C., *Catholicism and Political Development in Latin America*. Chapel Hill, 1971.

Vallier, Ivan, *Catholicism, Social Control and Modernization in Latin America*, Santa Cruz, 1970.
Vargas Urgarte, Rubén, *Historia de la Iglesia en el Perú*, Burgos (4 vols.), 1953–61.
——, *El Episcopado en los Tiempos de la Emancipación Sud Americana*, Buenos Aires, 1965.
Vergara, Ignacio, *El protestantismo en Chile*, Santiago, 1962.

Wayland-Smith, G., *The Christian Democratic Party in Chile*, CIDOC, Cuernavaca, 1969.
Willems, Emilio, *Followers of the New Faith. Culture Change and the Rise of Protestantism in Brazil and Chile*, Vanderbilt University Press, 1967.
Williams, E. J., *Latin American Christian Democratic Parties*, Knoxville, 1967.

II. South Africa

Albertyn, J. R., *Kerk en Stad-Verslag van die Kommissie van Ondersoek van die Gefedereerde Nederduitse Gereformeerde Kerk en Godsdienstige Toestande in die Stede van die Unie van Suid Afrika*, Stellenbosch, 1947.

Batts, H. J., *History of the Baptist Church in South Africa*, Cape Town, 1920.
Baynes, A. H., *South Africa*, London, 1908.
Benham, M. S., *Henry Callaway. First bishop for Kaffraria*, London, 1896.
Boesak, Allan, *Farewell to Innocence. A social-ethical study of black theology and black power*, Johannesburg, 1977.
Booth, A. R. (ed.), *Journal of the Rev. George Champion, American Missionary in Zululand, 1835–9*, Cape Town, 1967.
Boshoff, C. W. H., Smith, P. E. S., and Crafford, D., *Swart Teologie?* Pretoria, 1972.
Bot, A. K., *Die Ontwikkeling van Onderwys in die Transvaal, 1836–1951*, Pretoria, 1951.
Brain, J. B., *Catholic Beginnings in Natal and Beyond*, Durban, 1975.
Brandel-Syrier, M., *Black Women in Search of God*, London, 1962.
Briggs, D. R. and Wing. J., *The Harvest and the Hope. The story of Congregationalism in Sourthern Africa*, Johannesburg, 1970.
Brookes, Edgar H., *The History of Native policy in South Africa, from 1830 to the Present Day*, Cape Town, 1924

Brown, W. E., *The Catholic Church in South Africa. From its origins to the Present Day*, London, 1960.

Cawood, L., *The Church and Race Relations in South Africa*, Johannesburg, 1964.

Christian Principles in Multi-Racial South Africa. A Report on the Dutch Reformed Conference of Church Leaders, Pretoria, 1953 (ed. F. J. van Wyk), Johannesburg, 1954.

Coetzee, J. C., *Onderwys in Suid-Afrika*, Pretoria, 1958.

—— (ed.), *Onderwys in Suid-Afrika, 1652–1860*, Pretoria, 1975.

Colenso, J. W., *Ten Weeks in Natal. A Journal of a First Tour of visitation among the Colonists and Zulu Kafirs of Natal*, Cambridge, 1855.

Cottesloe Consultation. The Report of the Consultation among South African Member Churches of the World Council of Churches, 1960 (ed. L. A. Hewson), Johannesburg, 1961.

Cox, G. W., *The Life of John William Colenso, Bishop of Natal*, 2 vols., London, 1888.

Danziger, Christopher, *The Huguenots (Looking at South African History)*, Cape Town, 1978.

Davenport, T. R. H., *The Afrikaner Bond. The History of a South African Political Party, 1880–1911*, Cape Town, 1966.

Davie, T. B., *Education and Race Relations in South Africa*, Cape Town, 1955.

Davies, Horton, and Shepherd, R. H. W., *South African Missions, 1800–1950*, London, 1954.

de Blank, Bertha, *Joost de Blank. A Personal Memoir*, Ipswich, 1977.

de Blank, Joost, *Out of Africa*, London, 1964.

de Gruchy, John W., *The Church Struggle in South Africa*, Cape Town, 1979.

de Jongh, P. S., *Die lewe van Erasmus Smit*, Cape Town, 1977.

de Kiewiet, *A History of South Africa, Social and Economic*, Oxford, 1941.

de Klerk, W. A., *The Puritans in South Africa: A History of Afrikanerdom*, London, 1976 edn.

de Vries, J. Lukas, *Mission and Colonialism in Namibia*, Johanneburg, 1978.

de Wet, C. J. H., *Ons Christelike Republiek*, Pretoria, 1940.

Desmond, Cosmas, *Christians or Capitalists? Christianity and Politics in South Africa*, London, 1978.

Dreyer, A., *Die Kaapse Kerk en die Groot Trek*, Cape Town, 1929.

du Plessis, J., *A History of the Christian Missions in South Africa*, London, 1911.

——, *The Life of Andrew Murray of South Africa*, London, 1920.

du Toit, S. J., *Christelijke School in hare Verhouding tot Kerk en Staat*, Paarl, 1876.

Eiselen, W. W. M., 'Gedagtes oor Apartheid', in *Tydskrif vir Geesteswetenskappe*, April 1949.
Engelbrecht, S. P., *Geskiedenis van die Nederduitsch Hervormde Kerk van Afrika*, Cape Town, 1953.

Ferguson, G. P., *The Story of the Congregational Union of South Africa*, Pretoria, 1940.
Florin, G. P., *Lutherans in South Africa*, Durban, 1967.

Gerdener, G. B. A., *Studies in the Evangelization of South Africa*, London, 1911.
———, *Boustowwe vir die Geskiedenis van die Nederduitse Gereformeerde Kerk in die Transgariep*, Cape Town, 1930.
———, *Ons Kerk in die Transgariep*, Cape Town, 1934.
———, *Recent Developments in the South African Mission Field*, London, 1958.
Gey van Pittius, E. F. W., *Die Staatsopvattinge van Calvyn*, Cape Town, 1958.
Giliomee, H. B., *Die Kaap tydens die eerste Britse Bewind, 1795–1803*, Pretoria, 1975.
God's Kingdom in Multi-Racial South Africa. A Report on the Inter-Racial Conference of Church Leaders, Johannesburg, 1954 (ed. F. J. van Wyk), Johannesburg, 1955.
Gray, C. N., *Life of Robert Gray*, 2 vols., London, 1876.

Hammond-Tooke, W. D. (ed.), *The Bantu-speaking Peoples of Southern Africa*, London, second edn, 1974.
Hanekom, Christof, *Krisis En Kultus. Geloofsopvattinge en seremonies binne 'n Swart Kerk*, Cape Town, 1975.
Hanekom, T. N., *Die Liberale Rigting in Suid-Afrika, 'n Kerkhistoriese Studie*, Cape Town, 1951.
Harington, A. L., *The Great Trek*, London, 1972.
Hastings, Adrian, *A History of African Christianity, 1950–1975*, Cambridge, 1979.
Hayward, V. E. W. (ed.), *African Independent Church Movements*, London, 1963.
Hellmann, E., *The Impact of City Life on Africans*, Johannesburg, 1967.
Hewitt, A. J., *Sketches of English Church History in South Africa*, Cape Town, 1887.
Hewson, L. A., *An Introduction to South African Methodists*, Cape Town, 1951.

Hinchliff, Peter, *The Anglican Church in South Africa*, London, 1963.
——, *John William Colenso, Bishop of Natal*, London, 1964.
——, *The Church in South Africa*, London, 1968.
Hoernlé, R. F. A., *Race and Reason*, Pretoria, 1945.
Hofmeyr, J. H., *Christian Principles and Race Problems*, Johannesburg, 1945.
Horrell, M., *A Decade of Bantu Education*, Johannesburg, 1964.
——, *Bantu Education to 1968*, Johannesburg, 1968.
Huddleston, Trevor, *Naught For Your Comfort*, London, 1956.
Human Relations in South Africa. Report of the Committee on current affairs adapted by the General Synod of the Nederduitse Gereformeerde Kerk, 1966. Cape Town, 1966.
Human Relations and the South African Scene in the Light of Scripture. Official translation of the Report 'Ras, Volk en Nasie en Volkerverhoudinge in die lig van die Skrif', approved by the General Synod of the NGK, 1974, Cape Town, 1976.
Hurley, D. E., *Apartheid: A Crisis of the Christian Conscience*, Johannesburg, 1964.

International Commission of Jurists, *The Trial of Beyers Naudé, Christian Witness and the Rule of Law*, London, 1975.

Jabavu, D. D. T., *An African Independent Church*, Lovedale, 1942.
Johanson, Brian, *Church and State in South Africa*, Johannesburg, 1975.
Jooste, J. P., *Die Verhouding tussen Kerk en Staat aan die Kaap totdie helfte van die 19 de Eeu*, Bloemfontein, 1946.
——, *Die Geskiedenis van die Gereformeerde Kerk in Suid Afrika, 1859–1959*, Potchefstroom, 1959.
Kane-Berman, John, *Soweto. Black Revolt, White Reaction*, Johannesburg, 1978.
Keet, B. B., *Whither South Africa? (Suid-Afrika—Waarheen?)* Stellenbosch, 1956.
Kleynhaus, E. P. J., *Die Kerkregtelike Ontwikkeling van die Nederduitse Gereformeerde Kerk in Suid-Afrika, 1795–1962*, Bloemfontein, 1974.
Kotzé, J. C. G., *Principle and Practice in Race Relations*, Stellenbosch, 1962.

Lea, A., *The Native Separatist Church Movement in South Africa*, Cape Town, 1926.
Lewis, C., and Edwards, G. E., *Historical Records of the Church of the Province of South Africa*, London, 1934.
Lovett, R., *History of the London Missionary Society, 1795–1885*, 2 vols., Oxford, 1899.

Lubbe, W. J. G. (ed.), *Die Sinode van die Nederduitse Gereformeerde Kerk van Natal 1865–1965*, Durham, 1965.

M^CCarter, John, *The Dutch Reformed Church in South Africa*, Edinburgh, 1869.

Malan, J. S., 'Religion and Development', in *Journal of Racial Affairs*, SABRA, Pretoria, July 1979.

Malherbe, Ernst G., *Education in South Africa*, Cape Town, Vol. I, 1925, Vol. II, 1977.

Marais, Ben, *Kleurkrisis in die Weste*, Cape Town, 1952.

Marais, J. I., *Geschiedenis der Nederduits Gereformeerde Kerk in Zuid-Afrika, tot op de Grote Trek*, Stellenbosch, 1919.

Marrat, J., *Missionary Veterans in South Africa*, London, 1894.

Mason, G. H., *Zululand. A Mission Tour in South Africa*, London, 1862.

Meintjes, Johannes, *The Voortrekkers. The Story of the Great Trek and the Making of South Africa*, London, 1973.

Meiring, Piet, *Stemme Uit Die Swart Kerk. Gesprekke met dertien geestelike leiers*, Cape Town, 1975.

Metrowich, F. C., *Development of Higher Education in South Africa, 1837–1927*, Cape Town, 1929.

Moffat, Robert, *Missionary Labours and Scenes in South Africa*, London, 1842.

Moore, Basil (ed.), *Black Theology. The South African Voice*, London, 1973.

Moorrees, A., *Die Nederduitse Gereformeerde Kerk in Suid-Afrika, 1652–1873*, Cape Town, 1937.

Muller, C. F. J., *Die Oorsprong van die Groot Trek*, Cape Town, 1974.

Natives of South Afrika, Their Economic and Social Condition. Ed. by the South African Native Races Committee, London, 1901.

Neame, L. E., *The History of Apartheid. The Story of the Colour War in South Africa*, London, 1962.

Neumark, S. Daniel, *Economic Influences in the South African Frontier, 1652–1836*, Stanford, 1957.

Northcott, Cecil, *Robert Moffat: Pioneer in Africa, 1817–1870*, London, 1961.

Oberholster, J. A. S., *Die Gereformeerde Kerke onder die Kruis in Suid-Afrika*, Cape Town, 1956.

Oberholster, J. J. (ed.), *Die Nederduitse Gereformeerde Kerk in die Orangje-Vrystaat*, Bloemfontein, 1964.

Oosthuizen, G. C., *The Theology of a South African Messiah*, Leiden, 1967.

——, *Post-Christianity in Africa. A Theological and Anthropological Study*, London, 1968.

Oxford History of South Africa, ed. Monica Wilson and Leonard Thompson, 2 vols., Oxford, 1971.

Paton, Alan, *Apartheid and the Archbishop. The Life and Times of Geoffrey Clayton, Archbishop of Cape Town*, London, 1974.
Paton, David M. (ed.), *Church and Race in South Africa*, London, 1958.
Philip, John, *Researches in South Africa. Illustrating the Civil, Moral, and Religious Condition of the Native Tribes*, 2 vols., London, 1828.
Pauw, B. A., *Religion in a Tswana Chiefdom*, Cape Town, 1960.
——,*Christianity and Xhosa Tradition. Belief and Ritual among Xhosa-speaking Christians*, Cape Town, 1975.

Randall, Peter (ed.), *Directions of Change in South African Politics*, SPRO-CAS publication no. 3, Johannesburg, 1971.
——, *Some Implications of Inequality*, SPRO-CAS publication no. 4, Johannesburg, 1971.
——, *Towards Social Change*, SPRO-CAS publication, no. 6, Johannesburg, 1971.
——, *Power, Privilege and Poverty*, SPRO-CAS publication no. 7, Johannesburg, 1972.
Ranger, T. O., *The African Churches of Tanzania*, Nairobi, 1972.
Ricards, James, *The Catholic Church and the Kaffir*, London, 1880.
Rosettenville Conference Report, *The Christian in a Multi-Racial Society*, Johanneburg, 1949.
Russell, Margo and Martin, *Afrikaners of the Kalahari. White Minority in a Black State*, Cambridge, 1979.

Sales, Jane, *Mission Stations and the Coloured Communities of the Eastern Cape, 1800–1852*, Cape Town, 1975.
Saunders, Christopher (ed.), *Black Leaders in Southern African History*, London, 1979.
Schapera, I. (ed.), *Western Civilization and the Natives of South Africa*, London, 1967.
Schimlek, F., *Mariannhill. A Study in Bantu Life and Missionary Effort*, Mariannhill, 1953.
Scholtz, G. D., *Die Geskiedenis van die Nederduitse Hervormde of Gere-formeerde Kerk van Suid-Afrika*, 2 vols., Cape Town, 1956.
Setiloane, G. M., *The Image of God among the Sotho-Tswana*, Rotterdam, 1976.
Shepherd, R. H. W., *Lovedale, South Africa: The Story of a Century, 1841–1941*, Lovedale, 1941.
Smith, C. S., *A History of the African Methodist Episcopal Church*, Cape Town, 1922.
Smith, N. J., *Die Planting van Afsonderlike Kerke vir Nie-Blanke Bevolkings-*

groepe deur die Nederduitse Gereformeerde Kerk in Suid Afrika, Stellenbosch, 1973.

Smuts, J. C., *Jan Christian Smuts*, London, 1952.

Spoelstra, B., *Die 'Doppers' in Suid-Afrika, 1760–1899*, Cape Town, 1963.

Steenkamp, L. S., *Onderwys vir Blankes in Natal, 1824–1940*, Pretoria, 1941.

Strassberger, Elfriede, *The Rhenish Mission in South Africa, 1829–1936*, Cape Town, 1969.

——, *Ecumenism in South Africa, 1936–1960. With Special Reference to the Mission of the Church*, Johannesburg, 1974.

Sundermeier, Theo (ed.), *Church and Nationalism in South Africa*, Johannesburg, 1975.

Sundkler, Bengt G. M., *Bantu Prophets in South Africa* [1948], second edn, Oxford, 1961.

——, *Zulu Zion and some Swazi Zionists*, Oxford 1976.

Taylor, J. D., *Christianity and the Natives of South Africa*, Lovedale, 1928.

Theal, G. M., *History of the Boers in South Africa*, London, 1887.

Thompson, Leonard (ed.), *African Societies in Southern Africa*, London, 1969.

Tödt, Ilse (ed.), *Theologie im Konfliktfeld Südafrika. Dialog mit Manas Buthelezi*, (*Studien zur Friedensforschung*, 15), Stuttgart, 1976.

van Broekhuizen, H. D., *Die Wordingsgeskiedenis van die Hollandse Kerke in Suid-Afrika, 1652–1804*, Cape Town, 1922.

van der Merwe, J. P., *Die Kaap onder die Bataafse Republiek, 1803–1806*, Amsterdam, 1926.

van der Merwe, W. J., *The Development of Missionary Attitudes in the Dutch Reformed Church in South Africa*, Cape Town, 1936.

van der Watt, P. B., *Die Nederduitse Gereformeerde Kerk*, Pretoria, vol. I, 1976, vol. II, 1977.

van Jaarsveld, F. A., *The Afrikaner's Interpretation of South African History*, Cape Town, 1964.

Vorster, J. D., *Die Kerkregtelike Ontwikkeling van die Kaapse Kerk onder die Kompanje, 1652–1795*, Potchefstroom, 1956.

Welsh D., *The Roots of Segregation. Native Policy in Colonial Natal, 1845–1910*, Cape Town, 1971.

West, Martin, *Bishops and Prophets in a Black City. African Independent Churches in Soweto, Johannesburg*, Cape Town, 1975.

Whisson, M. G., and West, M., *Religion and Social Change in Southern Africa*, Cape Town, 1975.

Whiteside, J., *History of the Wesleyan Methodist Church of South Africa*, London, 1906.

Wilkins, Ivor and Strydom, Hans, *The Super-Afrikaners. Inside the Afrikaner Broderbond*, Johannesburg, 1978.

Wilson, Monica, *Religion and the Transformation of Society. A Study in Social Change in Africa*, Cambridge, 1971.

Wirgman, A. T., *English Church and People in South Africa*, London, 1895.

World Council of Churches, *Christians and Race Relations in Southern Africa*, Geneva, 1964.

Index

222   *Index*